BUSINESS CASES
THAT MEAN BUSINESS

A PRACTICAL GUIDE TO IDENTIFYING, CALCULATING, AND

COMMUNICATING THE VALUE OF LARGE-SCALE IT PROJECTS

JIM MAHOLIC

DEDICATION

To my wife Maureen. A virtuous woman whose worth is beyond gold.

Proverbs 31:10

CONTENTS

SECTION THREE: EXPLORING FOR EVIDENCE

SECTION FOUR: ANALYZING YOUR FINDINGS

PREFACE

About the Author and the History of This Book

Like many authors, I didn't start out as an author. I began as a practitioner, building business cases in support of capital funding for Information Technology (IT) projects. During my career, I have twice been a Chief Information Officer (CIO). Both positions were in manufacturing companies. In this capacity, I frequently championed large IT projects to support the needs of the company. Years later I joined a software company and helped sales teams document and present business cases to our prospective customers. In my early days, I read dozens of business books, hoping to unlock the mystery of creating credible, compelling business cases. When I was faced with my first business case, I had to learn what a business case was and what it was supposed to achieve. I found some good material, but mostly I just found lots of consultant-speak. What I really wanted was a step-by-step guide to help me identify, calculate, and communicate the value of these expensive technology projects. Not finding what I wanted, I began keeping a journal of things that worked and things that didn't work in the creation and presentation of business cases. My successes grew, and software sales managers began asking me to help their customers create solid business cases. Word spread, and I was asked to teach these techniques not only to sales managers but also to sales teams. I have traveled across the United States, Europe, South America, India, Asia, and Australia teaching sales teams and customers how to succeed by focusing on the value of their solutions, rather than just the features of their products. That's how this journey began.

I have prepared and delivered over one hundred professional business cases in support of IT projects. I have prepared business cases for a variety of organizations including manufacturing companies, healthcare organizations, city governments, multinational defense contractors, top-tier shipping and logistics organizations, nationally known universities, global and regional retail chains, US military command, multinational energy companies, global financial services companies, telecommunications companies, restaurant and hospitality companies, and large public utilities. My business cases have been used to support capital project proposals for the acquisition of commercial software, large-scale consulting engagements, and factory expansion projects. All of these experiences give me a rich perspective on what separates a successful IT business case from an unsuccessful one. These principles are universal. They are relevant across all industries and across geographic boundaries.

I welcome your comments about the book. Has it helped? Was it lacking in a particular subject area? Such comments will improve the book for its next edition. You can connect with me on LinkedIn or reach me by email at:

BusinessCaseAuthor@gmail.com

Who Might Benefit from This Book?

Business Cases That Mean Business is written for those individuals and teams that must identify, calculate, and communicate the value of a proposed capital project. While heavily slanted towards technology projects, this book is written for anyone who must prepare a justification for a capital project, even if you've never created a business case before. Unlike other business case books, *Business Cases That Mean Business* provides more than just spreadsheets. *Business Cases That Mean Business* walks you through the process of gathering the right data, analyzing that data, and packaging it all into a credible, compelling business case. If you have a proposal for a project that requires capital funding, this book is for you.

Project managers must sell their proposal internally to receive funding. Likewise, sales teams that sell large, complex solutions also must frequently create financial justification for their proposals. This book will help you, regardless of whether you are an internal project manager or you are part of an external sales team seeking to justify a capital project. Capital investments are typically project-based activities and can be used for any large initiative. The capital investment you seek might be for computer hardware or software. It could be for software implementation services. While the references and examples in this book focus on capital projects for IT initiatives, capital projects are relevant in non-IT areas and could include business process re-engineering such as setting up a more streamlined call center or re-training and re-focusing the sales staff. Such projects could involve optimizing a distribution center or introducing new campaigns to attract new hospital patients for exploratory outpatient services. The list of possible capital projects is nearly infinite. However, they all share a common requirement:—they must be justified and approved by some executive committee. Whatever your particular project might be, the benefits and the costs required to achieve those benefits will be examined by an approval committee. To receive the approval of this committee—and also its funding—someone needs to prepare a well-organized, compelling business case that shows how spending these funds will be beneficial to the organization.

The goal of this book is to get you all the way to a completed document and executive presentation. Whether you are an employee seeking to gain approval for your internal project or you are selling large-scale capital projects, this book will guide you through the steps and considerations involved in creating and presenting a compelling and credible business case.

Abbreviations Used in the Book

In this book you will see abbreviations for common executive titles and business areas.

- IT stands for information technology. The IT department is the primary computing and data storage department in an organization.
- CEO stands for chief executive officer. This is the most senior executive in the company. In this context, senior does not mean oldest; it simply refers to the executive with the most power and authority. Not all companies name their most senior executive CEO. Some simply call that person President.
- CFO stands for chief financial officer. The CFO is the most senior finance or accounting executive in the company. Typically controllers and accountants work for the CFO.
- COO stands for chief operating officer. The COO typically oversees all operational and manufacturing areas of a company, but not sales and not finance.
- CIO stands for chief information officer. The CIO is the senior IT person in the organization.
- CTO stands for chief technology officer. The CTO is the senior IT person responsible for technical matters such as infrastructure, networking, and pure technology. Some organizations have both a CIO and a CTO. Other organizations may just have one or the other.

- KPI stands for key performance indicators. These indicators are used by executives to measure the efficiency and effectiveness of their organizations.
- Many of the financial measurements presented in the book are presented using the term "in dollars." If you live outside the United States, you could just as easily interpret this statement to mean "in your local currency."

An Introduction to Public Financial Data

Also in this book, we will explore financial data from publicly traded companies and compare this data to the data from privately held companies. A publicly traded company is a company whose common stock is traded on one of the stock exchanges. If the public company is headquartered in the United States, it is required by the Securities and Exchange Commission (SEC) to publish its financial results each three-month period, or quarter. These documents are available in electronic form, and can be found on the company's websites (usually in the Investor Relations section), you can access them freely. The three most common documents are the 10-Q, the 10-K, and the 8-K. Each will be explained in more detail below. These three documents often contain great nuggets of information. If you'd like to explore these SEC filings, you can also search and view them at www.sec.gov/edgar.shtml.

If you are not familiar with financial statements, or if you are not familiar with the most common business terminology, you can find helpful definitions on the web and in print. One helpful website with great definitions of business and finance terms is Investopedia, located at www.investopedia. com. For a printed reference, I recommend *Reading Financial Reports for Dummies*, by Lita Epstein.

In her book, Epstein explains these three documents. She begins with an overview of the 10-K:

> The 10-K is the annual report that provides a comprehensive overview of a company's business and financial activities. Firms must file

this report within 90 days after the end of their fiscal year (companies with more than $75 million in assets must file within 60 days). In addition to the information included in the glossy annual reports sent to shareholders, investors can find more detailed information about company history, organizational structure, equity holdings, subsidiaries, employee stock-purchase and savings plans, incorporation, legal proceedings, controls and procedures, executive compensation, accounting fees and services, and changes or disagreements with accountants about financial disclosure. (pg. 14)

She explains the 10-Q as follows: "The 10-Q is the quarterly report that describes key financial information about the prior three months. Most companies must file this report within 45 days of the end of the quarter (firms with more than $75 million in assets must file within 40 days). This form includes details about the company's market risk, controls and procedures, legal proceedings, and defaults on payments" (pg. 14). Each year you would expect to see three 10-Qs and one 10-K. The year-end filing only requires a single document, the 10-K, so companies do not prepare both a 10-K and a 10-Q for their final quarter.

Finally, Epstein explains the 8-K: "The 8-K is a periodic report that accounts for any major events that may impact a company's financial position. Examples of major events include the acquisition of another company, the sale of a company or division, bankruptcy, the resignation of directors, or a change in the fiscal year. When a major event occurs, the company must file a report with the SEC within four days of the event" (pg. 15).

We'll explore how to get the most of the 10-K and 10-Q in the Hypothesis section of this book.

Privately held companies are similar to publicly held companies in most respects. The primary difference relates to their treatment of common stock. The common stock of privately held companies is held by private parties. It is not available on any of the stock market exchanges. Privately held companies are not required by the SEC to post quarterly or annual results, and they are not required to conduct public quarterly earnings calls. Accordingly, getting access to quarterly or annual financial information from privately held companies will be more challenging.

SECTION ONE
START STRONG

Chapter 1

An Overview of the H.E.A.R. Method

The objective of this book is to help you become a more persuasive and effective leader. Leaders have a vision for the future and develop road maps to get their organizations to that future. Such road maps typically require new projects. Those new projects require funding. Effective leaders know that projects can transform or streamline an organization, and they know that they must create a compelling justification for the organization's executives to invest in that project. To be a leader you must plan your presentation methodically. Additionally, the methodology set forth in this book will provoke you to think strategically when seeking approval for your capital project. Too many proposals think tactically. A sound tactical approach is necessary to execute the project, but it is strategic business thinking that gives the project its vision and gains senior executive support.

The core of this book focuses on the H.E.A.R. method. The H.E.A.R. method is my time-tested approach to identifying, calculating, and communicating the value of a large-scale project proposal. It is no coincidence that the acronym is the word *hear*. Listening, as you will learn in the Evidence section, is a fundamental skill if you want to elevate the effectiveness of your proposals. The letters stand for:

H: Hypothesis
E: Evidence
A: Analysis
R: Recommendation

The intended outcome of this approach is a compelling, credible business case that advances your proposal through the chain of approval. This book will explain each of these steps in detail. For those readers who wish to know what our end-game looks like and want to know how this all comes together, the agenda for the final presentation is found in chapter 51, "Packaging Your Recommendation." For now, here's a quick overview of the H.E.A.R. method.

HYPOTHESIS

According to *Webster's Dictionary*, a *hypothesis* is "an unproved theory." The first step in any capital proposal is to clearly understand the problem at hand—what problem are you trying to solve? For an executive committee to even entertain your premise that a project must be initiated, they must be convinced that a need exists and that your potential project addresses that need. We refer to this need as a business pain. Examples of common business pains are:

- Inventory levels are too high.
- Expenses are too high.
- Revenues are not growing as they should.
- Our employees are not as productive as they could be.

To succeed, you must first start with the hypothesis that some business pain exists. Then you must show the approvers that there is more value in solving that pain than it costs to solve it.

EVIDENCE

Webster's Dictionary defines *evidence* as "something that makes another thing easy to see or perceive." In the Evidence section of this book you will learn how to collect evidence that supports your hypothesis. It's one thing to suggest that your organization's expenses are too high. It's something much more powerful to be able to provide credible evidence that the hypothesis is correct and that expenses are, in fact, too high. We will explore many available sources of evidence from both inside and outside your organization.

ANALYSIS

Again looking to *Webster's Dictionary*, we see that *analysis* is defined as "to examine in detail." Once you collect the evidence that supports your hypothesis, you must analyze it to ensure that it stands up to scrutiny and objectively supports your position. The Analysis section will introduce concepts of maturity modeling, adoption rates, and the timing of benefit realization. Activities that are described in the Analysis section often occur concurrently with activities that are described in the Evidence section.

RECOMMENDATION

Finally, you'll need to compile all of your notes and analyses and produce a compelling, articulate business document. In the Recommendation section you'll learn about document preparation and effective presentation techniques that will give your proposal an advantage when presented to senior executives.

Success often depends on coming to the presentation hoping for the best but having planned for the worst. When you finish this book, you should feel confident in your ability to initiate, create, and present a credible, compelling, professional business case in support of your proposal.

Chapter 2

Understanding the ROI Calculation

A business case is a formal method of demonstrating that your proposal to spend a large sum of money on a specific project delivers more value than it costs the organization. In essence, you are presenting the return on investment, or ROI. However, ROI is one of the most overused and misunderstood terms in business. On the surface, its definition might seem as simple as "return on investment." Unfortunately, it is not that simple.

Some financial terms have universal definitions, such as Internal Rate of Return (IRR) or Net Present Value (NPV). IRR and NPV, however, have specific equations that are universally understood by finance professionals. Conversely, ROI does not have a universal definition.

For those seeking a specific equation for ROI, the generally accepted formula is:

$$\frac{\text{Project Benefits minus Project Costs}}{\text{Project Costs}}$$

But this equation lacks so many critical variables that financial professionals consider it unreliable. Here are the problems with this equation:

- No defined timeline (for instance, are the costs for the first year or for the next ten years?)

- No specific scope of what is included and what is excluded from costs
- No tax consideration (expense savings carry a different tax treatment from revenue benefits, which carry a different tax treatment from asset benefits. Incorrectly presented tax effects are a pet peeve of finance professionals, and remember that you'll need the support of these professionals when you put forward your financial estimates)
- Often blends balance sheet and income statement items in the same calculation (another pet peeve of financial professionals)

If ROI is so deficient, why is it always used as the benchmark term? It is simply a common understanding of a bigger issue. Most capital projects require some form of justification before the approval authority will release funds to execute the project. The approval authorities typically demand information that will allow them to understand the value of the project. Not the cost, but the value. They want to know what they will get in return for the money that they're spending, hence ROI.

For the remainder of this document, we will move away from the term ROI, and instead replace that concept with the term "business case." For the purposes of this book, we will define a business case as "any document or presentation that identifies, calculates, and communicates the value of a proposed capital project."

Chapter 3

Strategic Persuasion and the H.E.A.R. Method

A business case is like a court case. To persuade the jury, you, as the advocate, must state the reason for your position, present evidence that supports your position, analyze the evidence in a way that compels the jury to respond favorably and present all of the relevant information sufficient to obtain a verdict in your favor. This book will walk you through very similar steps in your quest to receive funding for your capital project. You will learn how to identify project drivers, collect relevant evidence, analyze that evidence, create a sound financial spreadsheet and package all of that material into a compelling executive presentation. A business case, therefore, is much more than a single spreadsheet or a diagram of a future business process. A business case is the entire story. A business case makes the case for change.

Presenting a persuasive argument in order to seek approval for capital funds is a sales activity. You might not be a sales professional. You might, instead, be an engineer or an accountant or a human resources manager. Regardless of your education and current position, if you are seeking approval for capital funds, you are selling. You might resent being seen as a salesperson. For that reason, this chapter is entitled "Strategic Persuasion." But don't kid yourself. If you want capital funds, you are selling. You are selling the idea that your project is worth the money that you are seeking. You are attempting to convince executives that they should allocate precious funds to launch your idea. So, if you haven't considered it before, you need to come to grips with the idea that this activity is a sales activity.

Take a trip to any commercial bookstore and you'll see hundreds of business books about sales and sales presentations. Within the sales category, many books have been written about strategic selling. At the risk of oversimplifying things, these books fall into two broad categories—strategic and tactical.

Tactical selling could best be described as department-level, transaction-based sales activities. For example, you know that your organization has a problem with its inventory. You may already have a budget to address this problem, and you know that your direct manager has the authority to draw upon those budgeted funds to address this problem. In this situation, no strategic selling is required. Simply initiate a request (a tactical activity) for the already allocated funds and present it to your direct manager. Once approved, you can begin your project. But what if your inventory project could be expanded just a bit? Perhaps the inventory problem is related to problems with the production schedule. What might happen if you explored solving both the production scheduling problem and the inventory problem as part of a bigger project? Looking at the opportunity this way could be seen as visionary leadership. Not seeking only to solve a single, isolated problem, you expand your scope to address a complementary problem because you have a hunch that it won't take that much more money or effort to solve both problems at once. That's what I want you to think about.

> A business case is the entire story. A business case makes the case for change.

Strategic selling is expanding the conversation to include the executive level. To include the executive level (what many business professionals call the C-level) you must think beyond the departmental perspective and take a broader, more strategic view. Doing so will frequently enable you to increase the size and reach of the project. The H.E.A.R. method will guide you through a very methodical process of discussing and presenting the bigger picture, often with an outcome that leads to bigger, broader, more high-profile projects. After all, since you'll probably have to write a justification for a small project, wouldn't it be worth it to invest a little more time so that you could be championing a much larger project? Of course it would!

Larger projects draw more attention and can often propel your career further than a series of smaller and often insignificant projects. It's important to recognize, though, that we're not seeking to make projects larger just for the sake of making them larger. Most business processes are interconnected. And these interconnected business processes are often served by overlapping technological solutions (e.g., hardware and software). Simply focusing on a narrow aspect of a single business process may lead you to a single, nonintegrated solution. This nonintegrated solution may eventually need to be integrated into the larger enterprise infrastructure. With that in mind, it is often quite beneficial to look beyond just the single, narrow business process and explore improvements in adjacent processes. Yes, it will make the project larger, but it might also make the overall enterprise run more smoothly, with fewer integration points (which means fewer potential points of failure). For this reason, it is valuable to consider expanding the scope of your potential project.

Effective strategic selling requires that you condition yourself to move a little slower, a little more deliberately through the approval cycle. You must approach the effort as though your initial entry point into a given project is not the full project, but merely the most acute pain point of a larger opportunity. Consider the possibility that, with the investment of focused time and effort, you will discover many more pain points that, cumulatively, can expand your project into multiple business areas. You will need to apply more effort and gain comfort with executive-level conversations, but once you master strategic selling, your effectiveness (and corresponding career potential) will improve. The H.E.A.R. method will help you elevate your game and enable you to move your executive persuasion skills to higher and better levels.

Strategic projects typically involve complex selling conditions. Complex sales do not behave like simple sales. Complex sales require numerous meetings, often spanning several weeks and involving a number of people from different departments and different levels within your company. In his book *Hope is Not a Strategy*, Rick Page offers some great insights into the complex sale. He writes, "Today's complex sale encompasses more than just multiple buyers. In the last ten years, the traditional definition of the complex sale has exploded to include new challenges that are overwhelming. Buyer preferences for integrated solutions, rather than products, require teams of multiple sellers both inside and outside the vendor organization to help clients discern benefits and differences in complex products or services. Multi-departmental buying committees create shifting requirements and politics in ever-changing competitive evaluations" (pg. 5).

An effective business case is often a great way to navigate this complexity and to elevate your standing within your company. A properly positioned and executed business case demonstrates your knowledge and ability to address large, complex business problems. It often opens the door into other executives' offices to learn their concerns. Ultimately, a well-developed business case elevates your standing from a mere employee to that of a business advisor. A business case also has a powerful, if subtle, advantage for you. It helps sell your proposal in your absence. In between every meeting that you have with other departments, individuals within those departments are selling this proposal. Some are selling for you; some are selling against you. The business case process is not a single reporting event. Be aware that each time you collect evidence, present drafts, and have follow-up conversations, internal selling is happening between various factions within your company.

One common weakness in books about strategic selling is the omission of practical steps to help you communicate the value message. For our purposes, we will define the value message as "any communication (written or verbal) that clearly conveys the tangible worth or benefit of your proposal." The value message—also called the value proposition—is something that strips out the technical jargon so common in proposals and aligns any recommendations to your company's key business objectives. The most frequent communication vehicle for this value message is a business case.

Before we explore the business case process in detail, we are going to discuss three background topics. First, you will be introduced to a working definition of strategic and tactical initiatives. Second, you will be introduced to the concept of art versus science, at least as it relates to business cases. And third, we will review—and debunk—seven common myths regarding the purpose and promise of sound business cases.

Let's begin with our working definition of strategic and tactical initiatives.

Chapter 4

Looking beyond Tactical Challenges

Throughout this book, you will be encouraged to think about your business case and your proposal in strategic terms, rather than tactical ones. Tactical challenges are those challenges that are limited to a single, or narrow business area. Strategic challenges are those challenges that look out over a broader horizon. For example, imagine that a company is struggling with excess inventory. A tactical initiative might focus on warehouse management and how items are stored, retrieved, and replenished in the warehouse. That might solve the tactical problem of excess inventory, but not much more. A strategic view of this problem would look beyond the warehouse and include business areas that interact with the warehouse. What other areas might play a role in improving inventory management? There could be several considerations. One might be manufacturing. Is this department producing too much finished product? Or it might be in the factory scheduling area. Are they not balancing demand effectively? Or possibly it's on the other end of the process, in the shipping area. Are they having difficulty shipping the finished product in a timely fashion?

> Corporate executives generally would prefer to contemplate the solution to a family of business challenges rather than pick them off one at a time.

Corporate executives want their businesses to run efficiently. They know that efficient operations generate more profit than inefficient ones. It can be tempting to seek to solve a single business problem with a single solution. Yet there are times when the single, noticeable business problem is only a piece of a larger business challenge. Solving the single, isolated problem might actually worsen the overall business environment because this approach can mean excluding, or even ignoring, a larger business difficulty.

Corporate executives generally would prefer to contemplate the solution to a family of business challenges rather than pick them off one at a time. This is especially true when the potential solutions are disconnected. As an analogy, consider a car that has seen its gas mileage performance degrade over time. Why does the car get worse mileage now than before? It could be worn-out spark plugs. In this case, a tactical solution would be to change out the spark plugs. You bring the car to a mechanic, and while changing the plugs, he notices an oily residue on the plugs. He could continue replacing the plugs and consider the job complete, or he could explore other systems in the car to determine why there was an oily residue on the plugs. Possibly there's a small leak in one of the gaskets that allows oil to penetrate the cylinder walls and contaminate the spark plugs (and the whole engine for that matter). If the mechanic simply changes the spark plugs, the root cause has not been addressed and the new spark plugs will fail soon because they, too, will be burdened with the oily residue. I'll admit this analogy has its limits (cars are not companies), but I hope you see the larger point. Individual challenges are often the result of upstream or downstream problems. And if you only focus on the immediate problem, you may miss an opportunity to solve a much larger issue.

Chapter 5

Art and Science

In this book, I will refer to a number of things as "more art than science." I use this phrase because I want you, the reader, to stretch yourself a bit. This book does not provide a foolproof, scientific method for business cases. Instead it provides a time-tested framework. But because it is not a scientific method, it requires that you determine certain variables for yourself. The book is a guidebook, but it is not a recipe book. Much of the success of your business cases will depend on your ability to adapt to changing variables (including moody co-workers). This book attempts to provide a framework, or set of guidelines, for building a compelling business case. Because each reader will have different requirements and will be seeking to solve different business challenges, it would be impossible to precisely prescribe each step and each outcome with clarity. Therefore, I will strive to give you the tools to build your own business case, using the most likely common challenges. It is my hope that you can build upon these tools to develop your own skills for future business cases.

To bring this point home a little clearer, let's contrast two types of musical arrangements—orchestral and jazz. First, we'll examine an orchestral score as shown below.

"Solway," written by John Blackwood McEwen. Reprinted by permission from the Sibley Music Library of the Eastman School of Music.

If you're not familiar with music, the vertical lines represent time boundaries. In this example, the space in between the vertical lines represents three beats. Within the vertical lines, we see that the composer has provided parts for seven instruments. Each instrument is assigned specific notes to play, at very specific times and for specific durations. The symphony sounds great when each musician plays her instrument precisely as written. The beauty of the music is in the conformity to the composer's wishes. Admittedly, the musicians are talented, yet their expression of musicality is confined to the notes the composer has predetermined to be the best for this passage of music.

Now, contrast the orchestral score to the jazz score shown below.

"Donut King," written by Nick Capocci, copyright 1986. Reprinted by permission from the composer.

In this jazz score, we see an entirely different musical expression. Again, the vertical lines represent a set number of beats; in this case the composer determined that each measure (that's the space between the vertical lines) is assigned four beats. Unlike our orchestral example, where the composer wrote specific notes and specific timings for seven different musicians, the jazz composer chose to write only one part. That part would be played by a supporting musician, not one of the soloists. The soloist would make up his notes on the fly, using only the chords as his guide. If you look along the top staff by the "C" notation, you'll see Am and Dm markings, which mean A minor and D minor, respectively. The soloists who play this piece are given a lot of liberty. They can fill the space with a lot of notes, or they can choose to fill the space with only a few notes. The only constraints that are imposed are the chords. The musician must choose notes within the stated scales (A minor and D minor, in this example). Musicians in a band that are playing this piece must communicate and determine who is going to perform a solo; they also must decide if one musician will perform the solo for the entire piece or if different musicians will alternate playing it. A jazz piece, at least in my view, requires much more art than the orchestral piece. Both require musicianship, but it is possible that the jazz piece will never be played exactly the same way twice because the soloists have the freedom to alter the notes played each time the song is performed. This gives jazz its inherent liberty. It's also the very thing that creates anxiety in many orchestral musicians.

This book is more like the jazz score than the orchestral score. You will be given guidelines. Within those guidelines, you'll be introduced to concepts and then urged to adapt those concepts to your specific situation. That is, the ideas in this book depend on equal parts art and science. As you progress through the book, you'll gain confidence in your artful interpretation.

As we begin the journey, we will explore one more foundational topic—common myths about business cases. Successful business cases aren't created using textbooks; they're created using sound principles. The building blocks of good principles include experience and wisdom. Some of that wisdom comes from learning what to believe and what not to believe. This is especially true when it comes to common myths about business cases.

Chapter 6

Seven Myths about Business Cases

When I first began preparing business cases, I was naïve. I made some assumptions about business cases and, more importantly, about the contribution they would make toward receiving executive approval for my projects. These assumptions were based on myths—commonly held misperceptions about business and business cases.

Here are seven myths that I've encountered time and time again. Since I've heard these so frequently, I suspect you might have believed one or two of them yourself. For example:

1. A business case is nothing more than a pretty spreadsheet.
2. A good business case guarantees project approval.
3. A good business case converts skeptical executives to your way of thinking.
4. A business case can be prepared without the company's numbers.
5. The more you investigate, the more benefits you'll find.
6. Every proposal pays for itself.
7. A powerful business case paves the way for a higher-priced project.

Myth # 1. A business case is nothing more than a pretty spreadsheet.
    A business case is just that, a case. Consider a courtroom drama. The attorneys do not simply present a single alibi for the defendant. Instead they tell an entire story that is intended to persuade the jury. For your

efforts, a spreadsheet will be one piece of evidence, but your business case will consist of more than just a financial spreadsheet. Your business case must tell a complete story. We'll explore this comprehensive story throughout this book.

Myth # 2. A good business case guarantees project approval.

A good business case is certainly helpful to the approval process. In many instances, a business case is required for the approval process. If you are diligent and professional, and if you incorporate a sound methodology, your effort should result in a well-constructed business case, which should improve the likelihood that it will be approved. But...

Business cases project future events, but they do not guarantee them. The only guarantee in a capital project business case, assuming your company approves your recommendation, is that your company will be writing a large check to some vendor or consulting firm. Your business case can propose benefits, but it cannot promise that your company will realize those benefits. Savvy executives know this. They assume that your business case is susceptible to your biases and that, naturally, your business case will recommend the acceptance of your proposal. This doesn't mean that your efforts are wasted. It simply means that you should know that a business case is not, by itself, a magic wand to guarantee project approval.

Myth # 3. A good business case converts skeptical executives to your way of thinking.

I'm always intrigued by what I find when I begin a business case. Maybe I'll walk in and discover that all of the executives in the company are eager for this project (there's always a first time). Typically, when considering a request for capital funding, executives can be grouped into three camps: they are for it, they are against it, or they are undecided. Sorry to be so obvious, but that's my experience. And within each category there are degrees of enthusiasm. Some executives may support a project enthusiastically; others might favor the project but would not call themselves enthusiastic supporters. The same gradual scale can be applied to those who are not in favor of this project—some may be strongly against it, and others will be mildly against it.

A strong business case will likely energize those that already support it and may persuade some that were previously undecided. Those that are antagonistic will likely not be moved by your presentation. You have to accept that certain things are going on behind the scenes that existed before you began to develop your business case and will continue after you conclude. Your business case will help rally additional support but will likely have little effect on the staunch skeptics.

Myth # 4. A business case can be prepared without the company's numbers.

You will encounter this issue most frequently when attempting to prepare business cases for privately held companies. I have experienced it with a few publicly traded companies but not very often.

When creating a business case, your objective is to show the tangible, financial benefits your company will realize by implementing your proposal. In order to determine these benefits, you will often need to see and analyze your company's financial numbers. If your company's management resists, there is not much you can do. And it may be impossible to prepare a financial justification. Consider this scenario:

After meeting with the purchasing manager at a local hospital, you make the case that your purchasing software can help make the whole purchasing function more efficient, paying for itself in less than twelve months. In order to explore this further you ask the purchasing manager to provide you with his hospital's annual spend numbers (a common request that a CFO could typically answer). The hospital CFO resists and says, "We only provide such numbers on a need-to-know basis." Now you have a challenge. The purchasing manager wants to proceed with the project and his manager requires a reasonable justification for the expenditure. You want to give the manager a credible business case to justify the project but cannot since you have been denied access to the necessary data. So, while you could tell the purchasing manager, "Industry research, and our own customers confirm, that solutions such as ours can reduce the amount you spend by 2 percent" you would have to add, "But without your hospital's specific spend numbers, I'm not able to show you how that computes to an annual savings for your company."

You can see how we will have difficulty creating a financial comparison of costs versus benefits if we aren't given the financial numbers that we need to make our calculations.

Myth # 5. The more you investigate, the more benefits you'll find.

It has been my experience that the first wave of exploration yields a workable list of benefits and a reasonable range of their value to the business. Additional investigation may yield a few more benefits and a few more dollars of value. In chapter 9, "Building a Successful Business Case Template" I will discuss the Pareto principle, also known as the 80—20 rule. This principle certainly applies here. But what I have found, unfortunately, is that the more we explore, the more the management presents exceptions to our calculations. Management may accept that our proposal can cause a reduction in overall expenses by 1 percent. But as management evaluates and dissects the information, they begin to whittle that number back. They might say, "Your proposal is not going to have any impact on the rent or utilities figures, so subtract them from the total expenses before you apply your 1 percent benefit." The more thorough your investigation, the more likely additional exceptions will be introduced and your benefit pool will shrink, not grow.

That's not always a bad thing. There is a very grand benefit that can come from additional investigation, even if it results in some trimming of the total benefit value. That benefit is credibility. As you fine-tune the scope of your benefits, you demonstrate a richer understanding of the challenges and a more compelling statement of benefits. So, while the number might become smaller as you dig deeper, your credibility increases as you explain what is, and what is not, within the scope of your benefit assessment.

Myth # 6. Every proposal pays for itself.

This is not true. It's especially false in smaller companies. Capital projects carry a basic cost. For example, to implement a payroll solution for a company of five hundred employees requires a certain investment in time and money: it will be necessary to build basic employee profile information, build supporting database tables, set up various categories within the database, transfer in the employee data, and possibly purchase new hardware to support the new system. Does it take one hundred times longer and is it one hundred times more expensive for a company with fifty thousand employees? Probably not. It is therefore easier to justify such a project for a larger company than a smaller one. So, even though your proposal might be very easy to justify to a larger organization, the same proposal may be very difficult to justify if you work in a smaller one.

If your business case does not show a clear financial benefit (that is, the benefits greatly outweigh the costs), that doesn't mean that you shouldn't build a business case. It simply means that your business case may have to place more emphasis on non-financial benefits such as timeliness or accuracy of tax reporting or the ability to add or reassign employees more easily. Non-financial benefits are covered in chapters 18 and 47.

Myth # 7. A powerful business case paves the way for a higher-priced project.

This myth is a commonly held view by vendors. The truth is that these two items are unrelated. An effective business case means that the project is viable and worthy of funding. Once the value, or worthiness, is determined, the cost of the project enters a negotiation phase. The negotiation of a project's price is not affected by the power of the business case. I have seen numerous developers of business cases attempt to persuade decision makers that the business case shows enough value to deflect the focus away from the cost and onto the perceived benefits. Executive decision makers are stewards of their company's resources. As stewards, they are not going to award the contract to a vendor without regard to the cost of the project. Bear in mind that most executives have a financial incentive to demonstrate frugality and cost-consciousness. It is in their best self-interest to negotiate effectively during the negotiation stage. The business case is helpful, but it is not going to provoke them to award the project to a higher-priced bidder.

So, there you have seven common myths about business cases. The takeaway from these seven myths is this—business cases are not magical. They are a necessary step in obtaining approval for a capital project. To be effective, your business case must be professional and credible. Don't forget that selling your idea is still required, regardless of the effectiveness and impact of your business case. You must apply the effort that enables this document to sell in your absence.

Chapter 7

Understanding the Purpose of a Business Case

Capital funding decisions are rarely made quickly and are not made on impulse. Sales books that teach you to memorize a few clever phrases, promising that such cleverness will, by itself, help you gain approval for large, complex projects, are misleading and irresponsible. Capital funding decisions are made by committees. Executive buyers are sophisticated, rational, and thorough. Today's hypersensitive, litigious, regulation-intensive environment demands that all capital decisions be subject to a rigorous due diligence process. Shareholders are more demanding, executives are more demanding, and government decision makers are more demanding—they're all more demanding because they must prove with certainty that they did not act in haste or with undue favoritism. As Bill Stinnett states in his book *Think Like Your Customer*, "Let's not be naïve. Companies don't buy on impulse. In fact, that's the main reason companies institute buying policies that require a documented evaluation plan, multiple bids, a cost justification, and an elaborate approval process" (pg. 37).

Gaining capital project funding approval in today's business environment requires that you present sound, prudent recommendations and that you demonstrate that you followed a methodical, professional approach in arriving at your proposed conclusions. The consequences of the wrong decision for your company are a significant capital investment and possibly business disruption if the company has to undo what it did by adopting a poor recommendation and then start over with a different solution.

Therefore you must understand that these decisions are huge and often produce anxiety in the minds of your management. As the purchase price and scope of the proposal increase, there is a corresponding political risk to the decision makers. That risk may be real or imagined. Either way, your ability to mitigate that risk and soften their concern through your due diligence will improve your chance of success with the approvers.

Soon you may find yourself presenting a recommendation to a group of senior executives. Whether you know it or not, they will likely have several questions on their mind. Some of those questions might be:

- We have a limited pool of money for capital projects, so why is your project more worthy of those limited resources than another project?
- Why should we do anything?
- Why should we adopt your recommendations?
- Why must we act now?

As you might expect, you must prepare for this meeting before you ever begin your presentation. You must present a compelling case to these executives, including your best attempt to address their concerns and objections. This means you must anticipate these concerns and objections and be ready to deal with them. You must be organized, thorough, and professional. Your presentation must be coherent and, in most cases, must show a financial benefit that exceeds your requested investment. To demonstrate that you have conducted due diligence, and are not just requesting funding on a whim, you will need a business case.

How do we measure the success of a business case? A business case is considered a success when management grants funding and allocates resources to the proposed project. As a side note, there are rare projects that can launch without any funds (such as an upgrade of systems using your own staff). But even these projects frequently require a business case to justify the time that will be invested by your staff. As a general rule, if you need to justify your proposal, the approvers in the evaluation process will expect something like the business case model presented in this book.

A business case is about business. Business is about money—making more than we spend and spending effectively so that we either make

> A business case is about business. Business is about money—making more than we spend and spending effectively so that we either make more money or spend much less money.

more money or spend much less money. One of the big challenges for project managers is thoroughly identifying all of the benefits of a proposed project and ascribing credible, tangible, financial value to those benefits. This is critical to a successful business case.

Nearly every business manager can sit down and estimate the cost of a project. For example, a software project will have several common cost components, each of which we can compute. There is the cost of the software, the cost of requisite implementation services, the cost of training the users how to effectively use the software, the cost of annual support, and possible additional costs for hardware necessary to run the new software. Likewise, if this is a construction project, we can estimate the cost of materials, the cost of labor, even the cost of potential temporary business disruptions as we transition from one facility to the next. Once you have made your estimates, you will have a firm grip on the cost of the project. Let's say that your proposed project will cost $750,000. It is critical to present an incentive to spend that $750,000. To create that incentive, you must identify tangible, financial benefits that the organization will realize if it successfully implements this project. This is where many business cases fall flat.

Most business cases are good at computing the costs and at narrating various benefits, but they often fall short on providing crisp, credible financial benefit numbers that stand up to scrutiny. You'll recall from an earlier comment that you must write the business case in such a way that it is an effective selling tool in your absence. Part of that effectiveness is derived from having the benefits expressed in financial terms, not just in narrative terms (more about that in the Evidence section). If, on the benefit side of the ledger, we only come up with good narrative benefits (e.g., employee productivity will be improved, customer satisfaction will be improved, etc.) our business case will appear to have little tangible value (or return) against a list of very tangible costs (investments). This makes our ROI uninspiring and therefore our business case will likely fail. The challenge is to present benefits, especially the value of benefits, in a way that is credible, measurable, and supportable.

For years, business case developers have talked about hard benefits and soft benefits. Hard benefits are those benefits that are expressed in dollars (or other local currency) and presented in a way that is viewed as credible and sound. Soft benefits are those things that are difficult to express in financial terms but represent a benefit to the company. Likewise, there are soft costs. Soft costs are also difficult to express in financial terms, but they are those factors that could interfere with your business case and, ultimately, with a purchase decision for your solution. Soft costs include fear, uncertainty, and doubt surrounding your recommendation. They include the risk to individuals along the decision path (and are commonly masked or not openly discussed). An example of a soft cost would be the risk that a manager feels when considering whether or not to recommend your solution if he fears the project might not succeed. Are there people in the organization waiting in the wings with a big "I told you so"? To calm their nerves, your business case must be thorough, it must anticipate reasonable concerns, and it must provide some thoughtful, yet not defensive, commentary. Don't fall into the trap of believing that merely building a spreadsheet, regardless of how elaborate it is, will yield the positive response you need.

Think of the business case as a key component of the selling activity to people that are beyond your immediate reach. There will be executives involved in the decision and approval process that will not be able to participate in any of your interview or workshop activities. They may be unaware of your thoroughness and your methodological approach. This document, then, can be used to educate as well as persuade these executives. This is the document that sells your proposal in your absence. Anticipate all of the anxieties that might be expressed in the decision committee meeting. Has the software company's support been suspect? That becomes a soft cost. Is management concerned that your proposal will grow without restraint due to unknowns like scope creep? That's another soft cost. Anxieties, fears, and uncertainties such as these can interfere with your successful sales process. The business case is the ideal vehicle to help you address these concerns.

As you read through this book, you'll learn several techniques that can help you build and present a sound business case. You'll find several optional components that you can add that can boost your own credibility and blunt the anxiety of your project's approvers.

> Approach your first business case with the belief that this will be one of many that you will create over your career and that each one should be better than the last

FIRST BUSINESS CASE CONSIDERATIONS

If this is your first business case, it will be your most difficult one. It will be difficult because you won't yet have created any of the tools you'll need; everything that you'll ultimately need must be created from scratch. Approach your first business case with the belief that this will be one of many that you will create over your career and that each one should be better than the last. Also, keep this thought in mind—a business case should tell a story; it should have a flow. It should not just be a collection of PowerPoint slides and spreadsheets.

First-time business case developers often operate with a common but flawed assumption. That assumption is that your business case approvers, whom we'll simply call approvers, are fully aware of the situation and fully aware of the problems and the headaches and the disruptions that this problem is creating. First-timers tend to assume that the approvers understand the alternative solutions and why one alternative is better than any others. Rookies also tend to assume that the approvers have a strong sense of urgency to act. All of these assumptions might be correct about the people who are on the front line of a problem and who feel its effects every day. But these people may not be the ones who will be approving the funding for your project. You must assume that at least one key approver has no idea of the issues or the potential impact. It is also reasonable to assume that among your approvers, at least one will favor a different use of the limited company funds; this individual will likely seek to minimize the benefits that you ascribe to your project, as they will believe that denying you funding will bolster their chances of having their pet project funded. You have a number of known and unknown obstacles to overcome in your quest to convince the approvers to adopt your recommendation and fund your project. That's the purpose of a business case.

Developing a business case should not be intimidating. You simply must approach the development of a business case with discipline and ample planning. This book is intended to be a road map to guide you through the creation of this document. Throughout this book you will read about the value of drawing on your past business cases for current and future success. If this is your first business case, your experience begins here.

The business case is an interesting paradox. Many new projects will launch without a business case. Many capital project requests will succeed without a business case. And a business case alone does not guarantee approval. But a bad business case will always compromise credibility, and without credibility your justification for the project is weakened, possibly even damaged. By bad, I mean a case that is poorly written and poorly organized and that does not reach the proper conclusions—one that looks as though it was thrown together. So, if you are going to create a business case for a strategic capital project, it is important that you do it well.

It is also vital to understand that a well-constructed, professional business case is just as much art as it is science. The science part is easy to explain. There are going to be certain calculations required, and your math has to be logical and accurate. Everyone attempting to build a business case should be comfortable with that. The art is more subtle and undefined. No two capital project requests are the same. Therefore, no single business case presentation is going to be universally applicable. You must apply professional judgment to each business case opportunity to know what to do and what not to do in each case. The purpose of this book is not to cover every possible contingency, but rather to provide you with a comprehensive framework that will work for a large percentage of your future business cases.

Consider that a typical business case is presented to group of decision makers. An assumption exists that these decision makers will evaluate this proposal, as well as numerous other proposals, and in the end, decide that some projects are worthy of funding and some projects are not. The business case should strive to address all known concerns and attempt to address any anticipated objections. These concerns might be heavily weighted on the financial analysis, but other worthwhile benefits should be included in the business case so that all noteworthy contributions are documented.

Business cases run the gamut from a few short pages to several hundred. Bigger is not necessarily better, and one size does not fit all circumstances. You have to determine how much information you need to convey and how thorough your business case needs to be. It needs to be the right size for you and for your project. Factors that influence the size of your business case are the complexity of the problem that you're trying to solve, the complexity of the solution that you're recommending, and the breadth of the supporting evidence that you'll need to make a compelling business case.

Before you begin constructing your business case, let's look at a few common elements that all business cases seem to share. There are three universal considerations that your business case must acknowledge and three basic questions that you should anticipate from your approvers. The next chapter is solely devoted to these considerations. First, let's review the three basic questions on the minds of every approver. They are:

1. Why should we do anything?
2. Why is your solution the best solution?
3. Why must we do it now?

Let's examine each of these questions in more detail.

WHY SHOULD WE DO ANYTHING?

Somebody has determined that something needs to be done. What is it that needs to be done? You have to address that. What happens if we simply do nothing? Does the company miss out on some perceived market advantage? You have to address that, too. Remember that you cannot assume that the approvers understand the issue and why it requires attention.

> Too often, though, business case developers overlook the single biggest competitor of every project—doing nothing!

When planning a business case, most business case developers evaluate the merits of possible alternatives and offer valid, rational arguments that logically recommend one approach over another. Too often, though, business case developers overlook the single biggest competitor of every project—doing nothing! Frequently, business case developers assume that the company simply must do something and that inaction is simply not an option. Do not be that naïve. Any time money is involved, someone will suggest that the best decision is simply to not spend the money. You must anticipate this and confidently explain why your solution is not only better than alternative solutions but why it is also better than doing nothing.

In answering this question, you need to create a baseline understanding. This might require a paragraph or it might require fifty pages. It is important that you present a clear, unemotional statement of the situation as it exists today. We'll address this in some detail in the Hypothesis section. Reference points (both internal and external) are presented in detail in Section Three, Exploring For Evidence. Gathering these reference points help you determine how your company compares to similar companies in your industry. How does your company compare to companies in its industry? Are they ahead or behind the curve? Is there a problem with being ahead or behind the curve? These are fundamental statements that will help you to answer this first question, "Why do anything?" Once you establish a reason for doing something, you can move on to addressing the second question.

WHY IS YOUR SOLUTION THE BEST SOLUTION?

This is another great question that requires careful consideration. It is very important, in the development stages of your business case, to bounce your ideas and assumptions off of another contributor. You are well served if you can find a supporter within your company who is well versed in alternative solutions. If such a person is hard to locate in your company, seek out a peer through a professional organization such the Institute of Management Accountants (IMA), the American Institute of CPAs (AICPA), or the Institute of Electrical and Electronics Engineers (IEEE). You may also seek out other professionals in various professional user communities dedicated to specific types of technology or business processes, such as PC user communities or human resource professional communities. Once located, this person can act as your antagonist as you build your business case. The antagonist may be someone who has deep knowledge of a competitive proposal or it may be someone who has a valued, if different, perspective. What you don't want, though, is to bounce your early, rough, unrefined ideas off of someone who wishes to see your project fail. You don't want a saboteur, just someone to play devil's advocate and help you strengthen your case.

WHY MUST WE DO IT NOW?

Few things are as frustrating as gaining approval for the first two questions and then being rejected here. Your business case must reveal the urgency of action. This is another delicate issue that requires care and balance. If you understate the urgency, you risk having your project deferred or rejected because it appears to lack a compelling reason to act now. Conversely, if you overstate the issue you run the risk of being discredited because your proposal will come across more like an apocalyptic alarm than a sound, professional business proposal. We will identify items in the Evidence section that can help you to create a compelling and professional reason for moving this project forward sooner, rather than later.

As you develop your business case, be aware that your ultimate audience will extend beyond the people with whom you interact—your project sponsor and project contacts—to include people at one or more organizational levels above these individuals. The challenge here is to present, with confidence, a compelling and persuasive case that your recommendation should be adopted in a timely manner. It must articulate the benefits in a way that executives can accept and support. Your presentation must be diligently crafted and show that you have followed sound planning processes and that you are confident your approvers will acknowledge your effort and agree to move forward. To succeed, your business case must be able to stand on its own without your participation. Once you make the presentation and present your document to your managers, there is a high likelihood that your manager will take it to one or more levels higher in the organization for final approval. To be successful, your business case must be able to carry that message forward in your absence.

THE BUSINESS CASE FILTER

A business case goes through a predictable sifting or filtering process (see diagram below). It begins with a hypothesis that you present to your manager. Your hypothesis states your view of the problem and offers your high-level educated guess about the potential value in solving that problem. You gain the attention of your manager, and the manager decides that your hypothesis is worth exploring further. Your manager encourages you to create a business case to support your hypothesis. You begin your business case by exploring for evidence. Using your evidence, you seek to confirm that solving this business problem would be beneficial to the company. As you collect evidence, you may uncover new information—or you may clarify information you've already gathered. In either case, you may need to change your original benefit projections, and frequently you will need to adjust the benefit numbers downward.

Consider this example: your hypothesis states that you believe your company can save a considerable amount of money by improving its purchasing capabilities. A common approach is to suggest that improved procedures, supported by technology, can yield an annual savings of 2 percent. Last year your company spent $500 million on various purchases, including raw materials that were used in production. A 2 percent savings on $500 million yields an annual benefit of $10 million. During your evidence-gathering phase, you learn that some of that spending is really not negotiable. As mentioned in Myth number 4 in chapter 6, it is common that items such as rent and utilities would be included in a company's annual expense totals. Upon reviewing your hypothesis, your manager might require that these items be excluded from your calculations in order to maintain credibility as these items would not generally be included in discussions involving discretionary spending. You discover that the company spent $30 million on those items last year. That brings your benefit source down to $470 million and reduces your potential savings down to $9.4 million. As you do further analysis, and as you present preliminary estimates to the head of purchasing, you realize that there is another hurdle. The head of purchasing is rather reluctant to agree to a $9.4 million annual savings (we'll discuss how to address this reluctance in chapter 44 titled, "The Delicate Act of Gaining Commitment.") The best you can get him to agree to is 25 percent of that number, or $2.3 million in annual savings. Finally, as you're preparing your final recommendation, he expresses further concern over your calculations and states that the most he can commit to will be an annual savings of $1.5 million. This is a common experience: as you go through the various stages of presenting drafts of your business case, managers will likely reduce, or filter, the proposed benefits. This filtering is to be expected. In this example, what you might have thought was a legitimate $10 million annual benefit is now, at best, a $1.5 million annual benefit.

A good rule of thumb for business case development is to shoot for benefits that represent ten times the anticipated cost. For example, if you have estimated that your proposal will cost the company $4 million, you should shoot for $40 million in initial benefits. The benefit filter, as illustrated below, often reduces the initial benefit projections by as much as 90 percent. So if you begin with an initial benefit projection of $10 million, as in the previous example, you could end up with a much smaller $1.5 million after all of the filtering has occurred. Initially shooting for ten times the needed benefit amount enables you to avoid a possible awkward situation and at the same time help you to achieve your objective. Setting a lofty goal will allow you to realize your actual intended goal by accounting for the loss of benefits due to filtering, as well as potential added costs as the full project budget is prepared.

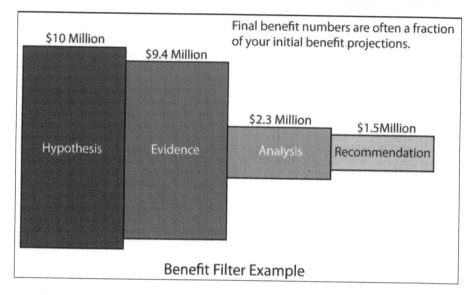

Benefit Filter Example

As stated previously, the business case is part art and part science. Its purpose is to help rational people reach a rational conclusion that your proposal is worth funding. There is no one right method, but there are many wrong ones. Understanding the dynamics of the business case filter will help you focus your efforts on identifying and presenting the most credible benefits package that your research can support.

Chapter 8

Three Universal
Considerations

There are three universal considerations for any business case. Your business case must align with these three universal considerations or your business case risks failure. The Three Universal Considerations are:

1. We must be true to our mission.
2. We must find ways to increase revenue.
3. We must find ways to be more effective and efficient.

All organizations, regardless of their purpose or customer base, must focus on these three universal considerations. When you begin your business case, invest the time to learn your organization's mission.

Let's look at three very different organizations and review their mission statements. The University of Chicago Medical Center states its mission is "to provide superior healthcare in a compassionate manner, ever mindful of each patient's dignity and individuality." Southwest Airlines states its mission is "a dedication to the highest quality of customer service delivered with a sense of warmth, friendliness, individual pride and company spirit." The Coca-Cola Company's mission is contained in three simple statements: To refresh the world; to inspire moments of optimism and happiness; and to create value and make a difference.

Every organization has a purpose. Some, like these three examples, are clearly documented. Your business case work should include a review of your organization's mission statement. While not every project will have a direct correlation to your organization's mission statement, no project should knowingly run counter to that statement.

> While not every project will have a direct correlation to your organization's mission statement, no project should knowingly run counter to that statement.

While these three universal considerations apply to all enterprises, to make your business case compelling, you must also invest time and effort to determine the specific issues that your company faces. It is helpful to do some research into your company's industry. You'll get an introduction into business research in the Hypothesis section. Talking about earnings per share is irrelevant to a local county government. Charitable organizations, as an example, will invest in projects that advance their mission to the community, but a manufacturing firm does not generally consider community outreach to be its driving issue. To make your business case credible, you must demonstrate that you are aware of the unique challenges facing your organization. Even within a given sector, things will not be uniform. For example, a manufacturer of automotive parts faces different challenges from a manufacturer of medical devices. A nationally acclaimed graduate school faces different challenges from a rural community college. The two manufacturers will be similar in some respects, as will the two academic institutions, but each individual organization will face unique situations that, if understood and acknowledged, may give you an advantage when your proposal is submitted for approval.

Once you demonstrate that your proposed project is aligned with the organization's reason for existence, you will naturally wish to show that the proposed project help with one or both of the other two universal considerations: increasing revenues and driving efficiency. You may be thinking that your company also wants to reduce costs. Driving efficiency will reduce costs, but reducing costs does not necessarily drive efficiency. Therefore, driving efficiency should be viewed as the higher goal.

Combining the three universal considerations with industry-specific content will position your business case for success.

Chapter 9

Building a Successful Business Case Template

No two business cases are identical. That statement alone could lead you to believe that it might be too much trouble to create a template for business cases—that even if you created a template, you would need to rework it for every proposal because it would not have enough reusable content. Not at all. All business cases have some things in common. And if you have a specific focus or area of expertise, there is a high likelihood that, over time, your business cases will look very similar (and that's a good thing).

Building a business case template is an attempt to make your job much easier as time goes by. Your second business case should be easier than your first and the third one even easier than the second. Building the first one will be the most challenging. For that reason, begin your first business case with the idea that you will reuse nearly everything from this business case in your next business case.

We learn by doing, not just by reading. Reading gives us some information. It provides guidance and often gives us encouragement. It may even provide a structure, but until we begin to put this learning into practice, we never really grow and develop. The first time we employ a new skill we are awkward at it. The tendency for many people is to quit because they find it just too hard and they fear that they will look ridiculous. So it is with these techniques. In your first reading, this information will make sense and seem straightforward. Putting the information into practice for the first time will seem awkward. Stick with it. As you continually practice, you'll improve. And because new skills are awkward, and we feel vulnerable when we first display them in public, consider starting in a low-risk situation, say with a tactical, single-department project; in this type of situation, minor public gaffes, such as stumbling over your words, will not adversely affect your overall performance. If your first experience with these new techniques is with your most significant and important project, you may find that this awkwardness works against you. Even so, perse-vere. You'll quickly see your own skills grow as you practice and perfect your business case development and presentation skills. Striving to build a workable template for yourself will also be a valuable step in your own development process.

Several years ago, I was in a role that required me to generate a com-pelling business case about every five business days. In each case, I had to collect evidence, perform an analysis, and prepare a specific client report. Obviously, these were highly structured, tightly focused business cases. In my situation, the cases were specific to manufacturing companies and three specific benefit areas—inventory optimization, cash collection, and cost reduction of direct material purchasing. Creating a template gave me a highly repeatable process with consistent results.

Creating a reusable, repeatable template will pay dividends with each successive business case that you construct. The realistic universe of cred-ible, tangible benefits is somewhat finite. Notice I wrote, "realistic uni-verse of credible, tangible benefits." There are an infinite number of poten-tial benefits, but there are only a few that are credible and tangible. For example, if you seek to show how your solution increases revenue, there are only two credible, tangible benefits—sell more (goods and/or services) or increase prices. There may be thousands of benefits that you could propose, but if you want to increase revenue, these are the two primary ways to do that.

You may have heard of the 80—20 rule, also known as the Pareto prin-ciple. This concept was pioneered by Vilfredo Pareto (1848–1923). Pareto was an economist and philosopher. He first observed that roughly 80 per-cent of Italy's wealth was owned by 20 percent of Italy's population. As his work evolved, Pareto ultimately concluded that this distribution applied almost universally— that in many contexts, including business, 80 percent of the results will come from 20 percent of the effort. Using a variation on that principle, I have concluded that while some business cases may take six to nine months to complete, the vast majority of the known benefits are discovered and validated very early in the process. To put it another way, most of the likely and credible benefits associated with a business case will be discovered and vetted within the first few interviews and discovery workshops, often within the first few weeks. The remaining time does not add materially to the discovery of additional benefits or justifications. And it is the discovery and confirmation of potential benefits that makes a business case sellable.

Certainly each case is different. You may need to invest additional time to build consensus from various contributors. The scope of the project may be complex, and that complexity may require that you meet with people at multiple locations. The premise still holds true, though, that you would identify 80 percent of the benefits at a location or within a solution area during the first few weeks of focused, investigative discovery. It is that predictability that makes creating a template so beneficial.

I created my first business case template when I was in a sales support role, working with scores of sales teams all across the US. I would be called in on very short notice, often with less than a week to prepare. My assignment would be to meet with client management, assess the benefit opportunity, create a compelling business case, and present the business case to senior client executives. I had to do all of this as quickly as possible because the sales cycle was placed on hold until I could complete my assignment. To be efficient and effective I knew that I had to create a reusable, credible template.

To build an effective template, I started by organizing my work into categories. For me, the categories were inventory optimization, improved cash collection and savings from consolidating purchases. I first determined the repeatable aspects of each category. For instance, inventory optimization will always involve calculating the current inventory turnover. Cash collection will always involve calculating the current days sales outstanding (DSO). And direct material purchasing improvements will require determining how much is spent each year on direct material. Below is a sample of my first inventory template. It is very crude and basic. The purpose was to compute the customer's current inventory turnover, then suggest a future-state inventory turnover target, and finally determine the value of achieving that future-state performance. I would take the benefit number ("one-time savings") and include that in the business case.

Published Cost of Goods Sold	$887,304,000
Published average finished goods inventory balance	$145,000,000
Computed inventory turns	6.119
Desired inventory turns	7.000
Resulting finished goods inventory balance	$126,757,714
One-time savings	$18,242,286
On-going savings (cost of money * one-time savings)	$364,846

To expand upon my template, I collected articles from trade journals and web pages. I would refer to those quotes in my template. One article mentioned a company that had achieved an improvement of 5 percent, while another showed a company that had realized an improvement of 9.5 percent. Using those references, I created two or three paragraphs for each topic and I included them in my template. Then for each future business case I did not have to research these topics. I already had well-written content for that portion of my business case which I could simply cut-and-paste into my next business case.

Let's look further at inventory optimization. First, I had to evaluate the company's current inventory performance and determine a reasonable future state (you can see the specific inventory calculation, as well as other financial calculations in Appendix B: Common Financial Metrics). I spent some time with our pre-sales team since they were the ones who gave the demonstrations to our clients. I asked them some basic questions:

1. Why do our customers buy our software?
2. What do our happy current customers say about how our products have helped them?
3. What distinguishes us in the marketplace?

I took their responses and let that form the foundation of my template. I reviewed a number of whitepapers that I had seen on corporate websites.

I modeled the format of my template after them. I worked out a table of contents for myself, which looked like this:

Introduction

Purpose

Overview

Use of Third-Party Research Statistics

Forward-Looking Statements

The Business Case

Executive Summary

Individual Solution Areas

Inventory Optimization

    Cash Collection

    Direct Material Spending

Additional Considerations

And If Your Business grows?

Value-Added Benefits

Appendix

Understanding the Assumptions

The Benefit Spreadsheet

After creating several business cases, I was able to create a working template that served me well. It provided a basis for many future business cases and cut my preparation time significantly. Using this template, my typical business case document, when printed, was about thirty-five pages, and looked thorough and professional.

Here's what made creating this template so easy. The entire introduction section was standard boilerplate content, so I did not need to change it. (A sample introduction is included in the appendix of this book.) The business case section also contained a high level of reusable, boilerplate content. I was able to develop this boilerplate content over time from the many business cases that I had created. For example, in the inventory optimization section, I included quotations from some of our customers about their successful experiences. This rich content applied to every inventory deal that we did, so it fit nicely into the template. Likewise, I used content from our pre-sales team that highlighted specific competitive advantages of our solution. Inventory optimization is often achieved when obsolete and slow-moving inventory is managed more effectively. Inventory can also be optimized when the client's warehouse communicates better with its suppliers on replenishment and demand issues. These are common, reusable reference points. All that would remain would be a paragraph or two about each client's specific inventory status and how much value could be derived by improving their turnover—a simple, insertable calculation.

Once the template was complete, I could use it to create individual documents for specific clients. All I needed to do was spend a few days in discovery meetings with key client managers and line personnel and an additional few hours with a plant controller to collect some basic operational and financial information, and then I'd have everything I needed to prepare their specific case. A small minority of salespeople bristled at my document after they saw it for the fourth or fifth time. I dispassionately explained to them that while they had seen this template many times before and had, possibly, expected a fresh, unique document for this client, the client had never seen this document and so to them, it was fresh, unique, and, most importantly, credible. Better still, since it contained their information (and often their logo on the title page) it looked as though it was created expressly for them.

You may already have strong business case content that you use and prefer. If you don't already have such content, the guidance provided in the Evidence and Analysis sections will arm you to begin your own library of reusable content. Don't worry. By the time you finish this book, you'll be able to build your own successful, professional, compelling business case template.

Chapter 10

Credibility Is Fragile and Fleeting

Webster's defines credibility as "that which is reliable and believable." I'll state this over and over again because credibility is the Achilles heel of any business case—If credibility is ever compromised, it is very difficult to recapture. For your business case to achieve success, you must be aware of the precious commodity that we call credibility. Maintaining credibility should always be on your mind throughout the entire lifecycle of the development of your business case. You can injure your credibility if your hypothesis is too grandiose, if your evidence is inadequate, or if your analysis is less than thorough. Therefore, don't let your guard down. You must give each aspect of creating a business case your full concentration in order to avoid weakening both your own credibility as well as that of your business case. And finally, what you include in your presentation, and how you present it, will determine whether your business case is viewed as a credible document.

> If credibility is ever compromised, it is very difficult to recapture.

Proclaiming that you are creating a business case creates an air of credibility and an expectation of thorough research. In addition, everyone who hears your proclamation will have their assumptions about what a successful business case should include. That is to say, that a number of people will evaluate your finished business case, and if you have not met their expectations, they will be disappointed. Disappointment erodes credibility.

It's not hard to maintain credibility throughout the business case life-cycle. But it is necessary to be aware of the penalty you could pay if you lose credibility. The penalty would be twofold. First, you would likely not receive the funding that you have requested. That would be obvious. But just as significantly, you could also suffer a career setback if your work is viewed as haphazard and incomplete.

Remember that not every project requires a business case. If you choose to create one you need to invest the necessary time and effort required to create a very professional one.

Chapter 11

The Role of the Executive Sponsor

Imagine the following scenario: one or more members of your management team has suggested that there is value in solving an existing problem. In this case, you assume that these executives have the necessary authority to get this capital project approved. You are depending on them to help you navigate through the organization—both to discover information that supports the hypothesis and to gain allegiance from other constituencies. You are hoping that a groundswell of support will supplement your business case and ultimately provide approval for your proposal. You believe your business case will communicate the challenges that your organization faces and the value that overcoming those challenges provides. But beyond you, who really stands to benefit from this project? Typically, there is someone in the organization—preferably a mid- to senior-level executive—who has a passion for the prospective project. This person has garnered enough initial enthusiasm from his peers and executives to get the organization interested in exploring this project further. We call this person the executive sponsor. If there is no sponsor inside the organization and if the enthusiasm for the project comes solely from external sources (from the software provider

> There are three capabilities that make someone an effective executive sponsor: executive access, authority to assign resources, and political effectiveness.

or external consulting firm), it has relatively little chance of gaining the necessary executive approval.

Your executive sponsor must have more than just enthusiasm about this project. For you to succeed, your sponsor must have a reasonable amount of political clout within his or her organization. If your project sponsor is politically weak, you can expect difficulty in gaining access to the right people and difficulty in gathering allegiance from the right people. There are three capabilities that make someone an effective executive sponsor: executive access, authority to assign resources, and political effectiveness. You should be aware of these traits and be ready to adjust your selling approach if you believe that your sponsor is weak in any area. Let's examine each trait a little more closely.

EXECUTIVE ACCESS

Executive access is a primary reason you need a strong and capable executive sponsor. A well-constructed business case shows how your recommendations align with the key strategies of your overall corporate enterprise. Typical department leaders do not have an enterprise-wide perspective. That's what executives are for. And an effective sponsor can give you access to these executives. Even a fifteen-minute conversation with a key executive can really sharpen your perspective and position your recommendation much more powerfully. Inasmuch as your sponsor is assumed to be biased in favor of your recommendation, you need to hear the executive perspective from several executives and managers, not just your sponsor. In addition, your credibility improves when you can supplement your sponsor's enthusiasm with the input of his or her peers or managers. We will address particular executive-level questions in the Evidence section of this book.

RESOURCE ASSIGNMENT

One of the primary challenges in a multidepartmental business case is getting the company to assign the right personnel to assist you. To enlist the right participants, you will often require assistance from your executive sponsor. Your sponsor can introduce you to the right department leaders and can also help you to assemble an effective and diverse team to build your business case.

An effective business case is developed when multiple—and different—points of view can be heard. When a business case reflects only one or two points of view, this can compromise its credibility. This is particularly problematic when those two points of view are deemed to be the opinions of people from wrong (or at least not the most preferred) departments, or those who do not adequately represent the needs of the organization. When you have included inadequate representatives, you can expect the overseeing executive to ask, "Who, from my organization, did you include in your interview processes?" If you have included only one or two people from a single department, you run the very real risk of having that approver state, "Well, those people don't speak for my area. And if those are the only people that you talked with, your recommendations clearly don't address our concerns." Such a statement can be injurious to your credibility. You need to enlist the support of your executive sponsor to ensure that you include a range of participants from within the organization so that your recommendations are not discounted during your presentation.

As stated earlier, the reason you commit to investing your resources in a business case is that you believe that the project is beneficial to your company. You need your management to demonstrate that same level of commitment by authorizing you to build a business case team of the right people from the right functional areas across your company. If the project includes more than one department, you will require the support from the other department leaders. If you are unable to secure that support, the other department leaders can easily sabotage your business case by claiming that your hypothesis did not elicit comments from them and that your conclusions are suspect. They'll say things like, "If you had only talked with us we could have showed you the error in your thinking." Statements like that are fatal to a business case. To avoid this situation, you need a well-respected executive to lobby for their support. The capable executive sponsor will be effective at working behind the scenes to gain support, or at least acceptance, of your hypothesis and recommendations. The capable sponsor will work with you to ensure that the other department leaders step forward and vocally proclaim their support when you make your presentation to the key decision makers.

POLITICAL EFFECTIVENESS

I wish I could say that everyone in an organization sees things as you do and that they can all get along. Regrettably, most of us know that this is not the case. I have observed certain organizations where one executive does not want to see another executive succeed. It may be juvenile, but it's also real. Your project depends on the assumed goal of shared success. Projects that require multiple business units to work together must all want to see the project succeed for it to succeed. Your project sponsor must be effective at securing alliances with other executives in the organization to ensure that success.

Consider this example. In a typical manufacturing organization there will be a manufacturing or operations group that oversees factory operations, production, and shipments. There will also be a finance organization, of which controllership is an integral department. The controller's office focuses on cost accounting. If you are implementing a manufacturing system, you can expect these two organizations to be antagonistic. They are antagonistic because they are measured on things that, to them, seem inherently mutually exclusive: units of production and cost tracking. The manufacturing group must produce as many finished items per shift as they can. That is one of their key performance indicators (KPIs). They strive to eliminate all unnecessary work from their environment. Initiatives such as lean manufacturing and Six Sigma stress the identification and elimination of non-value-added work—work that does not add value to the product. By eliminating those unnecessary steps, the operations group can streamline their operation and produce more goods, of the same high quality and in the same period of time, making the department more efficient and the company more profitable.

On the flip side, at least according to the operations group, are the controllers. Controllers need to know exactly how many of each component are used and what each component and subcomponent costs so that they can effectively compute a total product cost and ultimately determine a competitive selling price. Controllers fear that using averages instead of actual usage amounts could cause an error in the cost calculation, which in turns could cause a potential under- or overstatement of the selling price—which ultimately affects the true profit of an item.

The conflict comes when the controller's office dictates that every fastener or washer or inch of copper wire be completely accounted for. This requires that the operations group either allocate time or allocate people to count each and every component before it goes into the final product. If the operations group allocates time to count each piece before they use it, production will be slowed down and fewer items will be finished per shift.

Likewise, if the operations group allocates more people to count each individual fastener before it is applied to an assembly, that raises the labor cost of the factory and, correspondingly, reduces the company profit.

Both groups have a legitimate issue. But some compromise must be reached to resolve the conflict. Your executive sponsor needs to be effective at navigating such issues and helping the parties reach an agreement through compromise while keeping the focus on the larger, strategic issues so that your business case can keep moving forward.

Finally, your sponsor must be skilled at blunting the effects of those who seek to undermine your proposal. In their book *The New Successful Large Account Management*, Miller, Heiman, and Tuleja put forth the concept of an "anti-sponsor." An anti-sponsor, in their view, works to promote your failure: "Like a Sponsor and Strategic Coach, an Anti-Sponsor is credible to the buying organization. He or she has authority in the account and may exert influence on how the account and its key players are thinking. And that's the danger, because the Anti-Sponsor, by definition, wants you *out* or someone or something else in. Whatever he or she may do in the account, as far as you're concerned the Anti-Sponsor's role is to *negate your efforts* to improve your position" (pg. 82).

For all of these reasons, an effective executive sponsor is vital to the success of your business case.

Chapter 12

Assembling an Effective Project Team

Most business cases can be created by one or two people. Some business cases, however, will require a project team because the scope or cost of the proposal is so large and complex. In those cases, you will need to assemble an effective project team. The elements of a successful team are straightforward.

The key elements of a successful business case team are as follows:

- Members of the team should be knowledgeable about the specific subject area. For example, if your business case will be focused on the payroll and benefits areas of your company, your team should be comprised of those people that actually know something about these subjects. New team members that are seeking to learn about payroll and benefits will hinder your progress. However, team members that are seeking to learn about building a successful business case should be welcomed, assuming they meet the first criteria.

- Members of the team should be empowered by their manager to speak for and commit their area. Continuing with our payroll and benefits example, the team members that you need are those staff and managers that can help you identify the issues, dispassionately discuss those issues, and then work to propose and adopt reasonable solutions to them. If your team member must always check back with his manager for every little detail, your progress will be slowed as you wait for each little item to be discussed and resolved outside of the team.

- Members of the team should acknowledge that an opportunity for improvement exists. They may not agree on your approach to realizing that opportunity, but you need people that acknowledge that improvement opportunities exist and that there is some value to addressing and resolving them. Healthy debate and dialogue is usually very productive for the team.

There are numerous books on the creation and management of a healthy project team. That topic is outside the scope of this book. If you need to build a team to create your business case, you should seek help from a seasoned project manager on how to build and manage successful project teams.

Chapter 13

Section One Summary

Persuading executives to approve a capital funding request for a project that involves multiple departments or divisions requires more than simple spreadsheet and better than average presentation skills. Capital funding for such projects is not granted on an impulse but is authorized by a committee after a careful review of the proposal, including its benefits and its risks. Often, funding approval requires the creation of a business case to help you articulate the value of your proposal to disparate constituencies. A business case is simply a document or presentation that conveys the business value of your project.

A business case is subject to certain myths and misconceptions. We reviewed and debunked the following seven myths:

1. A business case is nothing more than a pretty spreadsheet.
2. A good business case guarantees project approval.
3. A good business case converts skeptical executives to your way of thinking.
4. A business case can be prepared without the company's numbers.
5. The more you investigate, the more benefits you'll find.
6. Every proposal pays for itself.
7. A powerful business case paves the way for a higher-priced project.

A business case helps decision makers answer three common questions:

1. Why should we do anything?
2. Why is your solution the best solution?

3. Why must we do it now?

Additionally, a successful business case shows careful alignment to the three universal considerations for any organization. Those three universal considerations are as follows:

1. We must be true to our mission.
2. We must find ways to increase revenue.
3. We must find ways to be more effective and efficient.

Benefits that are identified during the business case shrink as the process marches along. We call this the business case filter. During the process, assumptions are challenged and initial benefit projections are often scaled back. Credibility is one of the most significant assets of your business case. If your assumptions and corresponding benefit projections appear credible, if it appears as though you followed a sound, thoughtful methodology, you can increase the likelihood of favorable results from your presentation.

Building a reusable business case template is a good way to compress the time it takes you to create future business cases. A sound template includes rich, relevant content, presented in a professional manner. Building a template is especially effective if your job role will require the frequent creation of business cases, as in the case of a sales support professional.

An executive sponsor is a vital contributor to your business case development team. An effective executive sponsor will be able to assist you with access to key executives; provide assistance in securing necessary staff participation, especially across departmental or divisional boundaries; and be an effective internal politician when complex situations and conflicts arise.

Most business cases can be completed by one or two people. In those cases where the scope of the potential project is very broad, or when the projected cost of the project is very high, it may be best to assemble a team to assist with the creation and presentation of the business case.

SECTION TWO

CREATING YOUR HYPOTHESIS

Chapter 14

The Value of a Strong Hypothesis

We create business cases for two reasons: we believe there is a problem that can be fixed, and we believe that there is value in fixing or solving the problem. The starting point, therefore, is a statement that a problem exists. We call this statement the hypothesis. According to *Webster's Dictionary*, a hypothesis is "an unproved theory." The hypothesis, or theory, of your business case is an opening assumption that a problem (or improvement opportunity) exists and that there is value to your organization in addressing it. A thoroughly researched and well-written business case will prove the theory. It's really that simple. By the same token, without a hypothesis, there's really no reason to request funding because there's no assumption that there is a need for this project. For example, you could hypothesize that your company could benefit from implementing new financial accounting software. A business case will confirm a worthwhile hypothesis with credible supporting material. However, a business case will not convert a flawed hypothesis into a sound one. You need to invest some effort into creating a compelling hypothesis. Decision makers are human and are influenced by typical human stimuli. They are often predisposed to either accept or reject proposals based on a variety of rational and irrational factors. The business case plays to their rational, deductive reasoning skills. If well-written and well-documented, the business case provides support to the decision makers who approach the evaluation process objectively. Unfortunately, where decision makers are not objective, even the best business case cannot overcome irrational reasons for rejection. Knowing that, we must strive to position our business case to appeal to even the most cynical and irrational audiences.

> A sound business case evaluates the issues in detail and isolates the root causes from the annoying—but uninspiring—symptoms.

To gain approval for your capital project request, you have to identify and position your solution to address a legitimate business need. A sound business case evaluates the issues in detail and isolates the root causes from the annoying—but uninspiring—symptoms. Consider this medical analogy. I have a pain in my back. Suggesting that I take an aspirin or other over-the-counter pain medication may garner my interest. But if you offer to isolate the cause of my back pain and completely rehabilitate my back muscles, I'm very likely to listen intently, even if the solution requires more effort from me and is more expensive.

Just walking in to an executive's office, unprepared, might yield a response of moderate interest—as with the aspirin example above. However, investing time to research your company and prepare an educated hypothesis of potential problems likely positions you as a business advisor. This investment of time highlights your thoroughness—your willingness to look beyond the obvious symptoms and to really examine the root causes of core business problems. This section will help you understand how to do that, and as a result, elevate your standing by helping you create a compelling hypothesis.

A valid hypothesis could be as simple as "Our business could significantly reduce its costs by optimizing our procurement processes." That's it. That could be your opening hypothesis. The business case could be launched from something that basic. You then achieve success by validating your hypothesis (the Evidence section), analyzing and structuring your evidence for effect (the Analysis section), and communicating the value of solving this problem or exploiting this opportunity (the Recommendation section).

It is also possible that your hypothesis is much more expansive than the above example. For instance, you could postulate, "The purchasing, warehousing, and distribution functions could be optimized, thereby yielding significant financial and operational savings to the company." Depending on the size and complexity of your organization, that hypothesis could either be presented as one broad hypothesis or as three (or more) smaller, separate, tightly focused ones. One size does not fit all circumstances.

Within every business case, there is an assumed declaration. The assumed declaration is, "The benefits of solving this problem significantly exceed the costs." In the next section we'll introduce the idea that not all benefits are financial. But make no mistake; it is a very rare project that receives its requested funding if the measurable, financial benefits do not exceed the costs. Even when many of the benefits are not presented in financial terms, there is an expectation that financial benefits exist and that they will exceed the costs of the project.

You may not have intended to explore other aspects of your company. You may have assumed or been content with the notion that your project would be confined to a particular business function. But building a business case correctly should open the door to other parts of the organization. By starting with a strong, compelling hypothesis, you ignite executive interest. Executive interest yields access. Access invites discussion across departmental and divisional lines, which highlights other opportunities and expands the size of your potential project. A strong hypothesis has two tangible benefits for you: first, it allows you to position your proposal throughout the enterprise; and second, it should open the door to higher levels within the senior management corps giving you improved access and visibility. In order to receive the necessary funding for your proposal, you'll need to talk to people that can speak for and commit the organization as well as those that set the vision and direction for the organization. A well-articulated hypothesis will grant you the right to speak to individuals at higher and broader levels within the organization. And since the key funding decisions are often made at the highest levels, it is advantageous for you to meet with the highest-level management possible to ensure your proposal receives favorable consideration.

Chapter 15

Financial Statement Overview

Understanding common financial statements and how these documents are used will provide a strong foundation for a successful business case. For some of you with accounting and financial backgrounds, this chapter may be a bit of a review. For those of you without such experience, this chapter will provide an introduction into key financial statements.

There are two primary financial statements that we will use for our research: the income statement and the balance sheet. Government agencies and nonprofit organizations don't have these documents as they do not seek to create a profit. They have documents called "Sources and Uses of Funds" that serve a similar purpose. For simplicity, I have chosen to focus this discussion on commercial enterprises and specifically the income statement and the balance sheet.

> Financial benefits fall into four categories: increase revenue, decrease expenses, optimize assets, and improve productivity.

In the next two chapters you'll learn that financial benefits fall into four categories:—increase revenue, decrease expenses, optimize assets, and improve productivity. The income statement looks at an organization's financial activities over a period of time and addresses the first two items—revenue and expenses. As Lita Epstein explains it, "The Income Statement is where you find out whether a company made a profit or took a loss. You also find information about the company's revenues, sales levels, the costs it incurred to make those sales, and the expenses it paid to operate the business" (pg. 92). In basic terms, the income statement shows how much revenue was earned through sales over a certain period of time, called a reporting period. The income statement also shows how much the company spent to make that revenue. It details such expenditures as the purchase of raw materials and many common factory expenses. You will also typically discover a summary of how much the company spent on general expenses such as rent, utilities, and office salaries.

Income statements are created on a set schedule. The common time frames are one month, three months (or a quarter), and one year. The income statement seeks to match expenses against the revenue that the organization generated. In this way, the income statement seeks to portray the profit or loss in that reporting period. For example, in a quarterly income statement we would expect to see the revenue (or sales) that happened during that period, and we would expect to see the expenses incurred during the same period. We would hope to see revenues larger than expenses.

Admittedly, income statements are much more complex than I am describing here. The accounting profession and government regulatory agencies have established guidelines for reporting income and expenses so that investors can measure company performance against standard definitions of performance. Those guidelines also facilitate comparisons of one company against another, since the standards of accounting are assumed to be universally followed.

Our goal is to create a hypothesis that is credible. Part of building that credibility comes from relying on publically available data as much as possible. So, if you've hypothesized that your proposed project can help your company increase revenue, you'll want to compute the value of that increase as part of your business case. Where do you find the revenue number? You find that in the income statement. Often the revenue number will be the very first line item on an income statement (which is why many financial analysts refer to this number as "top line revenue"). Most companies consolidate the income from all sources into a single line, frequently called "Sales from Operations." Other revenue might be earned from a company's investments, and that revenue is often presented as a separate line so that investors can determine how much of the company's revenue came from its primary business and how much came from other sources. It is rare that a company will break down its revenue into categories on the primary income statement. A company may have income from six different product lines or from eight different countries. The revenue from all of these would typically be consolidated onto a single line on the income statement. The company might provide supplemental explanations that separate the income by product or by geography. This separation is common for publicly traded companies; the breakdown of the revenue by category, if provided at all, would likely be within the 10-K.

In addition to increasing revenue, the other common goal is to reduce expenses. The income statement can also show us how much money the company has spent on its expenses. There are typically two major expense categories that companies publish in their financial statements: sales, general, and administrative expenses (SG&A) and cost of goods sold (COGS). Sometimes companies call the COGS expenses "cost of revenue." SG&A expenses refer to those items that are most often discretionary. For example, advertising and marketing costs are often in this category, as are payroll and benefits expenses for office workers. The payroll and benefits for factory workers are typically lumped into factory expenses in the COGS entry. These are the costs incurred in actually producing the products that are sold. For example, if a company makes automobiles, then the cost of steel and transmissions and tires would likely go here. Also, this category would likely hold the labor costs of the factory workers. These distinctions are important when you begin building your hypothesis. If your proposed project will make the factory more efficient, you might state that your proposal could reduce the cost of items in the cost of revenue category. If, however, your proposal will make the office workers more efficient, then you might state that your proposal would reduce SG&A expense. Of course, it is possible that your proposal could favorably impact both categories.

The other major financial statement that we use is the balance sheet. The balance sheet differs from the income statement in that it does not look at things over a period of time but rather at a specific point in time. The balance sheet lists the assets (the things an organization owns), the liabilities (the debts the organization owes), and the equity (the difference between the value of the assets and the value of the debt). The balance sheet "is a summary of the company's financial standing at a particular point in time" (Epstein, pg. 75).

The balance sheet looks at the balance (or value at the time of examination) of company's assets and liabilities. The mathematical difference between the assets and liabilities is called equity. It is hoped that the assets exceed the liabilities, which means the company has a positive equity.

Both financial statements, the income statement and the balance sheet, are prepared at the same time. If you look at the year-end financial statements for a company, you would see how much was sold during the year (sales from operations) and how much was spent (SG&A and cost of revenue). You would also see the value of the assets (cash on hand, accounts receivable, land and buildings, etc.) and the value of the liabilities (mortgages on buildings, lease obligations, accounts payable owed to vendors, etc.).

For all of the good information that the financial statements provide, they really don't provide much detail. For example, you will find a value for SG&A expenses, but not an individual breakdown by department. So, if your proposal seeks to reduce IT costs, you will have to get those specific departmental costs from either the IT management or the accounting department directly.

The good news for you is that you do not need to have a detailed knowledge of these documents in order to have a successful business case. You do, though, need to understand that these two documents drive executive decision making. An improved income statement and balance sheet can help to drive a company's stock price higher—and it also typically drives executive bonuses. Your business case will be successful if your project successfully improves one or both of these financial statements.

Chapter 16

Determine the Project Drivers

A project must have a valid business reason to receive capital funding. Your job is to articulate that reason in concise and compelling terms. We call this the project driver. There can be more than one project driver. Project drivers drive the need, and therefore drive the benefits, for the capital request. One of your responsibilities is to communicate project drivers in compelling terms. Common assertions such as "Our systems are so old, management has to approve their replacement" or "Because we have to have it!" are vague and uninspiring. Such statements do not drive capital expenditures since, by themselves, they are not substantiated by evidence. As you begin your business case, be prepared to hear nebulous statements such as these from individuals at all levels of the organization. Be equally prepared to press these individuals for specifics. Simply asking, "Why would that be a good reason to go forward?" can open the discussion and lead you to uncovering compelling, tangible benefits. Tangible benefits are excellent project drivers.

What drives the need for this project? What adverse impact do older systems create? Why do we have to have new systems? The answers to these questions will differ by job level. Frontline workers, such as clerks, operators, and supervisors, will often state tactical challenges or complexities. They will suggest that overcoming these challenges will yield tangible benefits. Executives, on the other hand, will seek strategic reasons to approve funding. Although you may wish to interview personnel at all levels of the organization, including frontline workers, one of the goals of the business case is to communicate the value earned by solving various challenges in terms that align with the strategic objectives of the executives.

> One of the goals of the business case is to communicate the value earned by solving various challenges in terms that align with the strategic objectives of the executives.

It doesn't matter whether you begin building your business case from the tactical challenges (e.g., it currently takes too long to create a purchase order) or from the strategic objectives (e.g., we need to improve shareholder value). Your job will be to bring these two worlds together into one, complete, compelling business case. It's relatively easy to identify the tactical challenges. Spending thirty minutes with the purchasing or accounting staff will provide you with several pages of notes. We'll discuss how to gather evidence in detail in Section 3, "Exploring For Evidence." The challenge is to communicate how solving those tactical challenges will result in a strategic benefit. To the degree that you effectively communicate a strategic benefit, executives will be more likely to approve and fund your project. The best places to look for strategic issues are the organization's operating financial statements. Ultimately, businesses seek ways to increase profit, which leads to improving the overall value of the business. Improving the value of the business pleases existing shareholders and attracts new ones. Bill Stinnett, author of *Think Like Your Customer*, explains this very simply. He writes, "There are three major ways that a company can increase profits or earnings: (1) increase revenues (sell more), (2) reduce costs (spend less), and (3) better utilize company assets (do more with less). Everything else they do, and every other financial measure they track relates back to these three objectives, to the profits these three contribute to, and to the equity and cash flow that results" (pg. 82).

Aligning project drivers to relevant financial documents is one key to success. Many consulting firms also have methodologies for helping companies communicate value initiatives and align them with key business performance indicators. One excellent example comes from Deloitte Consulting. Deloitte has prepared an elaborate diagram that they call the "Deloitte Enterprise Value Map." This diagram contains over seven hundred value areas. (At the time of this writing, the Enterprise Value Map is free from Deloitte Consulting. Their website address is www.deloitte.com. To find this particular document on their website, enter "Enterprise Value Map" in the search box.)

Deloitte's document is an exhaustive approach to identifying business drivers. We should begin, though, with a much simpler example by tracing their document to its very basic origins, the DuPont Model. In 1914, F. Donaldson Brown was an electrical engineer for DuPont and was assigned to the company's treasury department. While Brown was in that position, DuPont purchased a 23 percent position in General Motors. Brown's manager assigned him the task of optimizing and rationalizing GM's disorganized finances. Brown is credited with building a series of simple tools, including the diagram below, to ensure that all business initiatives were properly aligned with existing financial measures. Alfred P. Sloan, GM's chairman at the time, commended Brown for his insightful and straightforward approach to this task.

We can take full advantage of Brown's good work. Take a look at the diagram below and notice the two boxes at the top. You can see the income statement and balance sheet identified. We want sales to increase and expenses to decrease. Obviously, these are gross simplifications of a contemporary financial statement, but it is this simplification that works so well for our purposes.

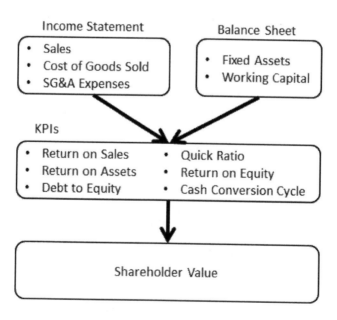

SIMPLIFIED DuPONT MODEL

In this simple diagram, we see the relationship between the two primary financial statements and the ultimate goal of increasing shareholder value. The two primary financial statements are presented at the top of the diagram. Determining the project driver(s) is often as simple as determining which of these key elements are improved by your proposed project. You will recall from chapter 8, "Three Universal Considerations," that all business cases must align with these considerations (initiatives must be true to the organization's mission, they must find ways to increase revenue, and they must find ways to be more efficient and effective). This diagram clearly illustrates where we find those items. Increasing revenue and reducing costs (e.g., becoming more efficient) are income statement items while optimizing assets (e.g., also becoming more efficient) would be found on the balance sheet. It would be very easy to create this same example for any type of enterprise—commercial, public sector, or non-profit. It is important to do more, though, than just mock up the two financial statements. You must show how favorable improvements to elements of these two documents will drive the much larger executive key performance indicators (KPIs). This approach is particularly beneficial when you are positioning non-financial projects. For example, a project team that is seeking approval for a database project is having a hard time getting the interest of the financial professionals. The finance team knows how to evaluate a proposal for payroll services, but how do they evaluate the value of a new database technology? This diagram can facilitate that discussion. If you are involved with technical projects, invest the necessary time to determine how these projects will impact the indicators listed here. The more effectively you define that impact, the more likely you will receive favorable feedback from the financial members of the approval committee.

This diagram is an excellent introductory image to present as part of your opening hypothesis. Note that this diagram does not provide insight into the potential line items where benefits may occur. That clarification will come after you collect that evidence in your upcoming discovery sessions (explained in detail in Section 3, "Exploring For Evidence"). Here, you're simply seeking to pique the executives' interest and get them to engage. You're hoping that they will ask you, "How will that benefit us?" or "In which areas do you anticipate the biggest benefits?" Such comments will indicate their interest.

In the expanded illustration below you'll notice that specific narrative benefits have been added for income statement items. This now becomes a very compelling conversation point. If your manager asks, "How does your solution increase sales?" you can respond, "By helping us identify key cross-sell and up-sell opportunities for customers, such as Amazon does when you purchase a book." Notice that these examples do not have dollar values. That comes later. This is just the first stage—the Hypothesis stage. We're trying to determine what drives management's need for this project. Once we determine the project driver(s) and determine that our hypothesis sounds reasonable, we are then ready to begin confirming our hypothesis by collecting evidence.

Income Statement

- **Increase Sales**
- **Reduce Cost of Goods Sold**
- **Reduce SG&A Expenses**

- Increase sales through cross-sell / up-sell driven by better customer information
- Use targeted market information to expand into new channels and new markets
- Bill for items that are currently, erroneously not getting billed
- Reduce cost of raw materials
- Reduce manufacturing cycle time
- Reduce unplanned factory overtime
- Reduce use and cost of expedited, in-bound freight
- Reduce MRO spending
- Reduce cost and aggravation of unplanned downtime
- Consolidate IT hardware, software, and infrastructure
- Reduce administrative staff
- Reduce HR benefit costs
- Reduce or eliminate use of outside services
- Reduce costs through implementation of shared service models

Chapter 17

Primary Financial Benefit Categories

Remember, a business case is about business, and business is about money. Your business case must show that your proposal produces benefits in excess of the costs of your proposed project. Using the DuPont Model as the basis for our discussion, we adapt Stinnett's three approaches to increasing profits, separating the third category ("better utilize company assets") into two. Once we've done that, our financial benefits will align in four general categories, which are:

- Top line revenue improvement
- Expense reduction
- Working capital improvements
- Productivity improvements

Appendix B, C, D, and E provide numerous specific examples, complete with equations, of benefits in the categories. For now, let's look at a summary of the primary financial benefits.

TOP LINE REVENUE IMPROVEMENT

All businesses desire more top line revenue. How do they generate more revenue? Typical commercial businesses can generate more revenue in two ways: sell more of their products or charge more for the products that they sell. The local government increases revenue by raising taxes or by offering fee-based services to the community. Nonprofit organizations can also increase revenue by offering fee-based services.

EXPENSE REDUCTION (or profit improvement)

Controlling expenses is another desirable goal for every organization. No organization generates as much revenue as it desires. Organizations always need more, and since they can't generate an endless supply of revenue, they must manage their expenses so that they spend less than they earn. There are many ways to control expenses. To be effective, your business case must explore those options and articulate the ones that are most compelling and relevant to your proposal.

WORKING CAPITAL IMPROVEMENTS

Another excellent way to show value is by improving working capital. Working capital involves things that are either cash or can quickly be converted to cash. Improving working capital, therefore, affects cash. The three most common working capital items that we might impact are accounts receivable (amounts owed to the company by its customers), inventory (materials that the company has purchased but may or may not yet have been converted into sellable finished products), and accounts payable (amounts the company owes its suppliers).

Optimizing accounts receivable is a fancy way of saying that your company collects its cash sooner. A simple equation for computing the value of improved cash collection can be found in Appendix E, but for now just know that there is value in collecting from your customers sooner. Likewise, there is value is converting your materials into sellable product sooner. The third working capital improvement area deals with vendor management and vendor payment. Prompt payment of trade payables (a term that refers to routine business purchases that were made on credit) is a good business practice. But there is a balance between paying too promptly and being delinquent. Your company might be able to benefit from delaying payment to vendors a day or two without injuring the vendor relationship. These three working capital items are often combined in a calculation called the cash conversion cycle. We'll explore the cash conversion cycle in more detail later in this section in chapter 21 called "Creating Your Sandbox."

PRODUCTIVITY IMPROVEMENTS

There are two primary ways to represent this benefit. The first way is doing more with the same resources. For example, assume that a typical purchasing clerk can process one purchase order every thirty minutes. If your solution provides an efficient method of entering purchase orders, possibly the typical clerk could process a purchase order in twenty minutes. In a typical eight-hour day, your typical clerk could now process twenty-four purchase orders instead of the previous sixteen. This benefit allows the organization to grow without hiring more people, thus creating a cost-avoidance benefit.

The other way to express productivity gains is doing the same work with fewer resources. This approach is much like the above example, only in reverse. If an average purchasing team has twenty-five clerks and they process sixteen purchase orders in an average day, they process a total of two thousand purchase orders in an average week. If your solution enables them to be more efficient such that each clerk can now process twenty-four purchase orders per day, instead of needing twenty-five clerks, the company will only need seventeen clerks to handle that workload. The elimination of eight clerks is a cost-reduction benefit.

There are notable difficulties with presenting productivity improvements. Productivity improvements are often called soft benefits. They are viewed this way because their quantification is somewhat suspect. Relying too heavily on them can often discredit an otherwise sound business case. Many productivity improvement hypotheses hinge on saving minutes per day multiplied times a large employee base to compute an enormously large benefit number. The weakness in this approach is that many executives do not consider this to be a tangible savings. Their reasoning is rooted in the financial statements. Their logic goes like this: "If I have ten employees today and I pay them $40 per hour, I pay my staff a total of $1,600 per week. If my employees can process purchase orders faster, but not fast enough that I can actually reduce my staffing level, then have I really saved any actual money?" This is often referred to as a "fingers and toes" benefit—saving a portion of a person's time but not enough to actually reduce the workload by a whole person. Some executives will embrace such productivity savings, but historically most will discard them as frivolous. You'll have to determine how your executives view such productivity benefits and proceed accordingly.

Chapter 18

Benefits Are Not Just Financial

Many project managers, when creating a business case, believe that the financial benefits are the only requirements necessary to gain executive approval. Based on past business cases, you could conclude that project managers believe if they build a decent spreadsheet, they will receive instant, even enthusiastic approval. Admittedly, financial justification is vital, and when a compelling case can be made solely on the basis of strong financial projections, the case is typically easier to sell, but there are many other supportable benefits that can bolster a business case that are not financially based.

The following four non-financial justification approaches, when properly documented and presented, can add rich credibility and salability to your business case. They are: strategic initiatives, operational efficiency, stakeholder value, and security, risk, and business continuity. Bear in mind that each of these non-financial categories also has the potential to be measured financially. Some executives will accept certain assumptions and permit these items to be included in financial calculations; however, since one of the main purposes of this book is to explain how to create a credible business case, I have elected to group these items under the non-financial category.

STRATEGIC INITIATIVES

Some projects must be done simply because the business is growing. Or maybe the competition has raised the bar and your company must upgrade its capabilities to simply remain competitive. Possibly your company has decided that now is the right time to expand globally. When thinking of strategic initiatives, consider these topics for inclusion—scalability (the business cannot grow as big as it needs to without upgrading its infrastructure); competitive positioning (we could lose market share or miss a key market window if we do not act upon this proposal); and high availability (our systems must be reliable and available 24 hours a day, 7 days a week, 365 days a year in order for us to maintain our competitive position or leapfrog our competitors). There are many more possible strategic topics. These are offered as a sample of potential discussion points to provoke your creative thinking. You can see how these topics might be hard to quantify, but you can also see how they can be quite compelling.

It is possible to quantify the value of building or adding these new capabilities. Frequently, though, such attempts depend upon the approval body agreeing to certain assumptions. Examples of such assumptions could be, "We will lose 5 percent of our business if we don't implement this project because our competitors will be better suited, and we'll fall behind." If this assumption is acceptable, you could quantify the benefit of implementing the project rather easily. Most executives, however, will question the validity of such an assumption because it is very difficult to prove such a thing. It would be reasonable, however, to state, "Our competitors have already adopted a similar initiative, and this places us at a competitive disadvantage in the marketplace. The longer we delay the more likely we are to lose business. How much business? That is not clear, but we will lose some business." That statement clearly conveys the value even though it does not quantify the value. And value statements should always be included in your business case when applicable.

I often share the following story when discussing strategic initiatives. The story involves a young couple. When they are young and childless, they buy a nice starter home that they can afford. They make improvements and enjoy the benefits of home ownership. In the passage of time they have their first child, and the house still seems adequate. However, the addition of a second child stresses their living space, and that stress often drives the couple to consider a larger home. We might call this a scalability issue—their family is growing, but their facility is not able to handle the growth. Accordingly, they select a larger home. The larger home is likely more expensive, not only in terms of mortgage payments but also in terms of monthly utility bills—a larger home costs more to heat. So, is the deci-sion to buy a larger home based on the results of a cost-benefit analysis? Typically not. Sure, there may be the cursory discussions about how the larger home will appreciate and the additional money will not be wasted. But the larger home does not increase revenue or decrease costs; it simply permits expansion, or scalability.

OPERATIONAL EFFICIENCY

A large number of business books published in the past ten years have touted the need for organizations to become more efficient, or lean. Typically this message is packaged as a number of component steps such as:

- Simplify
- Standardize
- Empower
- Integrate
- Centralize

Taking these steps can improve an organization's efficiency, but it's important to use them in a credible manner. Efficiency benefits are often measured and computed as saving a certain number of minutes or hours per day per affected employee. Such improvements are then multiplied by the average hourly rate (plus appropriate fringe benefit costs) and the number of employees involved in the benefit (typically a department or business unit), which yields comically large numbers. The message is an extension of our earlier discussion of productivity benefits and often sounds like this, "If we adopt this automated time-entry approach, it will cut sixty minutes per week for all of our employees, and since they earn an average of $35 per hour and since there are 15,000 employees at that facility, our proposal will save $2.1 million per year." Some organizations will accept this logic, but most will not. Most organizations will accept a benefit if there are actual, measurable reductions in expenses. This exam-ple will not reduce payroll costs by $2.1 million. The hour that these employees save will simply be allocated to other work. That reallocation is a valid benefit, but since credibility is our goal, it should not be carelessly inserted into the financial portion of the business case without much more concrete justification.

STAKEHOLDER VALUE

Stakeholder benefits are a little tricky. Benefits in this category have value to an individual stakeholder, but not to the enterprise as a whole. An example would be implementing an expensive new email marketing system simply to reduce the cost of postage. If the only benefit is the reduction of postage costs for a single department without a sizable increase in revenue from better marketing campaigns, then only the expense budget of that one department benefits from the cost of an expensive implementation. You could think of these benefits as annoyance or headache benefits. It is also possible that you could debate whether these benefits should more correctly be categorized as operational efficiency benefits. That's a case-by-case debate. Typically, these benefits are recorded when a stakeholder proclaims, "If I could solve this problem, it would really help me." The goal would be to work with the stakeholder to quantify and dollarize those benefits so that you could move them from this category into the more beneficial financial category. But some stakeholders are not willing to commit to specific numbers. We'll cover this more in our discussion of negotiated benefits in chapter 44, "The Delicate Act of Gaining Commitment," but as more organizations move toward incentive compensation models and as those organizations link the achievement of specific objectives to the payment of specific bonus amounts, many participants are reluctant to agree to specific benefit targets. These stakeholders will often be vocal in their assertion that this benefit is real and valuable, but will stop short of allowing you to actually dollarize the benefit for fear that achieving that specific new target will affect the incentive portion of their compensation. When this occurs, simply record the benefit, as best you can, in this section without the dollar targets.

SECURITY, RISK, AND BUSINESS CONTINUITY

Sarbanes-Oxley, the Gramm-Leach-Bliley Act, Federal Rules of Civil Procedure, Rules 26 and 34 for Records Management, FACTA, HIPAA, and other regulatory pronouncements carry very stiff fines and penalties when organizations are found to be out of compliance. Malicious intruders can hack into systems and steal personally identifiable information or corporate intellectual property. The potential threats facing today's organizations are real, frightening, and getting worse.

Your proposed project may do a lot to mitigate these risks and bolster an organization's ability to stave off threats and maintain operating continuity. How do you assign a value to that? Much as we discussed above, you would have to make assumptions about the cost or adverse impact of such a breach. If you have experience with breaches, or if your organization was recently cited and fined for a compliance violation, you have a credible, measurable, tangible benefit to present. If your company has not suffered such a breach, it may be very difficult to gain agreement on the potential adverse financial impact. All of the executives might agree that a breach would be costly, but they might not agree on just what the associated cost would be. Without verifiable financial numbers, any such benefits would then fall into one of these non-financial categories.

The table below summarizes the financial and non-financial justification approaches.

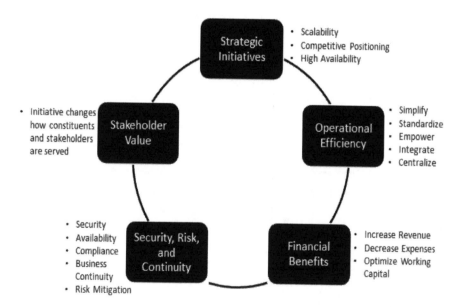

Chapter 19

Justifying Emerging Technology

Most of this book is devoted to projects that fit nicely into traditional accounting and financial categories. Such topics as improving inventory turnover, reducing overtime, increasing revenues, and cutting expenses are well covered in this book. Emerging technologies, though not called out specifically, need to be viewed through the same lens.

At the time of this writing, there are many emerging technologies that companies are evaluating on an enterprise scale. What should they do about mobility solutions (smartphones, tablets, etc.)? What should they do about social media (Facebook, Twitter, YouTube, LinkedIn)? Or cloud computing? Or advanced security considerations? These four are currently the focus of much attention, but there will always be new technologies on the horizon that will challenge corporate project leaders. At one time email was an emerging technology (seems like a long time ago!)

Advanced technologies are another business case challenge. How do you justify advanced technologies such as improved database technologies, business intelligence, middleware, and other cutting-edge

> From a business case perspective, integrating emerging or advanced technologies is really no different from constructing a new building. Any capital project requires justification. To successfully justify a capital project, you need to align your proposal with the common financial criteria.

investments? You justify them the same way you would any other capital project.

Keep in mind that, from a business case perspective, integrating emerging or advanced technologies is really no different from constructing a new building. Any capital project requires justification. To successfully justify a capital project, you need to align your proposal with the common financial criteria mentioned in the previous chapters.

To ensure that you align these proposals with the right financial categories, ask yourself these questions:

- Does my proposed project potentially increase revenue? If so, how?
- Does my proposed project potentially decrease expenses? If so, how?
- Does my proposed project potentially optimize assets? If so, how?
- Does my proposed project potentially improve productivity? If so, how?
- Does my proposed project potentially mitigate risk? If so, how?

If your project cannot be positioned to achieve any of these objectives, why would executives approve it? The simple answer is that they would not. Refer to the diagram of the DuPont model in chapter 16, "Determine the Project Drivers." All benefits should be able to line up with that diagram. You see, there is no magic justification method for emerging or advanced technologies. The burden rests with you, the business case developer. You must prepare a credible and compelling business case for your proposal. You must align your proposal with the customary financial considerations necessary for any capital project. Your proposal will ultimately request resources in the form of investment capital, staff, materials, and facilities. Your proposal will be evaluated against other, completely unrelated proposals for the use of those scarce capital funds. The better job you do in aligning your proposal with one or more of these key financial considerations, the more likely your proposal will advance to approval.

Chapter 20

Elevate Your Game
with Research

You have now been introduced to the value of creating a compelling hypothesis and the many considerations that contribute to a good one. You have also been introduced to the concept of aligning your hypothesis with key business financial documents—the balance sheet and income statement. Now let's explore another tool for aiding in the creation of a compelling hypothesis—business research. For the investment of a few hours, you'll receive the very rich rewards that come from potentially changing your status from that of a common employee to being a strategic business thinker. You have read about the need to identify potential business pain points. This chapter is devoted to walking you through basic business research that you can do before your first project discussions with your manager or the larger project team. If you weren't able to do this research before you started your project, don't worry. The information that you will gain during the research process will be valuable at any time during your business case efforts. This research approach will also yield dividends for you in the Evidence section, but we'll address those then.

Creating a compelling hypothesis requires an investment of time. It might take you two hours or it might take you twenty hours. The investment of time is required because you are going to do some research, followed by some analysis. This research will present you with numerous potential data points. The challenge is to sift through all of the data and to isolate the nuggets that can be used in your hypothesis. Remember this: not all data help you advance your hypothesis. Some data are merely data and must be set aside, at least for the purposes of your business case. Deciding which data contribute to your hypothesis and which data detract from it is part of the routine challenge of research. This is one of the areas where developing your business case requires more art than science.

I have chosen to narrate this chapter and the next as though I were teaching you in a class setting, using a case study. And just as though this were a class, these chapters will include my thoughts and musings as I progress through my research and learn what does and does not work in the case study. I have chosen to present you with an example from a consumer products manufacturing company. The approach that you'll learn will work for any business (e.g., manufacturing company, retail store, restaurant chain, financial institution, even a hospital or a government agency). In my example, I have chosen not to present a scrubbed and tidy version, but rather an example that walks you through just what you might find in a real-life scenario. I have chosen to include all of the decision points rather than provide you with a streamlined version so that you can follow my thought processes for this exercise. So, using this case study, we're going to see what, if any, hypotheses emerge when we look at a particular company.

Before we begin looking at the case study, let's consider the purpose of research, as well as some of the steps you might take in conducting it. When you begin to do research, your goal is quite simple: to collect data about your company and relevant peers or competitors. You can choose as many or as few competitors for this comparative analysis as you wish. For our case study, we will choose three. Before you begin, take a moment to identify three public companies that are in a similar industry to your own and, where possible, have annual sales revenue comparable to your own. If your company is a public company, this will be a rather straightforward exercise. US-based public companies are required to file their financial statements with the Securities and Exchange Commission (SEC). Most public companies make those filings available to the public on their corporate website.

Additionally, many public companies upload the audio portion of their quarterly earnings calls so that investors can also listen to them. I find earnings calls fascinating and enjoy listening to them because the listener gets to hear the executives in their own voice, complete with all of the passion or timidity that is absent from the written page. A typical earnings call lasts about an hour and is divided into two segments. The first segment is a prepared presentation by one or more of the senior executives. During this segment, executives share information about the most recently completed quarter, including sales performance, expense control, key sales wins, new acquisitions, and other interesting topics. Some companies will post the presentation notes on their website so that the listener can follow along as the financial data are discussed. This can be helpful because it is hard to follow columns of numbers without such an aid. The second segment of a typical earnings call is a standard question-and-answer session. During this segment, investment analysts are invited to ask questions of the executives. These questions are open ended. The topics might include stock repurchase considerations, asset disposal, planned acquisitions, launching of new products, and so forth. These calls can be very informative. To conduct a complete research effort, you should also listen to the earnings calls of your selected competitors.

If your company is privately or closely held, then public financial statements are likely not available and your approach to this research exercise will be slightly different. I encourage you to do all of the research that we will do below for your competitors and then seek to obtain financial statements from your own company's controller or vice president of finance. You can then plug those numbers into your spreadsheet and compare them against the competition.

Generally, we will not know whether your company is performing well or poorly by simply looking just at its data alone. We need to do parallel research into its primary and sometimes secondary competitors to determine whether the company is outperforming or underperforming in its market segment. Once the data are collected, we will need to analyze the data to determine where the company is underperforming (we will do much of that analysis in chapter 24, "Validating Your Hypothesis with External Evidence"). Generally speaking, it is easier to make the case that improvements are possible when your company underperforms and the case for improvements is tougher when your company already outperforms its competitors. Some opportunities always exist, but a company that is out ahead of its competition has likely already identified key issues and is already implementing strategies to be a market leader. Still, companies that outperform in some areas might underperform in others. And when we can identify areas in which they underperform, we might be able to position exciting new projects, assuming these projects can be shown to help boost their performance in those underperforming areas.

You might be asking yourself, "Why do I need to look for improvement opportunities? I already know that we're going to implement a new purchasing system." The reason that you'll want to do this research is to elevate your standing within the company and show yourself to be one who looks for ways to improve the overall performance of the organization. Doing this level of research and discovery will demonstrate that you look to address issues of strategic importance, not just tactical challenges. Since the company seems pre-disposed to spend some money to improve the purchasing function, consider reaching out to your colleagues in adjacent business functions such as inventory, manufacturing, and finance to see what opportunities might also exist in those areas. Possibly your project could be expanded to address challenges in those areas with only a little more effort. This is a much more strategic approach than to stay narrowly focused on just the obvious problem at hand. While each executive team views these challenges differently, most would prefer to address challenges from a broader, strategic perspective than with just a narrow—and possibly disconnected—approach of doing things piecemeal. This research approach will help you see the bigger picture that is confronting your executive team.

For our case study, we will look at a familiar consumer goods company. I am withholding their name because I don't want you to focus on the company; I want you to focus on the process. I have not personally worked with this company nor any of the companies listed as their competitors. That gives me some level of objectivity as I guide you through this exercise. For this exercise, we will use the publicly available financial data from their recent annual financial statements. Don't concern yourself thinking that the data might be stale. Financial analysis for this exercise is more about the process. The financial figures may change from year to year, but the process by which the analysis is done can be applied to any company at any time.

The first step in any analysis is to learn about the company. To find their main external website, I simply searched for the company's name via an Internet search and learned the URL of their corporate home page. From the website I can see that they separate their products into three product families, which are consumer, medical, and professional. When you do your own research, if you are not familiar with all that your company does, take the time to navigate all around the site and make notes about what you read. Typically, companies have an "About Us" section of their website that provides interesting background data. You may learn about new initiatives, new product announcements, or big sales wins where your sales team beat their competition. Just to remind you, you are on a journey of discovery. You don't know what you will find, and you don't yet know what conclusions to draw. Just begin the journey and take copious notes along the way. You may return to these notes and discover some real beneficial nuggets later. You may discover that previously unconnected dots now connect to tell a fascinating story.

Reviewing the website is interesting, but it's only part of what we need for our exercise. We need to find out what challenges the executives are facing and how the company is performing. To learn that information, I navigate their site until I find the "Investors" or "Investor Relations" link. On that page I will likely find great treasure. Here's what I'm looking for—webcasts (often under an "Events" or "Presentations" link), SEC filings and recent press releases. The first thing I will do is locate and download two documents—the most recent 10-K (which is only produced annually so it may be a bit outdated) and the most recent 10-Q. The 10-Q is the quarterly filing. The 10-Q is just like the 10-K except that it only shows the results for the most recent three-month period, or quarter.

Each publicly traded company is required to publish one annual 10-K and three quarterly 10-Q documents with the SEC. These documents, while tedious, are worthwhile reading. In every 10-K, you should read the first section, often titled "Part 1, Section 1, Business." This section tells you a lot about the business in general terms and then lays out specific risks facing the business and potential lawsuits in which they are engaged. This can be fascinating reading. To do the research thoroughly, you should read this section for your company and their main competitors. You should see similarities, but you should pay particular attention to the differences. Do they all mention the same risk factors, for example? If your company writes or omits something that is included or omitted from your competitors or peers, you should note it. Such a difference might be a worthwhile discussion point for your meeting with your executive sponsor. Such a conversation might go as follows. You could say, "I see that our company's 10-K states that the uncertainty of the supplier market creates a risk for our ability to meet demand, yet our competitors did not mention this. What disadvantages do we have that our competitors do not?" This could be the beginning of a rich conversation that could open new opportunities for improvement within your project's scope. It could also be that the other companies face the same risk but simply did not consider it worthy of a mention in their 10-K. Either way, doing the research gives you a piece of knowledge that might come in very handy in your discovery work. And thorough research will likely yield many such nuggets. You won't find them if you don't look for them. And it takes time and focus to find them. But the investment of your time pays big dividends as you begin to show yourself to be an employee who sees the bigger picture and wants to arm your company to compete effectively.

The 10-Q document is a quarterly filing that also has interesting information. About midway through the 10-Q, you'll find a section entitled "Management's Discussion and Analysis of Financial Condition and Results of Operations" or something similar. This section will explain what has happened over the past quarter that has either strengthened or weakened their financial condition. This is a great supplement to reading the 10-K because this will be much more up-to-date.

Press releases and trade publication articles are another great source of company information. A simple Internet search of your company and key executives frequently yields a rich catalogue of articles. Also searching investor websites (Motley Fool, Yahoo Finance, and investor.reuters. com, to name just three) often yields two big scores—research about the company and research about the industry. Search for your company's name and possibly the name of your president or CEO. You may find articles that also provide great data points for your business case. Subscription-based research services often offer richer analysis. Examples of subscription-based services include hoovers.com, onesource.com, morningstar.com, and valueline.com. Whether you use the free research tools or choose to subscribe, the investment of your time will always make you more prepared for your sponsor meeting and elevate you in the eyes of your management.

Through all of this research you are seeking information that confirms or expands your hypothesis. As my background is in management consulting, I look for data points that help me sell my services to a client. For example, if a company has recently acquired another business I suspect that they have several challenges such as integrating the business software from the acquired company into their own. There may be a number of security items involved with this acquisition such as getting password access, building access, and integrating personnel (and their respective personnel records) into the new company. There may also be layoffs as they consolidate functions and eliminate positions. There may be purchasing opportunities as they now seek to consolidate suppliers. The list goes on. We will continue our case study in the next chapter.

Chapter 21

Creating Your Sandbox

As you begin collecting data and begin some rough estimating, you will need a place to hold that data. I refer to that temporary spreadsheet/work area as my sandbox. It's not meant to be a formal, highly refined spreadsheet. It's meant to be a place where you can run some what-if calculations and ratios; where you can test your ideas about the data that you discover. You'll likely move select pieces of your data from your sandbox to your final presentation, but that happens later.

Many organizations use Microsoft Excel as their spreadsheet of choice. Excel is used in all of the examples in this book. For those wishing to explore alternatives to Excel, three free alternatives are available and they are Apache OpenOffice, LibreOffice, and GoogleDocs. OpenOffice is available for download at openoffice.org. LibreOffice is available for download at libreoffice.org. You can access GoogleDocs by going to docs. google.com.

Building the spreadsheet involves three key activities: collecting the data; calculating the ratios, key metrics and trends; and comparing the results against representative peer companies. Here's how I do this. I start with the most recent 10-K, which would be the most recent year-end SEC filing by the company. This document is frequently several hundred pages long and includes, among other things, the annual income statement and year-end balance sheet. As indicated previously, the income statement lists sales, expenses, and net income. The balance sheet shows the assets and liabilities of the company. In the first diagram below, you will see the data that I routinely collect. This is broken down easily by category in the 10-K.

Referring to the actual financial report, I then enter in four years' data (if four years are provided).

As I create business cases quite frequently, I have a standard spreadsheet that I use to capture the data. To get the data, I will review the published 10-K for the target company and will use their published numbers to fill in my spreadsheet.

Data From Financial Reports

Income Statement
Sales (Revenue)
Cost of Revenue
SG&A
Total Operating Expense
Operating Income
Income Before Tax
Net Income

Balance Sheet
Cash and Short-Term Investments
Accounts Receivable
Inventories
Total Current Assets
Total Assets
Accounts Payable
Total Current Liabilities
Total Debt
Total Liabilities
Total Equity

Employees

Trends are often just as important as individual moments in time. For that reason, consider entering in four years' data to help you see things over a four-year horizon. Looking only at the previous year may not be representative for either your target company or their competitors. Below, you can see the four-year financial data for our target example. All figures are shown in millions.

Data From Financial Reports	Current year	1 yr ago	2 yrs ago	3 yrs ago
Income Statement (in USD)				
Sales (Revenue)	$19,115.00	$19,415.00	$18,266.00	$16,746.90
Cost of Revenue	$12,695.00	$13,557.00	$12,562.00	$11,664.80
SG&A	$3,498.00	$3,291.00	$3,106.00	$2,948.30
Total Operating Expense	$16,290.00	$16,868.00	$15,650.00	$14,645.40
Operating Income	$2,825.00	$2,547.00	$2,616.00	$2,101.50
Income Before Tax	$2,576.00	$2,289.00	$2,318.00	$1,844.90
Net Income	$1,884.00	$1,690.00	$1,823.00	$1,499.50
Balance Sheet Items (in USD)				
Cash and Short-Term Investments	$798.00	$364.00	$472.70	$360.80
Accounts Receivable	$2,566.00	$2,492.00	$2,560.60	$2,336.70
Inventories	$2,033.00	$2,493.00	$2,443.80	$2,004.50
Total Current Assets	$5,864.00	$5,813.00	$6,069.60	$5,269.70
Total Assets	$19,209.00	$18,089.00	$18,439.70	$17,067.00
Accounts Payable	$1,920.00	$1,422.00	$1,449.00	$1,205.60
Total Current Liabilities	$4,923.00	$4,752.00	$4,928.60	$5,015.80
Total Debt	$9,715.00	$6,976.00	$6,496.40	$4,395.80
Total Liabilities	$12,467.00	$14,211.00	$13,126.00	$10,969.60
Total Equity	$5,406.00	$3,878.00	$5,223.70	$6,097.40
Employee Count	53,000			

There are basic relationships that I look for as I reflect on any company. I look to see if sales revenue is growing year over year. Our sample company, which I'll refer to as our "target company" had a sales decline from last year to this year. I also look at SG&A expenses. This expense category contains most of the discretionary spending (salaries for office workers, advertising, travel expense, and so on). I see that their SG&A expenses went up. I also look at operating income. It has increased from last year to this year. By themselves, these data points really don't tell us a complete story. I won't know the complete story until I analyze this information using some basic business measurements. All of the business calculations that I consider important are explained in detail in Appendix B. Until I build in some equations to show trends and percentages I won't really know much. Also, from these data alone I don't know how this company compares to its industry. Are they outperforming or underperforming against their peers? I won't know that until I build a similar spreadsheet for the peers and then see what story emerges.

Now I take the data and build four more small spreadsheets with the same headings, but now I build equations to evaluate key potential indicators—year-over-year performance, evaluation of costs as a percentage of revenue, working capital items, and key financial ratios. In my Excel spreadsheet, I simply build these analytical spreadsheets further down the same page as the initial raw data. Placing the data on the same page makes it much easier to drag and drop numbers for equations, rather than building completely separate files. The first example is year-over-year performance.

	Current year	1 yr ago	2 yrs ago
Income Statement (Y-O-Y Percentage)			
Revenues	-1.55%	6.29%	9.07%
Costs and Expenses			
Cost of Goods Sold	-6.36%	7.92%	7.69%
Sales, General and Administrative	6.29%	5.96%	5.35%
Operating	-3.43%	7.78%	6.86%
Total Costs and Expenses	-3.43%	7.78%	6.86%
Income from Operations	10.91%	-2.64%	24.48%

This is a quick snapshot of our target company's performance. You'll notice that revenues declined from last year to this year by 1.55 percent. On the surface, that's a disappointing result. Likewise, we see that SG&A expenses increased 6.29 percent. So, sales went down and expenses went up. Not good. If we stopped here, we might think this is a bleak picture. Reading further, we see that this may not be a bleak picture after all. Cost of Goods Sold (COGS) declined 6.36 percent. As a percentage, it appears as though this decline is barely enough to offset the increase in SG&A expense. But if you look at the raw numbers from the previous spreadsheet, you see that while SG&A expense increased by $207 million, COGS (which typically includes costs related to manufacturing) has declined by $862 million. This difference is what produces the favorable change in operating income (here called income from operations). Operating income increased 10.91 percent, or $278 million from last year to this year.

What can we infer from this example? Well, it looks like the company is doing a good job of reining in the cost of manufacturing but could do better at controlling the discretionary costs in the SG&A category. So, if our project is aimed at the SG&A area, we have new information to bolster our hypothesis. But what if we are pursuing a manufacturing solution and the data shows that the company is already doing great things there? One suggestion is to capitalize on the initiatives that might already exist. The company has shown skill in reducing costs in manufacturing. That suggests (though it does not confirm) that they have previously examined those costs and have found some waste or other items that can be done for less money. Quite possibly, a solution in this area might accelerate those savings and add more to them. This is important because any real, sustained improvement requires multiple forces—forces such as improvements in processes (what some consultants call workflow) and the use of advanced technologies. It is possible that neither has been fully exploited. Could there be additional savings if new, more efficient technologies were deployed? Possibly. Could there be additional savings if the processes and procedures were further evaluated for efficiency, say with a lean manufacturing or Six Sigma initiative? Possibly.

The point here is that you should not presuppose an answer just because the data suggest a high-performing or low-performing financial result. You will need a different approach when your company is already performing at a high level than when it is performing at an underperforming level. When evaluating a high-performing company, I seek to understand the method by which they perform well. Some companies have made efficiency a high priority. They have invested time and money to eliminate wasted steps and optimize their workflows. Other high-performing companies have achieved their success through sheer manpower. Their approach is to muscle their way through inefficiency with more people. Both companies may have strong financial statements, but the first one is more likely to have a sustainable model. The second company has the potential to burn its people out, thus causing low employee morale, turnover, and likely weakening financial performance down the road.

The next spreadsheet that I build will help me evaluate costs as a percentage of revenue. It looks like the example below.

Sales and Costs	Current year	1 yr ago	2 yrs ago	3 yrs ago
Sales Growth	-1.55%	6.29%	9.07%	n/a
SG&A as a Percent of Sales	18.30%	16.95%	17.00%	17.61%
Cost of Sales as a Percent of Sales	66.41%	69.83%	68.77%	69.65%
COGS+SG&A as a Percent of Sales	84.71%	86.78%	85.78%	87.26%
SG&A Growth	6.29%	5.96%	5.35%	
Delta of Sales growth vs. SG&A growth	-7.84%	0.33%	3.72%	
Income from Operations (as a percent)	14.78%	13.12%	14.32%	12.55%

We would love to see that our company has had an uninterrupted string of sales growth, year over year. Unfortunately, we see that in the current year the company's sales fell by 1.55 percent when compared to the previous year. This could be a reflection of national or global economic challenges. When we build our peer comparison (in the Evidence section), we'll see whether or not other, similar companies had sales falloff or if it was just our company. It is important to consider that one company's numbers do not tell a complete story. Once we compare our company to its peers, we can see a much better picture unfold. And it is that broader picture that helps add additional credibility to our business case.

Let's look a little closer at costs. To be profitable, a company strives to spend less than it makes in revenue. Most companies devote some effort (many devote much effort) to containing costs, even striving to reduce costs year over year even as the business grows. For that reason, most businesses keep track of what percentage of their revenue they allocate to expenses. But when you begin to compare one company against another it can get a little murky. Consider the following explanation. Domestic and international financial accounting standards boards stipulate much of how a business accounts for its financial performance. Yet, even with all of their standards and oversight, much is left to the discretion of each individual business. For example, the cost of utilities (gas, electric, water, sewer, and waste disposal) can be a large number, especially for manufacturing companies. It takes a lot of electricity to power a large manufacturing plant. Some companies account for utilities as one item in their SG&A category, choosing to lump all utilities into a single bucket. Other companies choose to separate utility expenses for office facilities from manufacturing facilities. You must understand that either choice is acceptable. As you can imagine, then, a company that lumps all utilities into SG&A would likely appear to spend a higher percentage of their revenue on discretionary expenses compared to a company that separates out their factory utilities and accounts for them by placing them in the category called cost of goods sold, or COGS. The second company would then appear to spend a higher percentage of its sales on manufacturing costs compared to the first company.

The larger point is this: individual categories may not be uniform across companies. What is uniform, though, are the top and bottom lines. The calculation for revenue from operations is quite consistent across all companies, as is the calculation for operating income. The bottom entry in the above spreadsheet shows income from operations as a percent of sales. Whether a company is a million dollar company or a multi-billion dollar company, we can typically compare them on this metric since it filters out all of the options for categorization and leaves us with a simple result: revenue minus expenses equals operating income. That doesn't mean that we should forgo measuring the percentage of sales devoted to these expense categories. And when comparing an individual company against itself over a period of years, we could expect it to have accounted for its own expenses similarly each year. So, these measurements are worthwhile, even with their known limitations.

The third spreadsheet that I prepare highlights the working capital items. Working capital is one of the asset subsections of the balance sheet. A company has assets. Those assets generally get classified into short-term and long-term assets. Working capital refers to the short-term assets, or those assets that can be most easily converted to cash. One very common and powerful business metric is the cash conversion cycle. This is explained in detail in Appendix B. The cash conversion cycle computes the time it takes a business to convert its purchases into cash. There are three components to the cash conversion cycle: days in inventory (DII), days sales outstanding (DSO), and days payable outstanding (DPO). Each of these three components are also explained in detail in Appendix B. The table below shows how our target company performs in the working capital area.

Working Capital Items	Current year	1 yr ago	2 yrs ago	3 yrs ago
Days in Inventory	58.45	67.12	71.01	62.72
Days Sales Outstanding	49.00	46.85	51.17	50.93
Days Payable Outstanding	55.20	38.29	42.10	37.72
Cash Conversion Cycle (in days)	52.25	75.68	80.07	75.93

For manufacturing, distribution, and retail companies, the cash conversion cycle is frequently a major focus area. Days in inventory computes the time from purchase of raw material until the item is sold and shipped (basically the time to convert raw materials into manufactured finished products that are sold to the customer). For this reason, fewer days would be better because it would mean that the company had converted its purchased materials into sold, shipped products. Days sales outstanding computes the time from the creation of a customer invoice (typically the same day as the item is shipped) until payment is received in full for that invoice. Like days in inventory, fewer days are better because it means that the company's cash is collected from the customer sooner. The third element, days payable outstanding, computes the time from receipt of a supplier's invoice until the supplier's invoice is paid in full. For this element, more days are better because it means that the company has been able to hold onto its cash longer. There is an obvious balancing act because while the company seeks to retain its cash as long as possible, it does not want to risk injuring its relationship with key suppliers by taking too long to pay.

With that as background information, here is the real value of understanding this financial measurement. The value of a one-day improvement is remarkable, especially in larger companies. Using our target company as our example, a one-day improvement in days in inventory would represent a one-time balance sheet improvement of $34.7 million (a complete description of this calculation is provided in Appendix B.) Furthermore, a one-day improvement in the cash collection cycle (days sales outstanding) would yield a one-time balance sheet improvement of $52.3 million. Finally a one-day extension in payment terms (to boost days payable outstanding by one day) would yield a one-time balance sheet improvement of $34.7 million. If one-day improvements were achieved in each of those categories, the potential benefit would yield a one-time balance sheet improvement of over $120 million. You can see why this area would warrant a lot of attention from company executives.

The fourth spreadsheet that I build is the key financial ratio spreadsheet. Many companies rely on financial ratios as a benchmark for their performance. While I find this more common in financial services companies like banks and insurance companies, it is still useful for other business segments. The key financial ratio spreadsheet looks like the example below.

Key Financial Ratios	Current year	1 yr ago	2 yrs ago	3 yrs ago
Asset Turnover	1.02	1.06	1.03	1.96
Return on Sales	13.48%	11.79%	12.69%	11.02%
Return on Assets	10.10%	9.25%	10.27%	17.57%
Return on Equity	40.59%	37.14%	32.21%	49.18%
Return on Capital Employed	19.77%	19.10%	19.36%	17.44%
Debt to Equity	1.19	1.80	1.24	0.72
Quick Ratio	0.68	0.60	0.62	0.54

The key financial ratios are interesting, but unlike the working capital items, they themselves cannot be manipulated. These ratios are the result of other components being manipulated, and these ratios are the by-product of those actions. For example, return on sales is computed as annual net income divided by annual sales. Annual net income is computed by subtracting all expenses from annual sales. So, to manipulate return on sales, the company must actually increase sales or reduce expenses. Still, many companies compare themselves against their past and against their peers using the common key financial ratios.

My final spreadsheet looks at efficiency metrics. These are only available for the current year as these measurements depend on year-end headcount, and very few companies provide a history of headcount statistics. This information will be used to compare the efficiency of the target company with the efficiency of its peers for the current year.

Efficiency Metrics	Current year
Revenue per Employee	$360,660
Operating Income per Employee	$53,302

These two measurements are interesting and create another potential story line. These are easily computed—divide the number of employees into total revenue and into operating income. When you review these figures, and compare them against those of the three chosen peers, you might be able to make the case that your company has too many employees. Please note that use of this metric must be handled tactfully. If handled poorly, this metric can be incendiary and create friction within the company. If you know that your company is seeking to reduce the workforce as part of your project, this metric can support the view that fewer employees would make the company leaner. You could assert that boosting revenue or operating income would have the same effect—making this metric highlight improvements in corporate efficiency. That's true, but most readers of your business case will see this as a justification for reductions in staffing. You will see, in the Evidence section, how to tactfully discuss and position your hypothesis using this metric.

And so there you have a quick presentation of my sandbox and how I use the research data to begin to form my business case. Within this quick stack of data we find numerous potential benefit topics that can add to the professionalism of our hypothesis. We've covered a lot in this section. Applying these principles and guidelines will help you create a strong, viable hypothesis for your business case.

If you're not convinced of the purpose or value of collecting and analyzing the financial statements, just stay with it. In the Evidence section we will explore external evidence. As we explore external evidence, we'll look again at this target company, comparing it to three of its peers by using their financial statements. That exercise should provide you with a deeper level of clarity and confidence that this approach will enrich your business case.

Which brings us to the next section, Evidence. In the Evidence section we will search for evidence that confirms our hypothesis. We will search both internal and external sources to make our business case as credible and thorough as we can. We are on the journey to building our compelling story.

Chapter 22

Section Two Summary

Your project can only begin if there is a tangible business problem that must be solved. The hypothesis is a statement that theorizes that a problem exists and that there is value in addressing it. A carefully worded, thoughtful hypothesis can often spark interest outside of the original, requesting department, thereby granting you access to key executives in other areas. Such access can expand your investigation, which frequently leads to the discovery of additional opportunities for your solutions.

Each new project is driven both by a business pain and a business measurement. Aligning the project with traditional financial statements allows you to present your very technical solution to non-technical financial personnel. The DuPont model is a very effective communication tool for highlighting the alignment of your benefits to the specific traditional financial measurements employed by your client.

There are four common financial benefit categories. Those categories are top line revenue improvement, expense reduction, working capital optimization, and productivity improvements. In addition to these financial benefit categories, there are four non-financial benefit categories that can also enhance your business case. The four non-financial categories are strategic initiatives, operational efficiency, stakeholder value and security, risk and business continuity. Each of these non-financial categories can be quantified and dollarized, but frequently they are only narrated, and not computed, because they are difficult to quantify—and because often the quantification methods introduce more questions than they resolve. Such challenges can injure the credibility of the business case, which is why there is rarely an attempt to quantify these components.

Investing a few hours in focused business research can give you great insight into your business and can often reveal potential hypotheses for your business case. Building a working sandbox can make raw, boring data pop with rich headlines and typically leads to an even stronger hypothesis.

SECTION THREE
Exploring For Evidence

Chapter 23

A Basic Discovery Primer

Congratulations! You have drafted a hypothesis that suggests a business problem exists and that there is some perceived value to solving it. This section will walk you through the necessary steps to identify and develop tangible statements of value that you can incorporate in your business case. Building a credible story that demonstrates that the perceived value is realistic and achievable is one of the challenges of creating a business case. In his excellent sales book, *SPIN Selling*, Neil Rackham writes, "As the size of the sale increases, successful salespeople must build up the perceived value of their products or services. The building of perceived value is possibly the single biggest selling skill required for large, complex sales" (pg. 8). Rackham rightly calls this a selling skill because the value proposition is not intuitive to everyone. Many of your executives will have to be sold on the idea that your proposal provides value in excess of its costs.

In their book, *Selling to the C-Suite,* Nicholas A. C. Read and Stephen J. Bistritz state: "It's impossible to write a value proposition unless you know what to propose, and to get at this information, you must convince the prospect to disclose something about how her business operates, where the dysfunction and costs reside, and what her vision is for an alternative. You then map your capabilities onto her requirements and return to the prospect with a specific plan that proposes a way for her to solve her problem or achieve her vision by using your capabilities" (pg. 130). What Read and Bistritz call "convincing the prospect to disclose something" is done through a series of organized interviews and workshops. This section is devoted to explaining some of the most productive techniques for collecting evidence using interviews and workshops.

> Building a business case with the expectation of gaining approval for a capital funding proposal is a selling activity.

Remember, building a business case with the expectation of gaining approval for a capital funding proposal is a selling activity. In order to identify and present that perceived value, you must supplement your hunches with solid evidence that supports your project's hypothesis. You must seek to collect evidence from internal and external sources. Your ability to collect the right evidence is influenced by your ability to tactfully and skillfully request, gather, and organize information. Developing and mastering that skill is necessary when you work with large, complex projects.

I must emphasize that the collection of evidence and the analysis of that evidence often happen simultaneously. For purposes of this book, though, these two activities are addressed separately to provide ample coverage for each topic individually.

Your goal for these two stages (collecting evidence and analyzing evidence) is to achieve three specific objectives:

- Validate your hypothesis
- Demonstrate that solving this problem aligns with key organizational goals
- Show that your solution returns a higher value than it costs,

Many business case developers want to demonstrate their knowledge and expertise about certain topics. This can manifest itself in several ways. First-time business case developers are often quick to jump to an instant conclusion when they hear of a potential business problem. They might hear a fellow manager say, "We have too much inventory." Immediately—often because they believe they need to assert that they have expertise in a certain area—they jump right on that statement and attempt to offer solutions that solve that isolated problem. This can be interpreted as a lack of maturity and skill. Consider this hypothetical example. Imagine that you walk into a doctor's office and say, "I'm having acute pain in my knee." Imagine, then, that the doctor makes an immediate snap judgment, saying, "Great, we can get you into surgery tomorrow and we can replace your knee with a new composite prosthetic knee joint." Now imagine that you only bruised your knee and that the right therapy would be to elevate the knee for a few hours, take a couple of aspirin, and apply ice every twenty minutes. Obviously you would question the thoroughness of the doctor who jumped right to an invasive surgical solution before understanding all of the considerations surrounding your sore knee. Likewise, you must show restraint and not jump to conclusions before you explore all of the symptoms associated with a business problem. The symptoms may point to excess inventory, but the root cause might actually be in another area of the business altogether, such as inefficient logistics or poorly managed warehouse practices. So, before you jump headlong into an incomplete recommendation, take a few moments and plan for a productive, objective evidence-gathering activity.

With this in mind, this section is intended to guide you through those objectives by gathering evidence using a process called discovery. In this chapter, we'll start with an overview of five topics:

- Validate your hypothesis
- Align your hypothesis with corporate goals
- Organize yourself for success
- Confirm the project's beneficiaries
- Understand the common discovery methods

VALIDATE YOUR HYPOTHESIS

One of the first things that you must confirm is that the hypothesis is valid and reasonable. Confirming your hypothesis requires you to engage in dialogue with managers and staff in the affected business areas and press them for specific pain points that they believe demonstrate that this problem warrants a solution that you might propose. A helpful perspective for the concept of "any affected business area" is to include your primary focus area plus those areas that provide inputs to your chosen area and any areas that receive outputs from your primary business area.

Consider the following diagram:

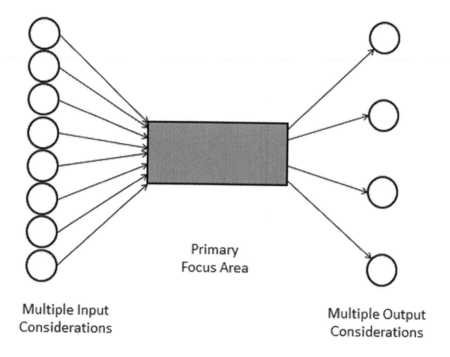

Primary
Focus Area

Multiple Input
Considerations

Multiple Output
Considerations

This diagram seeks to highlight the interaction between business areas. If your primary focus relates to a factory performance issue, you should include business processes that provide data to the factory (input considerations) and business processes that receive data from the factory (output considerations). For example, you might include sales as an input consideration, since sales creates demand for the factory to make something. You might also look at purchasing as an input consideration because they buy the materials that are used in production. And you might look at finance as an output consideration because they account for the costs and profit of manufacturing the products. You could add purchasing to the output consideration list too, if product quality indicates that inferior materials are causing some of the factory problems. Simply focusing on just the factory, without regard to the incoming and outgoing processes, may, therefore, provide you with an incomplete and narrow view of the true challenge that needs attention. We'll explore this more, later, when we cover the group workshop discussions in chapter 30, "Collecting Evidence Using Group Workshops."

ALIGN YOUR HYPOTHESIS WITH CORPORATE GOALS

Earlier, in chapter 8, you were introduced to the three universal considerations. In addition to ensuring that all projects align with those three universal considerations, all projects must also align with the organization's contemporary goals and objectives. Contemporary goals and objectives can change over time. Your company's goals and objectives might change because the company has just come through an aggressive acquisition spree, which may create a need to assimilate and integrate all of the new organizations while aggressively seeking cost reductions. Or the company may have new executive leadership, and that new team might have declared certain new objectives as the focus for the next two years. Whatever the case, you need to determine what the current goals and objectives are, and you must strive to align your solution to the achievement of those goals. One of the best times to determine or confirm the current corporate goals is during your individual interviews with key line-of-business executives. If you can't seem to get a definitive list of current corporate goals, you can always fall back on the DuPont Model. It is a great starting point for executive discussions. All businesses seek to increase revenue, reduce expenses, optimize assets, and mitigate risk.

ORGANIZE YOURSELF FOR SUCCESS

The discovery process requires the collection of a large volume of notes and reference documents. This process is best compared to mining for gold. Gold mining is difficult. It requires the removal of a lot of earth, then sifting through the dirt and rocks to uncover some gold. Sometimes the miner's work yields a handful of gold, and sometimes it yields a truckload. It is unreasonable to embark on a gold mining venture and expect to only find gold. To leave the site with gold, the miner must do the hard work of first digging through tons and tons of earth and then sifting it to reveal the treasure. The same is true for your business case discovery efforts. You should adjust your expectations accordingly. Your interviews and workshops will provide you with much more data than you ultimately need. And once the data are collected, you'll have to spend some time sifting through all of the data to determine which pieces are the irrelevant dirt and which pieces are the true gold. And because you're going to be collecting a lot of information, you should determine, in advance, just how you will organize all of this information.

The discussion of organization would not be complete without a discussion of your note-taking methods. Do you write things out in a binder or journal? Or do you type directly on your laptop during meetings? There is no single, universally preferred method. The best method is the one that enables you to capture as much of the dialogue and discussion as possible. Any method that you find comfortable—and thorough—is the right method. Additionally, you'll likely collect documents during your discovery sessions. For example, you might collect diagrams of business processes or flowcharts detailing the approval workflow. How will you catalog those collected pieces of evidence? If you are working alone, you can collect them all in a three-ring binder or a series of manila folders. If you are working as part of a team, you must determine how you will share and collaborate. Do you have access to a scanner? Scanning the documents, though time-consuming, ensures that you can preserve them electronically and share them with others as the needs arise. How will you share these documents? Does your company have a file-sharing capability on the company intranet? If so, you can post these documents in a secure folder and make them available to your team. If not, you will need to establish a manual procedure for sharing documents via email or USB thumb drives. Furthermore, if you are working as a team and you divide your interview and workshop sessions between team members, collaboration is vital to your success as scheduling conflicts will likely keep you from personally attending each interview session or workshop. You should spend a few moments considering how you will collaborate with your team and how each team member will archive their evidence for future use.

Just as important as your approach to organization is your approach to overall meeting preparedness. As you consider various information-gathering techniques and their effectiveness, keep this in mind—the caliber of your questions will determine the caliber of the contributor's answers. If you invest the time to prepare insightful, well-crafted questions, your interviewees and workshop participants will observe that you take this task seriously and will most likely engage with you in a way that is beneficial to your assignment. But if you neglect the planning and don't prepare thoughtful questions, you risk appearing unprepared and possibly even incompetent. If that happens, you will have compromised your credibility and may find it hard to enlist support or receive acceptances to your interview requests. Planning and personal organization will help you present an organized and professional image of yourself and your business case efforts.

CONFIRM THE PROJECT'S BENEFICIARIES

You need to prepare a list of potential interview and workshop participants. As you create this list, you should consider ways to expand beyond your initial area of focus and branch out into other departments and other divisions (refer back to the Input-Output diagram earlier in this chapter). To do that, you might need to educate your sponsor that building a business case often requires consensus and multidepartment support. (Remember, if the sponsor could write the check for the project herself, without further executive approval, why would she commit to creating a business case? But if she cannot fund this out of her own departmental budget, she's going to need other executives to affirm the need for this project; that is why you need to include these individuals—each with their own sphere of influence—in your business case.) Seek to determine which departments or divisions stand to benefit the most from your proposal.

This next point may not be on your radar, but you should also seek to understand which constituencies, if any, might be adversely impacted if your recommendation is adopted. Their input would prove helpful, as they could undermine the ease with which your project gains approval. Analyzing all interested parties, both advocates and adversaries, will help you create a prospective participant list for your upcoming discovery sessions.

UNDERSTAND THE COMMON DISCOVERY METHODS

Collecting evidence would be easy if you could simply circulate a list of questions to a few prospective project participants asking them to comment on the necessity for your project. And it would be great if they would thoroughly and honestly answer your questions and even provide you with their concise analysis of all real or imagined benefits. It doesn't work that way. You have to go exploring. Within your potential pool of participants you may encounter a variety of personality types and conflicting agendas. Some people will gladly give you helpful information, others will resist your requests for information, others may not have relevant information but will gladly take your time and distract you by volunteering their opinion—and some might be downright rude. This is another example where the business case requires more art than science. You will have to become effective at dealing with various discovery situations in order to collect the necessary data.

Let me illustrate this point using a common hobby—photography. In photography, what you see and how you see it depends on the lens through which you view your subject. Additionally, the resultant photograph can also be affected by placing specialized filters on the end of your lens. Different filters mounted on the same lens can produce very different results. Each filter creates art in a special way. Diffusing filters make harsh, contrasting objects appear softer. Green or red filters enhance or mask certain colors when used in black-and-white photography. This same perspective can be applied to business cases. When we begin a business case, it is appropriate to look at each business issue through a variety of lenses. We'll want the wide view to ensure that we grasp the context of the issue. We'll also want a close-up lens as we delve into specific details of a potential benefit. Furthermore, we need to be careful about placing filters on our perspective. It is enticing to seek out only those individuals who agree with our hypothesis. But such an approach filters the answer. As noted above, we need to solicit input from both agreeable and select disagreeable sources. You might think that inviting the disagreeable sources to participate is akin to opening Pandora's box. The problem is a little more complicated than that. If you selectively omit comments from those with dissenting opinions, they may elect to withhold their support from you when the approvals are requested. They can easily approach their managers and say that they were excluded from the interviews or workshops. Admittedly, this sounds juvenile, but it happens frequently when people are excluded from the discovery activity simply because they don't agree with the hypothesis or don't openly support your project. Therefore, be careful not to apply filters to your discovery, whether intentionally or unintentionally.

> You have to interview a lot of people because it is rare that one person will have all of the information that you need to support your business case.

The discovery process is similar to the discovery process that attorneys use to gather evidence before a trial. You have to interview a lot of people because it is rare that one person will have all of the information that you need to support your business case. One notable difference between the attorneys we see on television dramas and our approach is simple—we are not trying to uncover secrets or trick someone into sharing things they would prefer not to share. We are exploring for observable, verifiable evidence that confirms our hypothesis. We are exploring for evidence that the interviewees will willingly share. It is possible, even likely, that two different people will offer different perspectives about the same topic. For example, if you wish to understand why a new solution is desirable, you might get different and even contradictory opinions. This can provide a beneficial forum for the exchange of ideas.

Over the next several chapters we will dig deeper into actual discovery methods. Here we are going to introduce the three basic data collection methods: workshops, interviews, and questionnaires. In the workshop setting, we can gain a lot of insight by introducing common pain points and letting the group debate their severity, or even their merits, with us in the room.

Gathering relevant evidence is critical to creating a credible, compelling business case. Stating that you think there is a problem (or opportunity, if you prefer that term) frequently evokes the following response: "What makes you think that?" Skeptics will often add, "Don't you think you're exaggerating this, just a little?" Without evidence, it is more difficult to confirm your hypothesis, to prove that a problem exists and that it requires the attention you recommend. You may wish to consider an additional resource, *Let's Get Real or Let's Not Play*, by Mahan Khalsa and Randy Illig. This book offers an excellent and thorough approach to discovery. Though the book was written for sales professionals, we can apply its recommendations in our quest for information that we can use to build a credible, professional business case. Khalsa and Illig's book is available online from www.franklincovey.com.

The most time-consuming method by which you will gather information will be through question-and-answer interviews and group workshops. Engaging in these two types of discovery can be either highly productive or highly frustrating. That will depend on both the quality of your preparation and the willingness and knowledge of your participants. You can't control the participants' knowledge or willingness, but you are in complete control of the quality of your preparation. As noted above in the section

"Organize Yourself for Success," it is paramount that you know what questions to ask before you begin your discovery activities. In chapter 28 you'll learn about high-yield questions. That chapter will give you many suggestions that will enrich your discovery activity and produce meaningful results for you.

> Your interviews will be the most productive when you've done your homework in advance and come to the interview with a list of reasonable, relevant questions.

The interview format is excellent for drawing out individual contributors and hearing individual concerns. The interview format is typically the only way that you'll get to hear executive comments. Executives rarely attend two-hour workshops, but they often permit brief individual interviews (twenty to thirty minutes is often all the time you can get on their busy calendars). Your interviews will be the most productive when you've done your homework in advance and come to the interview with a list of reasonable, relevant questions. Common consultant-speak questions such as "Tell me what keeps you up at night" suggest laziness and a lack of planning. Instead of that question, you might start with a focused question regarding your project, such as "We are talking to the executive team regarding a potential project for cost containment. We think that this project can save the company a fair amount of money. Just how much we'll save will be explored in some upcoming workshops. From your perspective, which areas do you believe contribute most to the struggle to contain costs?" A good follow-up question to this would be, "If you were responsible for tackling this challenge, where would you look first, and why?" If the initial responses are brief, you might ask a probing follow-up question, such as "Can you elaborate?" to draw out more information. This approach helps set your conversation on the desired track and keeps you from wandering too far away from your primary objective—validating your hypothesis and seeking to identify the value of solving the stated business problem. We'll explore this topic further in the chapter 28 titled "Elevate Your Game with High-Yield Questions".

The group workshop format is often very educational for you, as the leader, because it is aimed at front-line and middle-management personnel who know the issues best. First, you'll learn about the issues in more detail.

Next, you'll learn a lot about your company and your fellow employees. You will observe interactions and alliances. To effectively use the workshop method, you must be a capable facilitator. Facilitation is one of the skills necessary for leading effective group workshops. You may have to act as referee as well as serve as pseudo psychologist. In a group of five or more, you need to ensure that you get vocal input from all represented constituencies. Just because someone attends one of your workshop sessions does not mean that she agrees with the points that were made or that she believes that all of the relevant issues were voiced. It is important to observe who is being most vocal. If you have a participant who is being silent, attempt to draw him out by asking if he has anything to add to the discussion, to ensure that his voice is heard and his perspective is noted (even if his perspective is not aligned with your hypothesis). We'll discuss how best to gently steer clear of unproductive or irrelevant conversations when we explore the parking lot concept in chapter 31 titled, "Executing Successful Workshops."

Questionnaires are the third common data-collection method. Questionnaires are most effective when limited to collecting basic financial and operational data, such as number of units shipped per month or the average monthly accounts receivable balance. Questionnaires are less effective when they attempt to elicit emotional or political information. You may find yourself frustrated if you circulate elaborate questionnaires to managers asking them to provide pages of narrative explanations of processes. This is rarely effective. Managers and executives have neither the time nor the energy to interpret elaborate questionnaires. For such information, you are best served collecting that information through a workshop or individual interview.

Many first-time developers of business cases frequently use the evidence-gathering activity as a way to collect feature-and-function information that will help them in some future demonstration of their preferred solution. Though the two activities may involve similar questions, the goals are different. A business case strives to quantify the value of proposed solutions. Feature-and-function discovery is aimed at clarifying the features that the customer desires in a new solution. Feature-and-function guidance is generally not helpful for a business case. For a business case, the evidence-gathering activity needs to appear independent of any specific solution, or what many call "solution agnostic." If you start with the narrow objective to simply affirm that your company has a need for a specific payroll solution from a specific vendor, you may not be completely objective. This lack of objectivity can cause you to miss other issues or alternative solutions during your discovery. When you start with your completed recommendation you essentially have blinders on. You run the risk of only hearing those things that conform to your predetermined answer rather than exploring to uncover all of the issues and as a result, possibly expanding your proposal to address a much larger problem for your company.

Knowing where to start your journey of discovery is frequently one of the harder tasks of a business case. Where do you find benefits? If your executive sponsor is supportive, he or she may offer some good suggestions on where you might expect to find benefits and possibly how you might quantify those benefits. If your sponsor doesn't offer suggestions, you'll have to seek out someone else so that you can put some real dollars to these benefits. There are a number of specific benefits presented in the appendices of this book.

Chapter 24

Validating Your Hypothesis with External Evidence

External evidence is helpful to your business case because it allows you to compare your company to other, similar companies. External sources consist of two basic categories: peer comparisons and published works (articles, books, press releases, etc.) By comparing your company to its peers, you will better understand where and by how much your company outperforms or underperforms in common financial areas. Such empirical data will add credibility to your business case and strengthen your presentation.

There is no single, best way to begin the research for financial metrics and benchmarks. Your research will depend on the resources to which you have access. If your company subscribes to benchmarking services, you might be able to tap into that resource for the specific one or more benchmarks that you desire. If, like most companies, your company does not subscribe to such services, your research will be limited to the basic public data available to all of us.

Let's assume that you do not have access to subscriber-based research analysis. Your work, then, will begin by conducting a basic financial peer analysis. First, select three other companies that are similar in size and market to your own company. You will want to select publicly traded companies so that you can find some meaningful financial data. The most relevant comparison is against your company's closest, direct competitors. Once you've chosen the comparison samples, locate and print the financial reports from their annual 10-K documents. If you're not familiar with how to do that, it's actually quite simple. Execute an Internet search on the company name and find their corporate website. Typically there will be a link on their site labeled "Investors" or "Investor Relations." Somewhere on that page you should find a link for Securities and Exchange Commission (SEC) filings. The 10-K is the annual report filed with the SEC, so navigate that page until you locate the most recent 10-K report. Usually it will be posted in PDF format and you can simply download it. Then, build a spreadsheet to capture the data, just as you did for your own company's data in the earlier Hypothesis section. In the Hypothesis section, you created a spreadsheet to hold the data for your company (or our sample company). You'll find it easy to add three new tabs to that original spreadsheet that you created. Label the tabs with the name of each company that you will be using for your comparison. Then, with those spreadsheets available, enter in the data from the corresponding companies' financial reports. Finally, create a fourth new tab, which you will use to visually compare the results of your company against these peers. Refer to the example below.

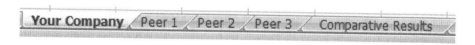

Within published financial reports, we can only expect to evaluate common, high-level metrics, such as inventory turnover or the growth of sales over the past few years. Nevertheless, these metrics are often the most compelling because they come directly from the audited financial statements and are, therefore, not subject to subjective interpretation. Metrics such as the efficiency of a single process, say the time necessary for a single clerk to create a single purchase order, are helpful but often are viewed as less significant because their improvement does not present itself directly on the financial statements. An improvement in sales growth is readily observable on the income statement. For this reason, financial statement metrics are always seen as the most desirable metrics.

Referring to the example from the case study we examined in the Hypothesis section, we will explore the financial results of three peer companies. Again, I have chosen to redact the names as they are not relevant to our exercise.

Peer comparisons are extremely helpful in establishing credibility in your business case. Such comparisons enable you to clarify just how your company stacks up to its competition and peer group.

Peer comparisons are extremely helpful in establishing credibility in your business case. Such comparisons enable you to clarify just how your company stacks up to its competition and peer group. By selecting peers with identical or nearly identical product portfolios and markets, you highlight just how strong or weak your company is on any given metric. As you might imagine, this is more credible than simply selecting three well-known companies from unrelated industries. Comparing your company to Ford Motor Company, Microsoft, Coca-Cola, and JPMorganChase might be interesting but would not be as powerful or relevant as comparing your company to three carefully selected peers in your industry.

Let's begin by comparing some basic income statement items. Examine the table below. You'll see that we have compared six elements from our peers.

Sales and Costs	Target	Peer 1	Peer 2	Peer 3
Sales Growth	-1.55%	-0.02%	-3.33%	-2.90%
SG&A as a Percent of Sales	18.30%	34.46%	30.38%	31.99%
Cost of Sales as a Percent of Sales	66.41%	41.23%	49.22%	29.80%
COGS+SG&A as a Percent of Sales	84.71%	75.69%	79.60%	61.79%
SG&A Growth	6.29%	-1.10%	-6.13%	-7.86%
Income from Operations (as a percent)	14.78%	23.59%	20.40%	25.45%

What you see in this chart are the results from all four financial statements. To produce this spreadsheet, and the ones that follow, simply enter in the financial data from the selected company's 10-K and create similar ratios and equations like you did for your own company in our Hypothesis section. Once done, you'll have all four companies' results displayed in a single place and ready for comparison.

In the sales and costs spreadsheet, we see several things. Our target company had a 1.55 percent decline in sales from last year to this year. But we also see that two of our peers actually suffered worse declines. This suggests that our company compared somewhat favorably to these peers.

Now we'll examine the common cost metrics. When we look at SG&A as a percent of sales, we see that our target company compared better than all of the listed peers. That suggests a strong focus on cost control, at least comparatively. Look next at the cost of sales as a percent of sales. Here we see that the target company compares unfavorably by a pretty significant margin. If you recall our coverage of this topic in the Hypothesis section, you will remember that some companies place certain manufacturing expense items in SG&A, while other companies may elect to place all manufacturing expense items in cost of goods sold (or cost of revenue). This makes it difficult to conclusively compare one company's SG&A percent against another company's SG&A percent. For that reason, you will find it helpful to combine the SG&A and COGS numbers to compute a combined percentage of sales for these two costs, as shown in the spreadsheet above. When we look at the combined number we see that our company spends a much higher portion of their revenue on these two items than the peers listed on this spreadsheet. That suggests a potential benefit discussion—reducing costs. What this does not show, however, is where those excess costs might be. For that information, we will use our workshops and group interviews to zero in on this potential benefit discussion. For example, if your project has anything to do with factory expenses (or factory efficiency), you can use this comparison to bolster your claim that costs are too high, at least when compared to your peers. That means that those companies have found a way to spend less for the same level of performance. And as we look further at our spreadsheet, we see another telling metric—SG&A growth. This metric compares how much we spent last year compared to this year in SG&A. Investment analysts would expect to see SG&A grow at a slower percentage rate than sales. Our target company, however, had shrinking sales but had growth in SG&A. Furthermore, we see that all of the selected peers were able to shrink SG&A expense and that their SG&A expenses grew at a lesser rate than their sales. Our target company, then, stands alone as particularly unfavorable on this metric. Accordingly, this can become a great discussion point for our executive interviews and group workshops.

Finally, we look at income from operations. Here we see that our company had the smallest percentage of income compared to these peers. That is not surprising since it seems as though our expenses are much higher.

From this first spreadsheet we now have several worthwhile discussion topics and likely benefit areas. If your project seeks to impact any expense category, you can begin to align your hypothesis with these financial facts.

Moving on, let's now look at working capital items. Below we have our company's data and that of our three peers.

Working Capital Items	Target	Peer 1	Peer 2	Peer 3
Days Sales Outstanding	49.00	38.72	26.95	56.88
Days Payable Outstanding	55.20	60.94	56.11	109.64
Days in Inventory	58.45	69.83	64.56	102.49
Cash Conversion Cycle (in days)	52.25	47.62	35.40	49.74

The cash conversion cycle is a common measurement for manufacturing and distribution companies and was introduced to you in the Hypothesis section. It is comprised of the three items listed here—days sales outstanding, days payable outstanding, and days in inventory. We'll unpack these one at a time. It is important to note that while most financial benefits can be presented as recurring year after year, improvements in working capital items are measured as one-time benefits. Once a working capital item has been improved, its benefit does not continue year over year. Let me explain. Working capital is a balance sheet item. You evaluate its value at year end and then again at the end of next year. If the balance in that asset has changed from one year to the next, that's your measurement, just as it is in your personal savings account. So, if you can simultaneously hold sales steady (or increase them) while at the same time shrinking inventory or accounts receivable, you will record a favorable benefit at the end of the year.

It works like this: assume the business is owed $100 by its customers at the end of the year. The $100 is not actually spendable cash. It is a debt that is owed to the company by its customers. If, at the end of next year, the company has maintained the same sales level but has an accounts receivable balance of $80, it means that it has converted $20 more into cash than the previous year. The $20 is the benefit. Inventory works in a similar way, and we'll explore that later in this chapter. Unless improvements are made in the process of producing inventory or collecting cash, those benefits will only be counted once—reflecting the year in which the improvements were made. If the balance stays the same for next year, there is not another annual benefit. If, however, the same effort is applied in the second year and the balance improves further in that year, then you will have recorded another year's benefits.

Let's examine our first working capital metric—days sales outstanding (often abbreviated as DSO). This measures the number of days from the time the company issues an invoice until payment is received for that invoice. Fewer days are better; most companies strive to hit the thirty-day mark. Here we see our company is taking forty-nine days. And we see that two of our peers actually do a much better job than us in collecting their cash. With that as background information, here is the real value of understanding this financial measurement. If our target company could collect its cash from its customers just one day sooner it would represent a one-time benefit of $52.3 million. That's a big benefit. The calculation for determining the value of one day's cash collection can be found in Appendix B. Here's how you might interpret this metric. We know that collecting cash one day sooner is worth a lot of money. We also see that our peers are able to collect cash sooner, in one case better than twenty-two days sooner. Now, it's probably safe to assume that our peers sell their products to our customers. That means that our peers are better at collecting cash from these same customers than our company. You can make the case that the marketplace supports a faster collection performance than our company currently achieves. So, how do we get our cash collected sooner? This will be part of your discovery process. During the interview and workshop sessions, you'll show the participants these facts and ask for their input. Do invoices have errors? That's important to know because invoices with errors often get paid later as the customer will withhold payment until the disputes are resolved. Remember, each day that our target company collects cash sooner is worth over $52 million. A five-day improvement would be worth over $250 million. And a five-day improvement would still mean that our company performs next-to-worst when compared to these three companies. I hope you see how this can help you to begin to form a powerful and compelling story line.

Our next working capital metric is days payable outstanding (often abbreviated as DPO). This is the reverse of DSO, as it measures the number of days from the time we receive an invoice from our suppliers until we issue payment for that invoice. In this metric, more days are better, as you want to hold onto your cash as long as possible. This metric is a delicate one. The relationship a company has with its suppliers needs to be strong and dependable. The longer a company stretches its payments, the more likely the supplier relationship will be injured. Taken to its extreme, the suppliers might decide that a company is no longer worthy to do business with because they take so long to pay their routine invoices. Suppliers would like to have their invoices paid within thirty days. Given certain economic conditions, that might not be feasible. With that in mind, let's look at our performance. Here we see that our company takes 55.2 days, on average, to pay its routine invoices. That seems high compared to the thirty-day expectation. Yet when we look at our peers we see that they all take longer than us. Just as we determined in our DSO discussion, we can assume that we buy goods from the same suppliers as our peers. If those vendors are tolerating longer terms, we might be able to stretch ours out by another day or two without injuring our supplier relationships. A single, one-day extension in DPO is worth a one-time benefit of $34.7 million. The calculation for determining the value of deferring payment for one day can be found in Appendix B.

Finally, let's look at days in inventory. Days in inventory (often abbreviated as DII) represents the number of days it takes to convert raw material purchases into finished, shipped product. Fewer days are better, and many companies strive to hit the thirty-day mark. A companion metric is called inventory turnover, sometimes shortened to inventory turns. This metric simply refers to the number of times in a year that inventory is refreshed or turned over. The two metrics refer to the same issue—convert raw material purchases to finished, shipped product as efficiently and effectively as possible. A company that achieves a thirty-day DII has an inventory turnover of 12.1. We arrive at this figure using the following equation: The company is refreshing its inventory every 30 days. By dividing the number of days in a year (365) by our 30-day DII, we see that we have a 12.1 turnover performance.

We can think of the potential benefit from optimized inventory in terms similar to those of the DSO example. Assume that the company has $200 in inventory at the end of the year. Like accounts receivable, it is a legitimate asset, but it is not spendable until that inventory is sold and cash is collected. So, if at the end of next year, assuming identical sales and cost numbers, the company has $175 in inventory, it means that $25 more was converted into cash than the previous year.

In our example, our company has a DII of 58.45. Unlike our other working capital metrics, the company outperforms its peers in this category. This is a good example for us, too. When this occurs, there is the tendency to think that there is no room for improvement and therefore no potential benefit from this vital area. But consider this: it is reasonable to expect that every company wants to improve and is not completely satisfied with its performance. We can look back in the Working Capital Table in chapter 21 and see the company's performance over the past few years. A quick review will show that there has been significant improvement in this metric (from 71.01 two years ago, down to 67.12 last year and down to 58.45 this year). With this in mind, it is often very credible to suggest an incremental improvement, even when the company performs well. Suggesting that the company could improve further, even by a single day, is worth a one-time benefit of $34.7 million. How would such an improvement be achieved? Again, that's what you'll explore in your interviews and workshops. You can uncover useful information through simple questions, such as "Do you think we could push inventory out the door any faster, even a single day faster?" Factory personnel know where inefficiencies exist and will usually offer a suggestion or two on how inventory can be pushed through the process quicker, without sacrificing product quality or safety. Armed with that, you'll be on your way to a strong business case.

Let's now move on to key financial ratios.

Key Financial Ratios	Target	Peer 1	Peer 2	Peer 3
Return on Sales	13.48%	23.08%	19.39%	25.45%
Return on Assets	10.10%	21.70%	9.64%	13.66%
Return on Equity	40.59%	90.95%	20.27%	26.35%
Debt to Equity	119.39%	102.12%	58.59%	28.74%
Quick Ratio	68.33%	70.01%	34.36%	133.78%

Key financial ratios are interesting, and many companies measure themselves against them. For a further description of each of these ratios, please refer Appendix B, —"Common Financial Metrics."

For business case purposes, you need to understand the calculations behind these ratios. However, your proposal will rarely impact a ratio. Instead, your proposal will impact the components of the ratio. For example, let's revisit our discussion of return on sales. Return on sales measures how much profit is returned for each dollar in sales. The higher the result the better. But the measurement itself is not something that is controllable. Only the components of this ratio are controllable. And the components are net income and sales. And net income is also a composite number made from subtracting expenses from sales. So, to improve this ratio, the company must find ways to either reduce expenses or increase sales. If either of these components are favorably impacted, this ratio will improve. This holds true for all other ratios listed here—improve the components and the corresponding ratios will improve. If your company measures itself against these ratios, it is important for you to know the individual components in these ratios so that you can show how your proposal favorably impacts the core components, and by deduction, favorably impacts these ratios.

Finally, let's review the efficiency metrics. By reviewing the published financial statements, you will be able to compute the following two efficiency metrics—revenue per employee and operating income per employee.

Efficiency Metrics	Target	Peer 1	Peer 2	Peer 3
Revenue per Employee	$360,660	$425,750	$585,400	$542,956
Operating Income per Employee	$53,302	$100,417	$119,430	$138,202

As we can see from the above table, our company underperforms in both categories compared to its peers. This can be the basis for another great discussion point. Like our other underperforming metrics, this example also lacks specific details of just what might be causing the inefficiency and which departments might be most inefficient. Such unanswered questions are great topics for interviews and workshops. As discussed above, these metrics are simply ratios made up of other, more direct components. Increasing sales or decreasing the workforce will favorably impact these metrics. What these metrics do not reveal is where any cuts should be made. For that, you need specific examples of inefficiency. And you would explore for specific examples in your interviews and group workshops.

It is common for managers to seek to evaluate certain efficiency measurements, such as how long it should take to enter a purchase order or how long it should take to reconcile the month-end financial statements. You might find it easy to determine those performance levels within your company, but how do you find that data for other companies or aggregated for an industry? As you create your business case, you will encounter people that hold the view that any and all metrics are publicly available and easily accessible. Say, for example, your hypothesis states that improved expense reporting procedures would streamline the process and boost accuracy for both employees who travel and those who administer expense reimbursements. As part of the confirmation that a problem exists, it is desirable to look outside of your company for established metrics. You might imagine that some research organization has compiled such metrics and published them somewhere. The reality is that while this metric (the time it takes an average traveling employee to accurately enter a week's expense report) may be available, it is unlikely that this metric is easily located and can be used for free. Consulting and research firms have entire divisions devoted to collecting and selling such data to companies seeking to do just this type of analysis. Many consulting firms subscribe to certain benchmarking services as they are engaged in this type of analysis routinely. If your employer subscribes to such services, you can request this information from the administrator of that subscription. If, however, your company does not subscribe to such services, you must pursue benchmarks the old fashioned way—through tedious research.

The most common place to start your search would be with your favorite search engine, such as Google or Bing. Type in the search criteria and see what you discover. Ideally you'll find something that states that a common performance for this metric is X and that companies can improve that metric by a certain percentage by following some specific path such as buying a certain software application or changing a certain internal procedure. Usually, though, what you'll find will be information that does not exactly align with your needs. Typically, you'll find a reference to a company that has realized an improvement of a certain percentage, but you won't likely know two important pieces of data—where they started and what the average is for a given industry or business process. With those pieces lacking, you still might decide to refer to this excerpt or benchmark as evidence that improvements can be made, but you'll need more evidence that this reference is relevant to your pursuit.

Here's an example of the art and science of external research from a recent search. After searching for the phrase "expense report efficiency," the search engine presented the following results: "Best-in-Class Companies Cut Expense Report Processing by 73%." This particular link came from a press release at PRNewsWire (http://www.prnewswire.com/news-releases/

best-in-class-companies-cut-expense-report-processing-costs-by-73-while-enjoying-36-higher-te-policy-compliance-62237417.html). In the article, the posted news release refers to a report produced by The Aberdeen Group that offers full details of their study. For the full study, The Aberdeen Group's website requires a payment of $399. With that in mind, if you were researching this topic, you would have to determine if you needed the full report or if you could infer sufficient information from the press release. This is always part of the challenge. Without the full report in front of you, you often cannot determine if the full report contains the real rich nuggets of evidence that you seek. Is it worth investing $399 to find that out? That's an individual decision.

Continuing on with the press release, we see that the article states that best-in-class companies were able to cut expense processing costs from $25 to $6.50. Here's part of the art over science. You could refer to that savings in your business case just as you read it from the news release (with proper attribution, of course), or even offer a variation on that statement, such as best-in-class companies have been able to cut their expense processing costs by over 70 percent. In some cases, executives will accept research based on a press release. However, in most cases, executives will demand to know the underlying variables that contributed to that improvement, such as how the actual costs were computed and whether those savings were achieved through headcount reduction or other cost-reduction measures.

When you are gathering external evidence, keep track of the source of every single quotation and reference. Posting the attribution of a source in your presentation gives the reader instant validation that you are not making your data up and shows a respectable level of due diligence on your part.

If your project involves the purchase of software or other business services, you can frequently receive assistance from the sales team in this same pursuit. Often sales teams have references, either from other customers that have accomplished what you are now trying to do or from articles and white papers that align with your hypothesis. All of these sources add additional credibility to your business case.

Perhaps the biggest challenge with external evidence is knowing when to stop researching. How much is enough? You might tell yourself, "If I search a little longer or read five more articles I might just find that elusive, very special nugget." This is an easy trap into which you might stumble, so consider this piece of advice: devote four hours to your initial research effort (thirty minutes planning how and where you will conduct your research and three and a half hours executing your research plan). After that, work on other aspects of your business case. If you determine that you still need additional external evidence, limit your additional exploration to two-hour time blocks. This gives you a path and a plan for additional research without making it open-ended and without consuming too much of your time chasing elusive needles in a haystack.

That should give you some idea how to locate and incorporate external evidence for your business case. Let's now move on to planning your discovery sessions, beginning with your executive sponsor.

Chapter 25

Gaining Your Sponsor's Perspective

The most important starting point for gathering your internal evidence will typically be your project sponsor. It is assumed that your sponsor is an advocate for this project and has given some thought to how such a project will benefit the organization. The more senior position that your sponsor holds, the more likely that her position is the prevailing opinion. You need to ask your sponsor specific questions to prepare for your upcoming discovery sessions. Below you will find common questions that you should ask your sponsor early in the development of your business case. Along with those questions are clarifying statements that will help illuminate the value of the initial responses. You will use your subsequent executive and manager interviews to confirm and strengthen the answers that you hear from your sponsor. If you hear contradictory statements to the same question, that merely signals that not all participants agree with your sponsor. This is not necessarily a bad thing. Remember our discussion of gold mining. You have to sift through a lot of dirt and gravel to find nuggets. You must also weigh the stature of the dissenter, as organizational politics frequently affect the outcome of such projects. That is to say that

> Your sponsor should be able to identify potential benefit areas and potential business units that can contribute to your case.

not all dissenting opinions carry the same weight when it comes time to decide on project approval.

Your initial sponsor interview is important because it sets expectations and boundaries. Your sponsor should be able to identify potential benefit areas and potential business units that can contribute to your case. Your sponsor may also do some advance work by alerting his or her peers that you will be heading up this business case effort and that you will need their support.

With that in mind, let's look at some key questions for your sponsor. When approaching your sponsor, you might try this tactic: state that to best serve her on this effort, you'd like to spend a few minutes talking through some basic questions about the project and learning her perspective. Before we dive into these questions, it must be stated that the responses that you could receive could be all over the map. Don't become offended if your sponsor turns the questions back to you saying, "I'm hoping that you'll be able to answer that with your business case." If you do get such a response, consider this gentle reply: "While I expect to fill in the details during the journey of the business case project, I was hoping that you would provide some general guidance to get me started on the right track."

Historically, journalism students have been taught to ask six basic questions when investigating a news story. Those six questions are: who, what, where, when, why, and how much. Using that as a basis, set an appointment with your sponsor to ask the necessary background questions. We're going to rearrange the sequence of those six questions to fit our purpose.

We'll begin with the "why" questions.

WHY SHOULD THE COMPANY DO THIS PROJECT and WHY SHOULD THE COMPANY DO IT NOW?

These questions help you understand some of the basic challenges, at least from the view of your sponsor. You're hoping to hear that some great opportunity will be missed if the project does not go forward. Or you might hear that the organization is aware that its current environment is too inefficient and costly and that moving to the proposed solution will help them gain efficiency and reduce costs. The answer to these questions will also help to determine the urgency of the project. If the answer is, "We don't really need this right now, but we should explore it anyway," you may not have as urgent a business problem as you had originally thought.

On to the "who" questions. There are two primary "who" questions:

WHO IS COMPENSATED TO FIX THE PROBLEM?

This is an often unexpected question, at least from the sponsor's perspective. Peter Drucker, the legendary twentieth-century management guru, is credited with saying, "What gets measured, gets done." Phrased another way we could say, "I will do those things for which I am compensated." If you become aware that certain managers perceive that a reward—whether financial or political—will accrue from the project's success, those are the managers with whom you'll want to meet. Typically, the project sponsor is one of those people. If there are others, you will want to note that and seek to meet with them for their perspective.

WHOSE INPUT SHOULD BE SOUGHT?

At the center of your business case is a business issue that requires attention. Often there are multiple interdependent and integrated business issues that require attention. There are numerous executives and managers that have opinions on the best approach to addressing these business issues. Your sponsor should be able to list the names of others that you should consult about the business case and the issues that it seeks to solve. It is likely that, among the potential contributors, there exists a difference of opinion on the best approach. It is beneficial for you to spend some time with various opinion leaders to document their thoughts, concerns, and recommendations.

There are three primary "what" questions.

WHAT ARE THE EXPECTED BENEFITS FROM THIS PROJECT?

We covered this idea at some length in the Hypothesis section, and it might seem exactly like the earlier "why" question. In most cases this question is similar to the "why" questions, but it is worth revisiting here. Your sponsor should be able to provide you with a list of expected benefits. It might be unreasonable, at this early stage, to expect that your sponsor can quantify those benefits. Still, she should be able to provide you with a list of benefit names. Such a list might include improved inventory turnover, reduced IT expenses, or improved sales of certain product lines. You can use the list to guide your upcoming workshops and interviews.

WHAT ARE THE SUCCESS CRITERIA FOR THIS PROJECT?

Typically, a project sponsor has given some thought to success measurements for this project. These success criteria should be aligned with the hypothesis of your business case. For example, if the hypothesis states that customer cash can be collected three days sooner by implementing this solution, you would expect that the success criteria will be just that—that the company will collect its cash from its customers three, or more, days sooner. If the success criteria do not align with your hypothesis, you should consider re-thinking your hypothesis. After all, what value will you receive if you think the project is successful and the sponsor thinks that it missed the mark? You need to understand the success criteria as you begin your business case.

WHAT ELEMENTS ARE EXPECTED IN THIS BUSINESS CASE?

There is no single, universal table of contents for a successful business case. Each sponsor has his or her own expectations. For you to be successful, you should seek to understand the components that your sponsor is expecting. In chapter 51, "Packaging Your Recommendation," you will see a sample agenda (or table of contents) that has worked in many situations. It might be perfect for your needs. However, your sponsor might wish to include or exclude items from that template if she has a specific template that has worked for her in the past. Verify what is expected so that you can build a successful business case in your sponsor's eyes.

WHAT HAPPENS IF THE PROJECT IS NOT APPROVED?

It is always possible that your ultimate recommendation, even with a sound business case, can be rejected. There might be some perceived penalty or missed opportunity that the company faces if the project is not approved. If you are told that no real adversity will arise if the project is not approved, you may find yourself with a project that is not a corporate priority. After all, if things will be fine if the company doesn't spend the money, why should they spend the money? That's why you should ask this question early.

Next, there are a couple of worthwhile "when" questions to explore.

WHEN WAS THE BUSINESS PROBLEM FIRST BROUGHT TO YOUR ATTENTION?

It is important for you to understand where you are in the process. Part of that determination will depend on how long the organization has faced this issue. For you, this is a brand-new business case. But it is possible that this issue has been fomenting in the executive suite for months or even years. There may even have been past unsuccessful attempts at resolving it. And if that's the case, it creates a certain dynamic that can place you at a disadvantage. Even though you have been newly assigned to this effort, the executives may view this as a longstanding problem. When you pick up this project, then, you are burdened with the unresolved frustrations of the preceding months and years. If that's your situation, discuss it with your sponsor to understand how to manage the executives' expectations and how best to proceed and succeed. You may also find that the executive team will be impatient with your proposed timeline. They may assert that they have already been on this journey for months or years and don't want to extend the timeline further. If this describes your situation, work with your sponsor and prepare a strategy to address this with the executive team so that you are not unnecessarily burdened with expectations arising from past unsuccessful efforts.

WHEN IS THE BUSINESS CASE DUE?

It is helpful to understand the parameters under which you are operating. Is this business case due by the end of the week, or is it due in ninety days? If your sponsor expects you to suggest a date for its completion, there are several factors to consider when building your timeline:

- *Scope.* How many business units, and how many business processes within each business unit, will you need to explore? Within each business process, how many people should be invited to each workshop? You can estimate the number of discovery workshops you'll need to schedule based on those parameters.
- *Data Analysis.* Once the workshops and interviews have been conducted, allow time to evaluate your notes and to build a first draft of your business case. A good rule of thumb is to allow an additional amount of time roughly equal to 30 percent to 50 percent of your

original discovery time. If you planned for six weeks of discovery, then, allow for an additional two to three weeks for data analysis.

- *Presentation Preparation.* You will benefit by allocating some time to create your final presentation. This commonly includes time to build PowerPoint slides, dress up your spreadsheets, and conduct a dry run with your sponsor. A good rule of thumb for this activity is to allow an additional amount of time equal to roughly half of your analysis time.
- *Complete Timeline.* Determine the total amount of time you'll need to prepare your case. Using this example, if you plan for six weeks of discovery, you should plan for your full business case project to take ten to twelve weeks.

WHEN IS THE FULL PROJECT EXPECTED TO BE COMPLETED?

This question seeks to understand when the finished project is expected. This is different from the completion of the business case. This question refers to the completion date of the project recommended by the business case. Understanding this date can help you understand other critical success factors, such as cost, level of effort, and so on. If the project must be completed within six months, this means that certain assumptions must be made about staffing, complexity, and so forth. However, if the expected completion date is five years out, that paints a different picture regarding staffing and complexity. A secondary benefit from this knowledge is that it provides you with an early reasonability test. Suppose that your project is estimated to take eighteen months. Now suppose that your sponsor believes that it can be properly completed in six months. You have a disconnect that must be addressed. It is always better to learn of these disconnects earlier rather than later. If you learn that you have such a disconnect, address this issue with your sponsor early. One effective way to address it is to lay out your assumptions and ask for her assumptions. You can discuss the pros and cons of the various opinions and likely reach a more workable common ground.

Next, there are a couple a worthwhile "where" questions to explore.

WHERE ARE THE LIKELY BENEFITS TO BE FOUND?

In a previous question we asked, "What are the expected benefits?" Here we are asking the same question, with a slight twist. With this question, we seek to understand the location or process where the expected benefits might be found. For example, the answer to the first question might be, "We expect to cut our expenses by 5 percent over the next three years." That tells us what benefits are expected. This question then asks, "Where might I find that 5 percent savings? In which departments and within which processes?" This helps you zero in on the benefit areas and helps you target your invitee lists for your interviews and workshops.

WHERE MIGHT I MEET RESISTANCE?

We would all hope to find willing and eager participants during the development of our business case. This is not always true. Your sponsor may be aware of such resistance, and if aware, can help you navigate those departments and individuals effectively. If your sponsor is unaware of any resistance, your question places this possibility on the table as a future consideration.

Finally, the "how much" questions.

HOW MUCH DO YOU EXPECT THIS PROJECT TO COST?

This is often seen as a chicken-or-egg question. Which is more important, knowing the cost or knowing the benefits? Well, they're both equally important. One consideration regarding cost has to do with computing sufficient benefits. If you learn that the proposed project will cost $5 million, you can be confident that you'll need to find well more than $5 million in benefits to justify the expenditure. If you combine this knowledge with information gained by asking other questions (such as questions about the likely benefit areas), and if you determine that the benefits are thin when compared to the costs of the project, you can discuss this with your sponsor to determine the best way to approach the business case, even if it offers potentially weak benefits.

Remember, you are building a business case to justify a capital expenditure. You need to know how much the project will cost to ensure that the benefits from your business case adequately offset those costs. Asking this question can invoke a variety of responses. For example, if your sponsor already knows the proposed cost of the project based on bids from vendors, you can be reasonably certain that your sponsor is prepared to request an amount similar to the bid amount when she prepares the final capital request. But if your sponsor does not have a true estimate for the cost of the project, she may assume that the project is significantly less costly than it will actually be. In those cases, you could be in for an unpleasant conversation down the road when you present a cost figure that is outside the range that your sponsor had envisioned. The risk of such misunderstanding is compounded in those cases when the sponsor has already shared her estimate with senior management and has set their expectations. To minimize the adverse impact of that future, unpleasant conversation, consider asking this follow-up question: "It's possible that the final project number will be higher than the original estimate, particularly if we discover that the project parameters need to be adjusted to deliver the desired project results. If that happens, how will we reconcile those different numbers and manage executive expectations?" Such a question establishes the guidelines for future conversations and sets the expectation that the original estimates might have been incomplete or incorrect. If this question is uncomfortable for you, then there's an even greater necessity that you ask it. Project sponsors often share numbers with their superiors at the outset of a business case. They want to gauge the willingness of their executives to fund the effort. If the bids from the vendors come back significantly higher than this first estimate, the sponsor may find herself in an uncomfortable conversation with her boss regarding the gap between the original estimate and the resulting bid. For that reason, you should lay the groundwork for handling these conversations early.

Now that you've met with your sponsor, you should know a lot more than you did when you were first assigned this business case. Using that new knowledge as a foundation, it's time to begin planning for your actual discovery work.

Chapter 26

Plan before You Explore

To effectively collect the necessary evidence, you need to draw up a basic discovery plan. This discovery plan lays out what you need to capture to add credibility to your business case. Done properly, it benefits you and your sponsor. As stated before, credibility is the hallmark of a successful business case. Your credibility is evaluated from the first meeting. You must appear professional, organized, and competent. Your sponsor would like to know that you have a plan for the creation of this business case. Even if your business case effort only takes a week, it should be a very organized and effective week. Nothing damages credibility like a disorganized interview or workshop activity. You must identify what you need to collect and from whom. Often you don't know who may provide the best information so you'll have to propose suggested participants based on position. For example, the head of accounting should be able to help with financial questions and the head of purchasing should be able to help with purchasing questions. Let's dive a little deeper into a very basic four-step discovery plan. The four steps are:

1. A rough cost estimate
2. An initial discovery approach
3. Focused data collection
4. A follow-up plan

STEP ONE—ROUGH COST ESTIMATE		
Elements	Considerations	Comments/Examples
Potential Cost Elements	• Hardware costs • Software costs • Software implementa-tion costs • Temporary labor costs	This list is a starter list meant to provoke your thinking. List as many project cost elements as you can imagine. Overlooking any could create a weakness in your business case.
Determine Ranges	• To be deter-mined after cost elements are listed	Estimate a range, in dollars, for each cost element above.
Determine timing	• To be deter-mined after cost elements are listed	For each cost element, consider when payment should be planned. Will all cost elements require payment at the start of the project or will some cost elements not require payment until sometime later in the project? The cost of many project elements ebb and flow during the life of a project. For instance, staffing demand can vary—both skills and time demands—as the project moves through it phases.

In Step One of your discovery plan, you need to establish a rough, initial cost estimate. This may seem terribly premature. It is not premature. All projects cost money. Building a business case is about financial justification. You need to know how big your justification must be so that you can succeed. Therefore, you should prepare some basic estimate. If your sponsor gave you a detailed cost estimate, you're well on your way. Unfortunately, it is not common to receive a detailed cost estimate from your sponsor early in the business case effort because specific costs may not yet be known. With that in mind, we must create one.

The first step in creating your cost estimate is to list all of the potential cost components. You don't need to know exact numbers at this early point in the development of your business case. You simply need a rough order-of-magnitude estimate. Determine the range of your capital request. Based on your knowledge—and possible input from others—is this project likely to cost $100,000, $500,000, $1 million, $5 million or more? That should be enough of an estimate to start your business case.

When making a preliminary cost estimate, it is important to consider that there are many forms of costs. Being thorough in this area starts you on the road to credibility. Take a software implementation project as an example. If your estimate only includes the cost of the software, most reviewers will dismiss your estimate as incomplete and uninformed. A software project commonly includes the initial license cost, the ongoing annual support costs, implementation and training costs provided by the software company or external consulting firm, possible temporary clerical fees for data entry personnel, possible overtime estimates for client staff that will be required to work longer hours during the implementation, and so on. While you might not know the numbers that correspond to each cost component, you should devote sufficient time to compile a thorough list of cost components.

After you create the list of potential cost components, you must determine a reasonable range of costs for each one. This is all aimed at ensuring that your business case is credible. It is fatal to your business case to underestimate obvious costs. Consider this situation: you estimate that it will cost the company $500,000 to license the software, and you omit any other costs. Armed with only the cost of the software you begin building a business case that justifies a $500,000 investment. Imagine how awkward it will be if you present a business case that shows a $1.5 million benefit for this $500,000 project only to learn later that the implementation costs will be another $750,000 and the annual support costs will be roughly $100,000 per year. In five years your project will have an estimated cost of $1.75 million with an estimated payback of only $1.5 million. What you might have thought was a slam dunk will become an underfunded project with little likelihood of approval. That is a failed business case. This failure could have been avoided by understanding all of the cost components and seeking to justify the full, true cost, not just the cost of a single component.

Once you have prepared a rough cost estimate, you must plan your discovery activities. To effectively collect the necessary evidence, you need to draw up a basic discovery plan. Step Two of your discovery plan has four primary questions:

STEP TWO—INITIAL DISCOVERY APPROACH	
Key Question(s)	Comments / Examples
Who must I convince that my hypothesis is valid and that this project is worth funding?	(This column is shown as a sample. Your list will likely differ depending on the scope of your project) • VP Finance • VP Marketing • VP Operations
To convince those persons that my hypothesis is valid, what information must I provide?	• Project cost estimates • Comparisons of our company with its peers • Benefit projections, with supporting evidence • Examples from other companies where these benefits have been achieved
Who are the internal people with whom I must meet to collect the right information? If I don't know the names, at least list the roles of the right people.	• Plant operations personnel • Corporate accounting • Purchasing department

What external sources should I explore to collect additional corroborating evidence?	• Annual reports of competitors • Earnings calls (our company and selected peers) • Industry analysis • Trade articles

This second step in your discovery plan is to help you think through the basic questions that you need answered. Bear in mind that mid-level and senior executives are busy people. Assuming that you can just pop in on them and have an unstructured conversation for thirty to sixty minutes is shortsighted. For that reason, you need to move to Step Three of the discovery plan, which is Focused Data Collection.

List each of the departments, and the specific roles within those departments, with whom you want to meet. List three pieces of information that you hope each can provide. The information you seek should either affirm or contradict your hypothesis.

STEP THREE—FOCUSED DATA COLLECTION		
Contributor	What Contributor Can Provide	Comments/Examples
Plant Controller	• Inventory figures • Warehousing costs • Labor costs	Inventory and cost data will be necessary to show trends. If costs are going higher, more discovery will be needed

Plant Manager	• Units shipped • Percent of shipments shipped on time • Overtime trends	Production and shipment data will help match output to costs. As a percentage, are costs rising or falling faster or slower than production output?

Once that rough outline has been put together, it's a good idea to present this plan to your executive sponsor and confirm that you are on the right track. The executive sponsor will review your plan and likely suggest some changes or improvements. The advantage of having the executive sponsor see this plan in advance is that it will help you to ensure that you're asking the right questions and seeking answers from the right people. Your goal, remember, is to create a credible, compelling business case. Getting the right data—but from the wrong people, or from people not deemed to be the right, best source for that information—can diminish your credibility.

You now have a discovery plan and a list of opening discovery questions. You should request a meeting with your project sponsor to discuss your hypothesis and circulate your list of questions to the appropriate people so that they can review your questions in advance of your discovery session. Once you have completed your first round of interviews, you should review your notes from those interviews. During the review you will discover things that are missing, such as particular details—who, what, where, when, why, and how much. For that reason, you need to schedule follow-up meetings when you conclude your first interviews. One effective method is to conclude all of your interviews with the following statement: "Thanks for giving me your time. This has been very helpful. I'm going to review my notes and, during that review, I expect some additional questions will surface. I may need another twenty or thirty minutes of your time to clarify some things we discussed. If I find that I need that additional time, I will contact you and check your availability." Using a table similar to the one below, you can fill in those follow-up questions as you review your interview notes.

STEP FOUR—FOLLOW-UP PLAN		
Contributor	What Else You Might Need	Comments/Examples
Plant Controller	• To be determined after initial discovery sessions	TBD
Plant Manager	• To be determined after initial discovery sessions	TBD

Investing the time to create a simple discovery plan will help focus your efforts and optimize your time with executives. Attempting to collect the data without a plan—by winging it—does not usually yield the best results. Often these attempts look haphazard and the data are less compelling because there wasn't a plan to capture the best data available. There is an old adage that goes like this: those who fail to plan are planning to fail.

Chapter 27

Boulders, Rocks, and Pebbles

As you begin to collect data, you will find it helpful to categorize or group potential benefits into categories. The following grouping idea has proved helpful in building understandable and well-received business cases. During each interview and group workshop, you're going to ask people to help you identify and quantify the value of solving a problem or enabling a new opportunity. In chapters 29 through 34, you will be given guidance on how to gather evidence in individual interviews and group workshops. Gathering people together is a big step, but that does not by itself help us compute the value of the benefits. It is rare that your participants, whether staff members or executives, can pinpoint the value of your potential project. They will generally have rough ideas, but rarely will they have solid financial data for you. The burden to quantify the benefits rests with you, the business case creator.

> It is rare that your participants, whether staff members or executives, can pinpoint the value of your potential project. The burden to quantify the benefits rests with you, the business case creator.

Several years ago, after trying a number of less successful analogies, I came upon an idea that I have found to be very, very helpful with my clients as we work together to build the value of the proposal. As I would listen to interview and workshop participants tell me that something might have value, or that something might be inefficient and very expensive if not solved, I would guide them to help me quantify the value. Most participants had a hard time quantifying value, so I would guide them using a very simple concept—boulders, rocks, and pebbles. Big benefits, or big problems, I classify as boulders. Boulders remind people of something immovable, something rock solid. Really small benefits or irritating little problems I classify as pebbles. Everything else is a rock. Rocks are small enough to hold in your hand and easily tossed aside. When trying to compute the value for my business case, I ask the participants to organize all of our value discussions around those three simple concepts.

To make this analogy more concrete, I ask them to imagine a giant two-sided scale, like the kind held by Lady Justice in those statues outside of courthouses. On the one side of the scale would be the cost of the project. I realize that we probably do not know the cost at this time, but we can pick a working range for this exercise. Let's say your project will cost between $500,000 and $1,000,000. The upper end of that range goes on the cost side of the scale. Then I ask my participants to help me offset that cost by throwing stuff on the benefits side of the scale. This is where this analogy really helps. Invariably I will hear of numerous potential benefits. Participants always want me to believe that any benefit that they suggest is always a boulder. I guess participants think they will receive some implied kudos when they have suggested a benefit or an opportunity that is significant. To help everyone view these things through the same lens, I offer these guidelines for their consideration.

A BOULDER IS ROCK SOLID

To be considered a boulder, a benefit or an opportunity must meet several criteria. These criteria are listed and explained below. It is a challenge to expect that each boulder will fully satisfy each of the following criteria. The goal is that the benefit meet as many of the listed criteria as possible—and that the criteria are met as fully as possible. How thoroughly a benefit meets an individual criterion is a subjective call made by you and your team. It is another example of art over science. However, if a benefit only meets a few of these criteria, it might be downgraded to the rock classification, or it might get eliminated altogether. You will make these decisions on a case-by-case basis. As a general rule, there are eight primary criteria for a benefit to qualify as a boulder.

Boulder criteria:

- Must be material
- Must be reasonable
- Must be measurable
- Must be observable (where applicable)
- Must be attainable
- Must be corroborated
- Must be indisputable
- Must receive commitment

It Must Be Material

In public accounting, accountants are very concerned about transactions, discrepancies, and irregularities that are material. Material does not refer to fabric, nor does it refer to tangible items such as inventory. In this context, material, as defined by *Webster's Dictionary*, means "important, essential, substantial." The first test for a benefit to qualify as a potential boulder is that it must be substantial. A good litmus test for materiality in this context is that the prospective benefit must yield at least 25 percent of your total necessary benefits. You may recall the discussion of the Benefit Filter that you attempt to identify and quantify benefits that yield *ten* times the cost of the project (see chapter 7, "Understanding the Purpose of a Business Case"). Do not get lulled into thinking a benefit is a boulder because it yields 25 percent of the estimated project cost. Such a number would only yield 2.5 percent of your necessary benefit total. So even if a benefit would meet all of the other criteria, to be a boulder it must be material.

It Must Be Reasonable

We have all heard of business cases that suggest a 20 percent rise in sales revenues would be possible if the client would simply implement a proposed solution for customer relationship management (CRM). That might be possible. But it is unrealistic. Assume, for instance, that you are preparing a proposal that hinges on the potential growth in annual sales. A common test to assess reasonability of such a proposal is to reflect on the past five years' business performance. If sales growth for your company during the past five years was averaging 5–8 percent year-over-year growth, you push the outer boundaries of reasonability if you suggest a growth potential greater than twice the historic performance. The largest top line revenue improvement that you could reasonably suggest would be twice that, or 10–16 percent growth. Remember, to be successful, the business case must be credible. Suggesting benefits that are unreasonably optimistic erodes the credibility of your business case.

It Must Be Measurable

During your workshops, you'll often hear someone offer a benefit, followed by the proclamation, "Just trust me, this is huge…" Statements like that should make you skeptical. Remember, your goal is to create a credible business case. I would not expect a senior executive to believe me simply because I said, "Just trust me." Evidence is required. The same is true for your eager participants. You must be able to measure things as they are today and present reasonable supporting documentation that your company can achieve your projected benefit target. You will have to work with your interviewees and workshop participants to determine the benefit measurement.

Some measurements are easy, but they can be difficult to quantify. Let me explain. It's easy to say that the warehouse is inefficient—and it may be easy for you to make such a statement as you observe the activity in the warehouse. But for this criterion to be meaningful, you must be able to translate that inefficient activity into some measurement. Then you must be able to suggest, with credibility, that your proposal will favorably impact those measurements. The burden for arriving at such a measurement, however, is upon you, not the warehouse manager. You need to work with him to uncover the benefit opportunity and to reach some agreement on its measurement. You must apply the effort to convert what you see into something that a spreadsheet can compute. A simple test for measurability is to ask, "If we improve this area, how will we know? What items or performance metrics will change that we can measure?"

It Must Be Observable

Many times you will hear that certain processes are terribly inefficient. Or you will hear that the warehouse is woefully overstocked. In this case, you must be able to see the problem for yourself. This is different from needing to be able to measure a process; you need to physically see the offending process or object. It is not sufficient for you just to take someone's word on

faith. You must personally observe that this item is worthy of boulder status—or you must diplomatically demote and reclassify your participant's
suggestion because it really does not qualify as a boulder. A simple meeting to observe the process in question can allow you to confirm its boulder
status. Schedule a time when you can go with the department manager to
observe the process and interview the workers. During your meeting, ask
the workers for their suggestions for ways to improve and streamline the
inefficient process.

It Must Be Attainable

This may seem like a redundant restatement of an earlier criterion, namely,
that the benefit must be reasonable. The difference is subtle yet noteworthy. It may be reasonable for your company to improve inventory turnover to eight turns per year, but is it attainable? That answer often comes
by comparing your company to its peers—either companies in the same
industry or companies of similar complexity. If no one in that sample group
is achieving an eight-turn performance, it would seem unlikely that your
company can attain that goal.

Or consider this: you suggest that your company can increase revenue
by 10 percent. Is the achievement of this goal merely as simple as implementing your solution, or does this incremental benefit push the company
into a whole new performance bracket? For example, to increase revenue by
10 percent at a manufacturing company, the company has two options. The
company could simply raise prices 10 percent or they could sell 10 percent
more of their product. But the two options require different infrastructure
support. To raise the price only requires that the market accept the higher
price without reducing consumption. But to sell more product, there must
be a corresponding increase in production. If the manufacturing capacity is
already at maximum utilization, the proposed increase in production may
require additional investment, such as the acquisition of several new production machines and possibly even the addition of another shift of workers
to meet the increase in production demand. Those costs might adversely
impact your overall benefit impact. Therefore, you must determine that
your proposed benefit can be attained without undue cost or burden (or, if
the benefits are quite impressive, you can identify the added infrastructure
requirements and still show a justification for the project based on your
projected increase in revenue).

It Must Be Corroborated

Many workshop participants will suggest that implementing a new solution or changing a specific procedure can produce a benefit. Such suggestions can be alluring, especially when they sound like they will generate a sizable benefit. In such situations, finding others to corroborate your benefit assumptions will enhance the validity of the prospective benefit. Consider a trial attorney. She finds a witness who will testify that her client was not at the scene of the crime. Imagine how much more credible her statement becomes when she can provide additional corroborating witnesses to support the whereabouts of her client. Likewise, you gain credibility when you can substantiate a suggested benefit from multiple individuals. Your benefit assumptions are further enhanced when these individuals represent different departments.

It Must Be Indisputable

This criterion is similar to corroboration but on the flip side. In developing your business case, you will have occasions when colleagues will corroborate on the presence and value of a benefit. You may find that enthusiasm begins to grow as this benefit is added to your list of potential boulders, only to have a subsequent interviewee inform you that this benefit is overstated and simply is not as grand as you have been told. Naturally, such a contradiction requires its own evidence. And it is important to determine what has motivated this person to contradict your original documentation. If, however, your contrarian seems reliable and forthright, you may have to eliminate, or at least scale back, your benefit before presenting it to senior management. When faced with contradictory evidence, often you can salvage a benefit by negotiating with the parties holding the opposing view. First, get him (or them) to at least agree that there is some value to solving the problem (or to implementing your solution). Don't start with a specific value in mind; just gain agreement that there is some value. Once you gain that agreement, you can attempt to nudge them toward agreeing on a specific dollar value, which might be lower than your original number but will still be higher than zero. If you cannot gain agreement on a specific number, you can still keep this benefit in your existing list of benefits, but you'll need to acknowledge that some disagreement remains on the specific assessment of that benefit.

It Must Receive Commitment

This is a stumbling block for many first-time business case developers. Frequently, first-time business case creators build a spreadsheet, enter in some of the company's numbers, and produce a benefit projection that is impressive. The downfall for inexperienced business case developers is that the projections are only projections. They don't become credible, prospective benefits for the business case until they are reviewed and supported by the business manager responsible for that area.

For example, if you project benefits in the purchasing area that suggest your project will enable the purchasing team to negotiate better prices and thereby save the company 3 percent off all of its raw material purchases, you must gain the agreement from the responsible purchasing manager that such performance is reasonable, possible, and even likely. Because without her confirmation that your benefits are realistic, and without her willingness to stand up and embrace those projections as her own, your business case could be discredited when presented to senior management.

Here is a common scenario. Let's say that you look at the figures and determine that the purchasing department can save $500,000 a year by implementing a certain solution. The accounting manager agrees that this seems reasonable. So, without gaining specific agreement from the purchasing manager, you proceed to include this benefit in your presentation. During the presentation, you advance the idea that the company can save $500,000 per year by implementing your solution. Many heads nod in agreement. And then the unthinkable happens. The senior executive in the room turns to Beth, the purchasing manager, and asks, "Beth, what's your opinion of those numbers?" If you have not gained commitment from Beth in advance, you run the risk of having her state, "I reviewed these numbers before, but I never agreed that such an improvement was possible or even likely in our area. My team already does a great job of negotiating with our vendors, and I think these numbers are too aggressive, so I cannot support them." Imagine the awkwardness as everyone begins to question your thoroughness and the credibility of your business case. Gaining commitment from the responsible manager is vital to the credibility of your business case.

> Approach each benefit as though the responsible manager will have his or her compensation adjusted to align with this benefit.

You should approach each benefit as though the responsible manager will have his or her compensation adjusted to align with this benefit. Make a conscious effort to talk with the most senior person responsible for an area and work to gain his or her support for the numbers. This is a give-and-take conversation, and you may find that you may need to retreat a bit from your preliminary numbers in order to gain more enthusiastic approval.

A common negotiation will go like this: you suggest that a 5 percent improvement is possible in a business area. You determine that 5 percent is worth $350,000 in annual savings. The manager hears this and immediately begins to think that if your proposal is approved, she will have to achieve that $350,000 in savings in order to continue to receive her bonus, so she pushes back and wants to reduce the number. A commonly used tactic is to accept that 5 percent may be ambitious and pull back. In this case, you might ask, "Let's say 5 percent is an aggressive improvement. Would you at least agree that this proposal will be beneficial to your area?" This question seeks to reaffirm that you have, in fact, identified a legitimate benefit. Once there is agreement on that point, reintroduce the specific number by saying, "Well, we agree that there is a benefit from this proposal. If 5 percent is too ambitious, what number do you feel comfortable with? Do you think you could support a 3 percent improvement?" What you are doing is seeking to pin this manager to a number that you can use with confidence. To the best of your ability, don't let the manager escape with an incomplete commitment. Agreeing that there is a benefit but not receiving commitment to a specific percentage or dollar figure would leave your benefit incomplete. When this happens, as mentioned above under "It Must be Indisputable," you are left with a benefit that lacks a specific dollar value. Since our goal is to show that our project returns more than it costs, it is necessary to quantify as many benefits as possible. In pure mathematical terms, one side of your scale will show the cost of the project in dollars. If the other side has benefits without dollars, how will the approvers have confidence that your proposal is financially sound?

As noted above, it is a very rare potential benefit that fully satisfies all eight boulder criteria. Even some very credible boulders may lack one or two of these. It should always be your goal to achieve as many of these criteria as possible for each of your stated benefits. Don't get discouraged if some of your benefits lack a couple of these criteria. Many potential benefits carry sufficient credibility even when a couple of these criteria are not obtained. You have to determine which criteria, if any, can be omitted while still achieving a credible business case.

ROCKS AND PEBBLES

Many of the benefits that lack the criteria stated above are still worth capturing and evaluating. By investigating such opportunities, you will obtain a lot of benefit information for which people may have a great passion. They might not be able to measure the benefit, and they may not be able to collect a broad range of support for it, but they will believe it's a benefit nonetheless. And many times that's worth presenting to the executives.

In many instances, you will be able to dollarize your captured benefits, but in others you will not. When you cannot dollarize a benefit, you must be able to identify and explain its non-financial value (we'll explore that in chapter 47, "Don't Forget the Soft Benefits"). Improved employee morale is one frequently raised benefit. What is the value of improved employee morale? Even if you were able to dollarize employee morale, most managers would question the validity of the financial measures you used to value it. Yet if you implemented a solution that honestly improved employee morale, there would be a benefit to the organization and, as such, it should receive proper recognition as a valid, if non-financial, benefit. Improved employee morale might help reduce employee turnover (turnover is costly in lost productivity and in recruiting and readiness training costs). Improved morale might contribute to reduced employee theft. It might reduce the number of sick days taken by employees. In the end, many executives will treat employee morale as a valid, yet soft, non-financial benefit. Because of this, there should be a section in your business case where you can articulate these soft benefits.

You need to invest most of your effort striving to quantify measurable, attainable, high-value benefits. Once you've done that, though, you are wise to revisit the lists of rocks and pebbles because you may find some great nuggets there (no pun intended.) In upcoming chapters you'll learn how to build your case on the boulders that justify the project and then learn how to supplement that strong case with a bulleted list of benefits that didn't measure up to the standards of boulders and that you have not dollarized. It isn't that the benefits are not quantifiable—if you apply enough time and effort all benefits can be quantified—it's that you simply were not able to quantify them within your time and resource boundaries. You will want to be selective in the rocks and pebbles that you include in your presentation. Try to select ten or fewer and attempt to rank them by significance, where possible. Including these items will demonstrate that you listened to the various suggestions and incorporated those potential benefits that seemed viable. You'll see how this all comes together in the Analysis and Recommendation sections.

Chapter 28

Elevate Your Game with High-Yield Questions

In the next two chapters we will explore the two most common internal discovery methods—individual interviews and group workshops. Regardless which of those two methods you use, or how heavily you depend on one versus the other, you must prepare carefully for each discovery session.

While it is not possible for me to anticipate every potential solution you might be proposing, and therefore, impossible to supply you with a complete list of questions for each and every potential scenario, it is possible to guide you so that your discovery sessions are as productive as possible.

> High-yield questions are a staple of productive discovery sessions.

The use of high-yield questions is a common tool. High-yield questions are a staple of productive discovery sessions. Their name says it all—these questions evoke better responses (have a higher yield) than less thoughtful questions. So what are these high-yield questions? Simply put, they are questions that require more than a single word answer. These questions often begin with "How" or "What," For instance, you might ask, "How would a new inventory system help you improve the efficiency and accuracy of the inventory function?" or "What are the biggest bottlenecks in your department's workflow and how are they costly or unproductive?" You can imagine how much richer the answers to such questions might be than if you were simply to ask, "Does your department have bottlenecks?" That question might only produce a "yes" or "no" answer. Not a very productive discovery session.

High-yield questions need to be prepared in advance. This is probably why they are used so infrequently. Most people hate to plan and falsely believe that they can just wing it. To elevate your own status as a professional and to harvest the very best out of a limited timeslot, you must prepare your questions in advance. A good starting point is to plan five good thought-provoking questions for each of your individual interviews. In preparing these questions, a simple method is this: take the time to identify the primary activities of each department that you will interview. Typically, the list of primary activities is relatively short. For example, the order management function might have the following activities:

- Receive request for quotation
- Convert quotation to order
- Verify order for completeness
- Obtain credit approval
- Route approved order
    o   To manufacturing, if items must be manufactured
    o   To fulfillment, if items are in the warehouse and available for shipping
- Invoice customer

Once you have identified the primary activities, you can adapt the following questions to explore the challenges in each department and within each of their primary activities.

Here are some examples of high-yield questions:

- [General]: What are the three biggest challenges with the ____ aspect of your department? (The underscored area would be the name of one of the primary activities of that department—such as obtaining credit approval).
- [If your proposed solution focuses on the human resource function...]: When a new company is acquired, what are the biggest challenges in integrating those new employees into our company?

- [If your proposed solution focuses on the sales function]: Explain your account planning and business development strategy. How do you prioritize your pursuits to optimize success?
- [If your proposed solution focuses on the manufacturing planning function]: What are the biggest challenges you have with the current production planning process?
- [If your proposed solution focuses on the finance and accounting function]: Month-end closing process is a challenge in most large companies. What are the biggest challenges facing your department regarding month-end processing?

Once you have explored the primary activities of this department, you should ask if there are other challenges that concern your interviewee that you didn't ask about. A common question would be to confirm that you have listed all of their primary activities. This simple follow-up question will ensure that you have given your interviewee a chance to voice those concerns that are of most interest to him or her.

The sample questions above are just the first step. Once you have asked those questions, and received and documented the response, there are at least two follow-up questions that you should prepare to ask, and you should ask them at every interview. First, ask, "What are the impacts of those challenges?" With this question you are hoping to hear that the challenges create inefficiency, additional cost, possibly some overtime, maybe even redundant steps. Any similar response is helpful to your business case. Take copious notes as you'll want to be able to refer to these conversations and specifically to the statements your interviewees have made about various challenges. Quoting these statements will support your hypothesis that your proposed solution will be valuable to the company. As you are engaging in this discovery activity, be sure to capture the interviewee's statements as precisely as you can. You may even need to have the interviewee repeat his or her statements to ensure that you capture them accurately. When an executive makes a strong statement such as "This single annoyance is easily costing us hundreds of thousands of dollars every year," you can add valuable credibility to your business case by quoting him directly by name.

For the next follow-up question, you may need to introduce the question with a bit of empathy and concern. You should certainly phrase this the way that works best for you. Here is one example. "Those sound like costly/nagging/disruptive challenges. You've probably given some thought to the cost of these challenges. What do you think would be the value of mitigating or eliminating them?" Again, be sure to take careful notes of what your interviewee says. Even though she may not be able to mathematically quantify the value of solving these challenges, she will likely respond with words that clearly convey value. Write down those statements. You can work on the specific math later. For now, especially in executive interviews, simply hearing the interviewee tell you that there is value in solving this problem will advance the credibility of your business case. In chapter 51, "Packaging Your Recommendation" you will learn how these quotes fit into your presentation and how they add strength to your business case.

As you consider your questions, be aware that certain easy-sounding questions can backfire and create unrealistic expectations. One question to avoid is this: "If you could wave a magic wand, what three things would make your environment more successful and more productive?" This question leads the interviewee into falsely thinking that you can actually deliver them their wish list. You may not think it does, but it creates an air of expectation that your solution will solve all of the current problems. So, as a general rule, do not ask hypothetical questions for which you do not possess the resources to deliver.

The final high-yield question is a general follow-up to any statement made during an interview or group workshop. The question is, "Can you please elaborate?" This allows the person to offer further explanation. Additionally, it allows you to explore deeper and keeps you from accidentally relying on your assumptions. You want to hear the individuals tell you, in their own words, the full scope and difficulty of a particular challenge.

Chapter 29

Collecting Evidence in Individual Interviews

An old, familiar story tells of the three apprentice scientists who were blindfolded and told to examine an object simply by touch. They did not know what they were examining nor did they know that they were all examining the same object—a circus elephant. One scientist was placed by the trunk, one by the tail, and one by one of the legs. They were each asked to examine the object with their hands and explain what they thought they were examining. The scientist who examined the trunk explained that he had a coarsely wrapped hose, like a fire hose. The scientist who examined the tail explained that his object seemed to be like a rope. Finally, the scientist examining the leg explained that his object was large and sturdy, like a tree trunk. When the blindfolds were removed they saw that they were all examining the same object, but from different perspectives. Additionally, it was clear to each of them that they did not have a complete perspective, merely a narrow one based on the limitations of their individual examinations.

This anecdote provides a good reference for us. As we discussed in chapter 23, your discovery work is similar to the discovery work performed by trial attorneys. And like them, you should expect to hear different perspectives about the same topic. One interviewee might state that the invoicing system is wonderful while another might state that it is inadequate to do the job. You need to accept that both may be right, at least from their perspective. You need to also understand that neither has the full perspective. Your objective is to collect evidence that confirms and amplifies your hypothesis. Evidence that contradicts or questions your hypothesis is also worth documenting. You may choose to reevaluate its value later, but always capture as much as you are able during your meetings.

One successful approach for discovery is to use brief individual interviews for the executives and to use group discovery workshops for the managers and their staffs. This is not a requirement; it is simply a method that has proven quite effective. Many of the questions and suggestions that you'll read in the next few chapters are not specific to a situation. You may find that certain high-yield questions that were introduced in the previous chapter are equally effective in both individual interviews and group workshops. Likewise, you might find some of the group workshop questions and suggestions found in chapters 30 and 31 might be applicable for you in your individual executive interviews. One size does not fit all. You must use your own judgment to determine where and when these suggestions are most helpful for you.

PLANNING FOR AND CONDUCTING AN EXECUTIVE INTERVIEW

Executives, by the nature of their role, will often know the high-level impact of issues, but may not know the granular details of specific problems. However, they will understand and wish to improve the big-picture items. So while executives may not know the exact technical details of the warehouse bar coding system, they will likely know if the warehouse is not as efficient as it is expected to be and if the inefficiency is costly in terms of overtime, slow shipments, or misplaced orders. Therefore, expect a different perspective from the executives when you conduct their interviews compared with the perspective that you will hear from managers and front-line workers on the same topics.

Executive interviews must be concise, well-organized and punctual. You can ensure that you achieve these objectives by following a simple three-step approach: planning, executing, and reviewing.

Step One—Planning

As stated in chapter 26, "Plan before You Explore", work with your executive sponsor to determine who should be interviewed. Depending on the scope of your business case, you'll want to suggest certain interview candidates by role (e.g., vice president of sales, vice president of human resources, etc.). Your sponsor will likely want to know what you hope to gain from each executive. Planning helps you demonstrate your preparedness to your sponsor and optimize your time with your interviewees.

> Before you sit down with an executive, you should know what outcome you expect from this interview.

In addition to the discovery plan that was introduced in chapter 26 you will find additional value when you invest the time to plan each executive interview and group workshop individually. One helpful element of your planning is to prepare a document listing the "Meeting Objectives" for each interview and workshop. This is a simple, brief document, often no more than one or two paragraphs, that lists the objectives you seek from these interviews. Before you sit down with an executive, you should know what outcome you expect from this interview. Don't begin your meeting planning five minutes before your meeting time; do it an hour or more beforehand so that you can devote adequate mental effort to planning your conversation. One key meeting objective for which you are responsible is to present a clear, concise overview of the proposed project. After you present the overview, you should ask your interviewee for his perspective on the merits of such a project. You do this so that you can gain this executive's unique outlook and interpretation. Another objective is to gauge the executive's enthusiasm or resistance to such a project. This knowledge may be helpful later as you seek to build a coalition for support of your capital funding request.

As you plan your interviews, pay some attention to timing and time management. Scheduling your interviews and workshops is a challenging task, and sometimes the need to complete them quickly interferes with completing them thoroughly. Some schedulers attempt to schedule interviews back-to-back-to-back, often only allowing a modest break for lunch. Using this approach, a planner can pack twelve or more interviews in a single day. I favor a different, more extended approach. When planning your interview sessions, plan for each executive session to last about a half an hour and plan the next one to start thirty minutes later. For example, start your first thirty-minute interview at eight o'clock in the morning and schedule the next one to begin at nine o'clock. If you are collaborating with other team members, you'll find it very beneficial to type your notes into your laptop or tablet while they are still fresh in your mind. You may also want to fill in the blanks in your notes—to input information that you were simply unable to write down during the actual conversation. During your review time, you might discover some follow-up questions that you want to ask. You might note additional executives that you'll want to meet that were not originally on your schedule. Allowing the thirty-minute buffer between interviews gives you a small amount of time to collect your thoughts before the next interview.

Step Two—Executing

Executing the executive interview can be intimidating for inexperienced business case developers. If you feel intimidated, consider asking your sponsor to attend the first one or two interviews with you to help you break the ice. His or her rapport with other executives should set you at ease and help you gain the confidence necessary to conduct the other interviews solo.

As you begin your executive interviews, thank the executive for meeting with you, give him or her a quick overview of your project and why you've asked for the interview, and then get right into your questions. Be prepared to take very good notes. You don't know when you'll get the chance to meet with this person again. As you ask your questions, be sure that you understand what the executive is saying. If any statement is unclear to you, politely ask him or her to clarify. Without clarification, you might just assume the wrong things and unintentionally undermine your own effectiveness. Authors Khalsa and Illig state this issue quite clearly in their book. In it they state, "To avoid guessing and assuming, it is helpful to listen carefully to the *key* words and phrases clients use, and then ask them what those words mean to them. It is astounding how often clients respond with something very different from what we expect, or at least something very useful and illuminating" (pg. 34). For example, suppose your executive interviewee stated, "The warehouse is a real problem." What do you suppose he meant? Did he mean that the pick-pack-and-ship process in the warehouse is inefficient? Or did he mean that the warehouse is bursting at the seams because there is too much inventory being housed there? Or did he mean that the labor force was struggling to learn the new bar code technology that was recently implemented? I hope you see the problem.

Without clarification you simply won't have the certainty of your assumption. Always ask for clarification of anything you don't understand. Don't nod in agreement if you are unsure. Such timidity will only weaken your business case when you later present your assumptions and find out that you are wrong.

Time management is an important consideration for the successful execution of an executive interview. When you request a time slot from an executive, be respectful of his or her time. If you request thirty minutes, do not overstay your welcome. When the thirty minutes have expired, conclude your interview and request an additional time slot if you need more data. By sticking to your allotted time you will be more likely to be granted a return visit. If you run over your time slot, it shows a disregard for the executive's schedule, and that is rarely appreciated. Remember, executives influence capital approvals even if they are not on the approval team. Being disrespectful to any executive is not a prudent act and punctuality is simply another aspect of respect.

Step Three—Reviewing

After each interview, you should spend a few private minutes reviewing the notes. This is an often overlooked or postponed step. It can be especially hard to review your notes if you have scheduled interviews back-to-back-to-back in the name of efficiency. Allowing half an hour between meetings might seem inefficient. It is not. You need that time to review your notes from the recent interview. Postponing the review activity has consequences. If you postpone this review, you risk forgetting what some of your cryptic notes mean. As more time passes, you'll find it more difficult to remember many of the nuances of the meeting. Do yourself a favor and schedule a solitary review time after each interview. This post-meeting review is just as important after the group workshops as it is for the executive interviews.

Planning, executing and reviewing are the keys to successful discovery interview sessions. Next, we'll explore evidence-gathering considerations for the group workshop format.

Chapter 30

Collecting Evidence Using Group Workshops

Group workshops are a great way to collect a significant amount of rich data for your business case. To be successful, you must give proper attention to two basic areas—planning and execution.

PLANNING FOR SUCCESSFUL WORKSHOPS

Like the previously discussed executive interviews, successful workshops require careful planning. There are five things you need to consider when planning your workshop:

1. Consider your desired outcome
2. Prepare an invitee list to achieve your desired outcome
3. Create a plan to engage the participants
4. Consider the logistics of your workshop to increase productivity
5. Execute the successful workshop (next three chapters)

Consider Your Desired Outcome

We touched on this in the last chapter, and it bears repeating. It is always beneficial to begin with the outcome in mind. This does not mean that you know the answers to all of your questions in advance. It means that you should have a good definition, at least in your own mind, of what a successful workshop should achieve. Here are a few examples of common, reasonable workshop outcomes:

- To understand the current state of the IT department including the challenges and costs associated with running the department (to include annual support contracts, IT payroll costs—employees and contractors, etc.);
- To understand the primary inputs, outputs and challenges of the shipping process;
- To understand the collaboration challenges between the sales and internal support teams;
- To understand the challenges of the HR department and to capture the value of improved access to better information.

Prepare an Invitee List to Achieve Your Desired Outcome

Once you know what you are trying to accomplish with your workshop, you can then begin to create a proper invitee list. You will want to invite people who can contribute to your outcome. It is best to limit your invitations to those who actually have a stake in the outcome and not just those who want to be heard. Workshop success is largely dependent on the participants. Let's assume that you are proposing a new purchasing system. One successful approach to participant selection is to use a simple "input-process-output" criterion. It works as follows. Which departments send information to purchasing? Who processes the information within purchasing? And to which departments does purchasing send information? This helps you understand all affected parties.

When considering exactly who to invite, consider inviting managers and directors rather than front-line staff. For business case purposes, we seek to keep our information at an executive business level. Though rare, there will be instances where front-line staffers seize the workshop setting as a venue to vent their frustrations with concerns that are less strategic and more tactical or administrative. Some of those concerns might be relevant to your business case, but frequently they can be disruptive distractions. We will discuss facilitation strategies to handle these disruptions in the next chapter, "Executing Successful Workshops." You will have to use your judgment as to which participants will be most likely to help you reach your desired outcome. Another cautionary note—sometimes you will become aware of friction or disputes between departments, specifically when one department serves another department. In those cases it might be helpful to schedule independent workshops to gather your first round of data. Keep in mind that our objective for our business case is to confirm our hypothesis and identify the value of solving the challenges presented in that hypothesis. Disputing parties can often attempt to focus on blaming others or defending an unpopular approach, which is usually not productive for our business case efforts. Seek guidance from your sponsor if you suspect disputes and friction on certain topics.

Create a Plan to Engage the Participants

Simply convening a meeting or workshop does not, by itself, inspire the participants to engage in helpful discourse. You must come prepared to guide the participants to engage. You must prepare to facilitate a productive workshop. A good starting point for your plan is to share the hypothesis with the participants and ask for their perspectives. Next, plan to share your desired outcome (as discussed earlier in this chapter). This helps the assembled participants align with your goals. This foundational work ensures that your workshop will be launched well and move in the direction in which you intend. Once the workshop expectations have been communicated, you'll want to consider how you move the discussion in such a way that you achieve your objectives. High-yield questions—along with the exercises in chapters 32 through 34—are great tools for getting workshop participants to engage.

Consider the Logistics of Your Workshop to Increase Productivity

Where and when you hold your workshop is not the most important variable in determining its success, except when the time and place are inadequate to do the job. These sessions are not lectures but working sessions where many people will be taking notes, retrieving documents from laptops, and so on. If the room is too confining, the participants will not be comfortable. And their discomfort could hamper your effectiveness in reaching your workshop goals. If you expect fifteen people to attend your workshop, you must secure a conference room large enough to comfortably accommodate all of these people and all of their meeting paraphernalia. Many people come to a meeting with their laptop, their cell phone, and possibly a notebook. Some will bring their coffee mug. If the room only seats fifteen people, it will be too small for your fifteen invitees if they bring all of their gear. A good rule of thumb is to book a conference room that has a capacity 30 percent larger than your initial needs. If you plan to have fifteen people, book a room that holds twenty. This allows for last-minute additions to the attendee list and allows each participant enough elbow room to work in the workshop.

Your meeting room should contain either a large whiteboard or several flipcharts. You're going to be writing things down for everyone to see. It's necessary for the participants to see the workshop notes in front of them. It's also very helpful to have a small point-and-shoot camera or a camera phone with a high-resolution lens. This is helpful as it allows you to take a picture of all of your notes on the whiteboard before someone accidentally erases them.

Now that your workshop is planned, let's explore some effective techniques for maximum workshop success.

Chapter 31

Executing Successful Workshops

Workshops are a very productive method for gathering evidence. Workshops, when planned and executed effectively, will yield great value. But the results of a workshop are directly related to the amount of planning you invest before conducting your workshop. You have got to be prepared and you must be an assertive facilitator. You cannot approach workshops casually because you have too much to cover in a limited amount of time.

> Workshops, when planned and executed effectively, will yield great value. But the results of a workshop are directly related to the amount of planning you invest before conducting your workshop.

Without getting too prescriptive, workshops need to flow and, due to frequent time limitations, must be carefully managed. Part of the effective management of a workshop hinges on two key workshop roles—facilitator and scribe. The facilitator runs the workshop and the scribe captures all of notes, issues and action items that arise out of the workshop. Whenever possible, you should consider enlisting someone other than yourself to be the scribe. It's often hard to act as both the scribe and the facilitator. The role of the scribe is more than just taking notes in the workshop. Though note taking is the primary function, the scribe must also capture the names and contact information of each of the attendees, be assertive (while also being polite) to ask individuals to clarify statements made during the meeting (so that the notes are accurate), and assume the responsibility for distributing the notes to all appropriate recipients soon after the workshop concludes.

Facilitation, however, is the real key to a successful workshop. If you are not familiar with facilitation or not as well skilled as you would like, consider Roger Schwarz's the excellent book, *The Skilled Facilitator*. In his book, Schwarz states, "Organizations typically use groups to plan and implement change, and groups typically need some form of facilitation. In addition, facilitative skills have become more important as organizations try to openly and constructively manage conflict arising from the change they try to create. At the heart of improving group effectiveness lies the ability of group members to reflect on what they are doing, to create the conditions necessary to achieve their goals. Groups find it difficult to openly examine behavior on their own; they often need the help of a facilitator" (pg. 5). As facilitator, your role is to coax discussion and interaction out of the assembled workshop participants. The facilitator does not come with a certain answer in mind, with the hope of coercing the participants to agree with that answer. Rather, a good facilitator uses tools and skills to guide the participants on a journey of discovery—a journey that is kept within certain guardrails, such as maintaining scope, sticking to the workshop schedule, and seeking value statements for your hypothesis.

As facilitator, you'll learn that there is no single discovery method that ensures you'll capture every issue and uncover every benefit opportunity. This is another one of those art versus science things. Below, I've listed my three favorite facilitated exercises:

1. Creating a prioritized list of challenges (explained in chapter 32)
2. Leading a SWOT exercise (explained in chapter 33)
3. Charting the organization's capability maturity (explained in chapter 34)

Each of these three exercises work well in nearly every scenario and provide for highly interactive workshops. The value of these three exercises is that they provoke different discussions about different perspectives from your workshop participants. By using them as a package of exercises, you should be able to discover a great deal about your organization and where the potential benefits may be hiding.

As the facilitator, your goal is to guide the workshop attendees toward the creation of a prioritized list of challenges complete with an assessment of value for solving each challenge. You can use these three exercises to achieve this goal. For your workshop, consider adding a fourth exercise that summarizes the previous three exercises and documents the preliminary value of solving the listed challenges. Your workshop agenda, then, might look like this:

1. Create a prioritized list of challenges.
2. Capture the SWOT considerations for each challenge.
3. Assess your organization's current and future capability maturity levels.
4. Summarize and document the value of solving each challenge.

Typically, you'll plan for your workshops to last four to eight hours. Four hours is more common, since it has become difficult to get managers to allocate eight-hour blocks of time to be away from their other responsibilities. As you begin planning your workshops, consider time-boxing the major activities. Here's one suggestion for how you might break down your four-hour workshop (your specific time allocations will depend on the breadth of your discussion topic and the level of enthusiasm and engagement of your assembled workshop participants):

- First fifteen minutes—introduce the hypothesis, introduce the workshop participants, and establish the ground rules for the workshop.
- Next thirty minutes—produce the prioritized list.
- Next ninety minutes—facilitate the SWOT exercise.
- Next sixty minutes—facilitate discussion of your organization's capability maturity. You'll want to determine both your current capability and your desired future capability.
- Final forty-five minutes—summarize the previous exercises and define the value of solving these challenges.

Using this approach, you should end up with a good list of potential benefits and a good idea of their financial value to the organization.

Time-boxing the workshops in this way will require that you stay on task and that you help the attendees stay focused on the workshop objectives. It will be beneficial for you to inform the workshop participants that the workshop must move crisply through these topics. Workshops can easily take on a life of their own and, as facilitator, your job is to keep the workshop on task without dictating the results. It is also best to keep the Pareto principle in mind. That's the familiar 80—20 rule that we addressed in chapter 9, "Building a Successful Business Case Template." You'll find that you'll get 80 percent of the relevant content in 20 percent of the time if you focus and facilitate effectively. It is possible that any one of these workshop exercises could easily consume a full four hours, or even six hours. But the additional value from all of that extra time does not justify the excessive time commitment. If you are prepared, and if you facilitate properly, you'll get a wealth of value from a four-hour workshop.

USING A PARKING LOT TO KEEP YOUR WORKSHOP ON TASK

One of the biggest challenges in any workshop is keeping the discussion moving in the direction that you desire. It is your responsibility to keep the discussion moving forward to develop the prioritized list, discuss the SWOT considerations, assess the organization's maturity, and finally weigh in on the value of solving those challenges—all within the constraints of your allotted time.

Every workshop has the potential to go astray. One reason that these workshops go astray is quite simple. In today's very hectic and overscheduled business climate, peers are not often assembled together for meetings. When they get together, they seize the opportunity to discuss some tactical, less relevant issues that have been a nuisance for them. And when another of their peers agrees and continues the dialogue, before you know it, the conversation is out of your control. Another common distraction is the discussion of the potential software solution (when a new software solution is being considered). A frequent distraction will start rather innocently. A participant will ask, "Does the new software do X or Y?" Since your workshop participants may have a high level of interest in the future software selection, software functionality is an all-too-common distraction.

When any of these distractions arise, how do you smoothly return the workshop to the topic at hand? This is another key facilitation skill for which you should prepare. When the workshop veers off topic, another dynamic is at work. And that's the dynamic that if you rein the participants in with some clumsy approach, you risk offending them. If you ignore their discussion and simply change the topic, you open the door for one of them to tell their management that you did not listen to their concerns. (This behavior is more common than you might think.) To avoid this, plan to have a "Parking Lot." A Parking Lot is a simple facilitation tactic that allows you to capture off-topic issues without allowing them to distract you from your primary mission. Creating a Parking Lot is a simple thing. Either set up a separate flipchart or cordon off a section of the whiteboard as your Parking Lot. When issues arise that you determine are off topic, simply comment to the group that you acknowledge the concern and you acknowledge that this issue needs further discussion, but this is not the forum for that additional discussion. Then write the issue on the Parking Lot and appoint someone to be responsible for following up on that issue after the workshop. The interested parties can certainly have their own separate meeting to address these Parking Lot issues without involving you and your business case team. By using a Parking Lot, you ensure that any tangential discussions that arise during your workshop are properly captured and assigned, but you also ensure that you aren't squandering precious workshop time with discussions that are not relevant to your business case.

> The challenge of marching through all of these workshop activities and arriving at some statement of value for each challenge is mentally exhausting. You should anticipate that your workshop participants will grow weary.

ADDRESSING BENEFIT DEFINITION FATIGUE

One other topic that must be addressed is benefit definition fatigue. The challenge of marching through all of these workshop activities and arriving at some statement of value for each challenge is mentally exhausting. You should anticipate that your workshop participants will grow weary. Benefit definition fatigue sets in when you repeatedly ask the assembled group to burrow into the value of each benefit that you've identified. Initially the group is engaged in the activity, but after a few benefits the work seems tedious and the group quickly tires of the repeated attempts to explain and quantify the benefits. Commonly, group members will state their displeasure with such statements as, "Trust us, this is a real benefit even if we can't explain the value right now." They may even disengage by exclaiming,

"Determining the value is your job, isn't it?" While it is your responsibility to prepare the Recommendation, including the value of the benefits, you need the input and collaboration from these subject matter experts to add credibility and context for your final presentation.

To be a successful facilitator, you should anticipate this phenomenon (benefit definition fatigue) and, when you recognize it, plan to take a short break or park that benefit and move on to another benefit or another topic. You can always return to a difficult benefit later, or you can pursue it individually with the one or two key participants who might have the best perspective on that specific benefit and its potential value. The key is to press through and not let the fatigue dictate your schedule or diminish your resolve to accomplish your goal. However, you want to be careful not to be too eager to defer too many individual benefit discussions as you can create a mountain of extra work for yourself. You are better served if you can get the group to press through the fatigue and address the benefits while you are all together.

WORKSHOP SYNERGY—AN UNEXPECTED BY-PRODUCT

Workshops often yield an unexpected yet very productive by-product. It's a function of having different constituencies interact on the same topic. Some will identify one item as a problem, while others will point to that same item and declare that it is inconsequential. This often creates great dialogue. For instance, one group may not have known that another group was wrestling with a problem. When they hear about it during your workshop, they share how they have solved that problem with the other group. In this case, your workshop has facilitated synergy in the organization. This is another benefit of the workshop. The benefit is that you have provided a platform for this productive exchange of ideas. Admittedly, this doesn't directly help you towards your assignment. But it does help you as it elevates you to the role of trusted advisor. You're helping them (even though it may be more accurate to say that they helped themselves). They will associate you with these helpful meetings.

With that as a background, let's begin planning our workshop, starting with the creation of a prioritized list of challenges.

Chapter 32

Making Workshops Count: Exercise #1—Creating a Prioritized List

As workshop facilitator you must come to the workshop prepared to lead the discussion and lead the group to a productive result. Part of your advanced preparation is to create the straw man list of discussion topics. For our purposes, we will define a straw man list as "a list of reasonable discussion points that will be edited and refined by a group of subject matter experts." We will assume that our workshop participants represent the subject matter experts on the workshop discussion topic.

How should you prepare this straw man list, and what items should be included? For many of you, this is an unfamiliar exercise. With that in mind, follow this example. You'll start with some basic research. Find a few key executive magazines, business books, and Internet sites. You can usually find what you need at your local public library or via an Internet search. Focus your search on those resources that target executive audiences. You are looking for top ten lists related to your workshop discussion topic. Many magazines, books, and Internet sites survey their readers and collect the top things that executives worry about. That list will likely vary by industry. Manufacturing executives face different challenges from restaurant or health care executives. Some challenges will be the same, such as hiring and retaining top performers, but others will be unique by industry. In any top ten list, there will likely be items that are relevant to your project. Review these lists and create one of your own with eight to twelve good bullet points. You may also wish to spend some time with your executive sponsor and learn what, if any, additional items he might add to your list. This list will serve as your opening discussion slide in your first exploratory meeting or workshop. Let's walk through a real-life example.

For this example, you'll start with the hypothesis that there is value in upgrading the current human resource (or HR) software system. An HR system is a pretty broad topic. You're going to invite a number of HR managers and directors to a workshop to talk through the issues and, hopefully, produce a prioritized list of challenges. Later on, you'll work to determine the value—or benefit—of solving these challenges with your recommended HR software system. To make your workshop productive, you need to get the participants engaged in discussion. One method is to create a list of several common challenges for a business area (HR, in this case). Present that list to the workshop participants and facilitate some interaction and debate. For this example, I did a quick Internet search for "top HR challenges" and found several useful results. Among the common challenges were these four items:

- Retaining high-potential talent
- Making managers better coaches
- Making the onboarding process easier and more effective
- Preparing for mergers and acquisitions

As part of your preparation as the workshop leader, you would want to add other discussion topics to this initial list so that you had at least eight discussion points for your workshop. Your goal will be to list a number of points that seem like reasonable concerns or discussion topics to you. I will caution you to not get too invested in these topics. That's why this is a straw man. It's going to get picked apart by the workshop participants. And that's a good thing. You might be tempted to abandon this recommendation and just start with a blank whiteboard and ask the participants to list their concerns. Unfortunately, that frequently leads to two negative outcomes. First, you will look woefully unprepared. This diminishes your credibility. Second, you risk that the group will begin listing a number of complaints and nuisance items that will not produce a productive, prioritized list of strategic concerns. Such a turn of events poses the risk that your workshop will focus on tactical items and you'll find yourself deep in the weeds. As facilitator, invest the time to come to your workshop as prepared as possible.

At the end of the workshop, you need the participants to believe that the resulting list reflects their views, not just yours. With that in mind, you should create a list of eight to twelve reasonable challenges before you meet with your workshop group. If you are planning multiple workshops on different topics, invest the time to create individual, relevant lists for each planned workshop. The lists might be similar, but they should be unique to the area of focus for the workshop. Start with a list like the one above and possibly add a couple of additional points that you find through additional Internet searches. For example, you might assert that companies have challenges with benefit administration. That would be another bullet point. You might also discover that companies wrestle with HR policy documentation—ensuring that all managers know the company's policies and know where to find the most up-to-date documentation regarding those policies. You might benefit from a brief discussion with one of the executives from that business area to gain his or her perspective on the top challenges facing the HR department. Your role as leader/facilitator demands that you invest the time to lead a productive workshop.

FACILITATE A DISCUSSION THAT LEADS TO A PRIORITIZED LIST

When you convene the group, you will present your list in the following way: "Here are some common challenges that seem to concern HR departments." Ask the participants to review the list and pick out the three or four items that most reflect their challenges. The goal is to produce a manageable list that is specific to your workshop. Three or four challenges per workshop will be viewed as a success. Conversely, six to ten challenges, while seemingly more beneficial, will actually be detrimental to your cause. That many challenges will take too long to work through. If there are that many challenges, you may wish to choose half of the list for one workshop and defer the second half of the list for a subsequent workshop. There will likely be some discussion among the participants as different people will assert that different items are more relevant, and they all won't agree. You'll want to facilitate a discussion within reasonable time constraints to ensure that this portion of your workshop yields beneficial results within your defined timeframe. Your goal is not to have all participants agree that your list is complete or accurate. Your goal is to facilitate a discussion that results in a prioritized list of three or four items that can be translated into a list of potential benefits. Don't get discouraged if the participants reject several of your original bullet points. That simply means that they are engaged in the discussion and are helping you identify the real challenges that they face. It also means that your initial discussion points have been refined by the assembled subject matter experts and they are fulfilling their responsibilities as workshop participants.

Finally, never assume that any list that you present is complete. You should always position your list to be a starting point or a springboard for discussion. It could be that your list is wonderfully comprehensive. But don't assume that. Assume that there are issues that are unique to the participants that you could not have anticipated. Ask them for additions to your list. Even encourage additions by saying something lighthearted like, "Surely I didn't guess 100 percent correctly. What else should we discuss while on this topic?"

Once you have your list, you need to prioritize this list. Think back to our discussion in chapter 27 on boulders, rocks, and pebbles. You want your prioritized list to reflect the potential benefit of solving that challenge. Be aware that some challenges are real nuisances to your assembled workshop participants. But nuisances are often not strategic, executive-level concerns. You'll have to coach your participants to think through the value of solving a problem and you'll want to place the highest priority on those challenges that represent the highest value if solved. Some of the nuisance items will likely filter to the bottom of your list.

There are a number of ways to get the group to assign priority. Since we are only dealing with three or four items, you might simply ask the group if these items reflect their biggest challenges. Allow time for some discussion. You don't need to scientifically determine which is the number one challenge or which is the number three challenge. What is important is that your list of three or four challenges represents the three or four most challenging items in your participants' business area. If the group does not agree with the list that has been compiled, circle around again and solicit input for additional challenges. It is important not to be too eager to finish at the expense of being thorough.

Now that we have a prioritized list, let's proceed on to the SWOT diagram.

Chapter 33

Making Workshops Count: Exercise #2—Utilizing a SWOT Diagram

The second useful tool for gathering evidence is called the SWOT diagram. SWOT stands for strengths, weaknesses, opportunities, and threats. It is believed to have been first used (and possibly created) by Albert Humphrey while at Stanford University during the 1960s and 1970s.

Current	Strengths	Weaknesses
Future	Opportunities	Threats

Even before you employ this tool in your workshops, you might consider asking your sponsor to walk through a SWOT diagram with you.

Your sponsor's perspective will often give you a baseline from which to facilitate your workshop discussion. You could use your sponsor's comments as opening items for each of the SWOT sections.

Facilitating a SWOT discussion within your workshop will provide you with another perspective. This exercise will provoke a different set of discussion topics from the ones you gleaned from the prioritized list exercise. This additional perspective will be helpful because this discussion typically provokes a lively discussion and debate. The debate often reveals additional potential benefit topics.

Consider this possibility: user teams don't know when they're inefficient. You might find that statement outrageous, but follow the logic. Users have been living with their current environment for months, maybe years. They've learned to live with the weaknesses, complexities, and inefficiencies of their system. They've created suitable workaround steps, albeit often manual and inefficient, to accomplish their assigned tasks. You have to acknowledge that they are achieving their objective. If a team has been assigned the task of creating and mailing out invoices, they have found a way to do that, even if their current processes are terribly complex and inefficient. So when you talk about a new invoicing system, it may not be readily apparent to your users that they are working harder than they need to when they prepare and mail invoices. They may also not readily acknowledge that they have a need for a newer method or that there could even be a better way of doing such a routine and mundane task. They've become accustomed to the way that they are working. It may take some time—through individual and group conversations—for the collective light bulb to shine and for them to openly acknowledge that there is a better way. The effectiveness of your questions will help guide them down a path that allows them to discover for themselves that their current method is inefficient and that an alternate method is much better and more efficient. For this reason, our SWOT exercise can be very helpful and enlightening.

When you look at the SWOT diagram, imagine a horizontal line dividing the grid in half. The Strengths and Weaknesses sections refer to the current environment. The Opportunities and Threats sections refer to the potential future solution. When planning for a thorough SWOT discussion for a group, prepare to facilitate this discussion with thoughtful guidance. If you're casual and freewheeling with this exercise, it can easily consume several hours and yield few results. As you plan for your SWOT exercise, bear in mind that each section yields its own results. The questions that are relevant for the Strengths section are not typically relevant for the Weaknesses section. The same holds true for the Opportunities and Threats sections.

One approach in using the SWOT has proven to be highly effective. As you plan this exercise, you'll want to set some guardrails for the discussion. One good set of guardrails would be to list the business activities within the scope of this particular workshop. We'll use a technique I call the modified business flow SWOT analysis. The modified business flow SWOT analysis starts with a relevant business flow. Let's stick with our HR example from the previous chapter. What are the business processes in the HR realm? Here are a few that come to mind:

- Create formal job description
- Determine job compensation and benefit plan
- Post job opening on appropriate internal and external websites
- Recruit candidates
- Hire new employee
- Perform onboarding (including provisioning for appropriate responsibilities)
- Enroll new employee in benefits plan
- Maintain employee data
- Manage time and attendance
- Pay employee
- Report financial/payroll data (departmental and governmental)
- Manage regulatory compliance (EEOC, Vets, H-1B, etc.)
- Manage employee termination
- Perform offboarding (including all deprovisioning)

In your workshop, present a list like this to your workshop participants as the starting point for your discussions. Confirm with them that you have listed all of the processes that they execute in the course of their daily work activities. They might suggest a few other items, which you would add to your initial list. Now that you have a list of business processes, you can begin facilitating the SWOT discussion. Ask the group to begin brainstorming about the strengths within the existing business flows. You will find that it will be helpful to solicit their perspectives on the overall business area as a whole, and not at the individual process level. Attempting to do a SWOT exercise for each individual business flow would be too tedious and too granular, and it would introduce fatigue very quickly. Keep this at the overall business area level for this exercise.

Our goal for each of these exercises is to gather evidence that supports our hypothesis. We are not just collecting random lists of interesting bullet points. For the Strengths section, our goal is to understand the perception of the current environment (or technology platform, if our project is technology or software focused). One effective way to lead this effort is to run this exercise in two passes. In the first pass, you ask your scribe (or some other timekeeper) to set a particular time limit, say three minutes. Once you start the clock, you invite the participants to blurt out their perceived strengths of the current environment. Just write them down as they are stated. For example, one person might state that the current environment is well known by all of the users. Another might state that it has already been paid for, and so on. Your goal is to capture all of the strengths as they are presented. Don't try to analyze each one during this rapid-fire session. Just capture the comments and collect as many as you can in the brief time allotment. You may observe that this exercise reminds you of a game of charades where words and phrases are shouted in no particular order and you, as the facilitator, are writing their statements on the whiteboard as fast as you can. Keep in mind that for a brief time allotment, this apparent chaos is quite productive. Once the timekeeper tells you to stop, you should ask the group if there are any glaring items missing from the list. The group might suggest another one or two items.

Once the list is captured, you'll want to orient the list in some priority order. A common technique is to evaluate this list using a simple voting system. Tell each person that they have three votes. Instruct them to evaluate the list and select the three strengths that are of the greatest significance, from their perspective. Have each person walk to the whiteboard and place a checkmark next to the items that they believe are most significant. Some people will have a real passion for only one or two items, so feel free to permit them to use their three checkmarks however they choose. If they choose to place all three marks on one entry, so be it. This is not a scientific exercise. This is simply an exercise to help us determine the priority of items. After the entire group has done this, you'll quickly see which strengths the group has determined are the most significant. You can then ask the group if they agree with the outcome. Do those items with the most check marks accurately reflect the most significant items on the list? If so, you have your prioritized list of strengths. You can ask the group, now that they see the priorities that have been assigned, if they agree with it. Again, this is not a scientific exercise. We're not seeking to determine if the number one item is the number one item. We're seeking to confirm that the top three or four items are, in their opinion, the top three or four items—as a group. Later, when you begin preparing your Recommendation, you'll want to review these strengths. For your proposal to gain approval, your future benefits must outweigh the current strengths. After all, you'll be asking the organization to abandon this environment, with all of these strengths, in favor of your proposed solution.

Now we'll move on to the weaknesses. As you did in the strengths exercise, set a time limit and encourage the group to blurt out their opinions on the weaknesses of the current environment. Again, don't analyze this list while you're capturing it. Capture as many bullet points as you can in this first timed exercise. It is not uncommon for the weaknesses list to be much longer than the strengths list. It's human nature for people to readily call to mind a list of negatives, while it takes some mental effort to create a list of positives. Once you have a good working list, work with your workshop participants to rank the weaknesses in priority order. One good way to prioritize weaknesses is to rank them based on their boulder-rocks-pebbles consideration. You would choose this method rather than the voting method as you are most concerned with identifying the weaknesses that represent the greatest value if solved. Once the group has prioritized this list, you now must facilitate a deeper exploration of the weaknesses so that you can determine the value of overcoming them. Be prepared to take your time to explore this thoroughly.

Dig in and ask the participants to explain each stated weakness. For example, one respondent might state that one weakness of the current environment is its inflexibility. For this and every other response ask the respondent to elaborate. What is the problem with this inflexibility? Does it cost too much? Does it take too long to process certain routine functions? How does this manifest itself? Your goal for each weakness is to attempt, as best you can, to reduce each weakness to something measureable. While not part of the SWOT table, a common follow-up question is this: What is it worth to reduce or eliminate this weakness? While your respondent might not be able to quantify the answer, he or she should be able to express challenges that represent cost, inefficiency, or lost revenue (at least that would be your hope). The following supplemental questions can help you gain additional insight. You should ask each question for each high-priority weakness:

- Which person or department is most affected by this weakness?
- What makes this weakness notable? (you're looking for comments that can be translated into benefits for your future proposal)
- How would you classify this weakness—boulder, rock, or pebble?
- What evidence exists that confirms that this is a notable weakness?
- How important is it to fix this weakness?
- In addressing this weakness, how would success be measured?
- What does it cost the company if this weakness goes unchecked?

Like many discovery techniques, you will find it helpful to conduct this same SWOT discussion with different constituencies. This allows you to hear different perspectives on the same issues. Those individual perspectives can result in a rich set of discovery notes.

You will want to walk the group through a similar exercise with the Opportunities and Threats sections. Help the group understand that these two items refer to the future environment. It is reasonable that the group may not know precisely how their departments or areas will perform in the new environment. This portion of the exercise often degrades into a feature-function discussion, especially if your future environment involves new technology. Those discussions are best moved to the Parking Lot, as this is not the forum for discussing intricate software and hardware capabilities.

You should treat the discussion of opportunities in much the same way that you did the exercise on weaknesses. Maintain your patience. This workshop takes time, and you cannot appear weary or let the participants rush the process. If you only collect the opportunities and neglect to collect the evidence that confirms the benefits of realizing those opportunities, you will severely weaken your business case. Don't assume you know what is behind any of these ideas. You need the evidence you collect to be the group's evidence, not what you speculate to be their problems.

To clarify any of the listed opportunities, there are follow-up questions that should be explored to ensure that you extract as much potential benefit information as possible from the assembled group. For example, you might propose a possible solution to the problem, such as implementing a new system, and then ask the group, "What *opportunities* might present themselves as a result of moving forward with a potential new solution?" If your participants are not providing a lot of rich information, you can urge them along by asking variations on this question, such as, "What cost saving opportunities might arise from the new system?" Or, "What market advantages will the new system provide for us?" The following supplemental questions can help you gain additional insight:

- What individual or department benefits most if this opportunity is fully realized?
- How would you measure success if this opportunity is fully realized?

Again, facilitate a discussion to prioritize your list of opportunities.

Finally, you must examine the threats—or what the group perceives to be threats. Such a discussion might include an assessment of the risks or threats associated with moving forward with the new proposal, including an examination of what might go wrong if the proposal was implemented too hastily, or not quickly enough. Common threats include controlling project costs, the effectiveness of training and keeping current with one's existing job responsibilities while devoting sufficient time to assisting with the new project. Identifying and clarifying the perceived threats may take some time so be patient and keep your attendees focused. Like before, once the initial list is documented, invest some time to prioritize the list before moving on to other topics.

Completing this exercise will give you additional evidence in support of your hypothesis. Now we will move on to our third workshop exercise, assessing the maturity of various capabilities.

Chapter 34

Making Workshops Count: Exercise #3—Assessing Capability Maturity

The previous two exercises were helpful in collecting evidence and discovering potential benefit opportunities. This exercise has a different objective. This exercise will help us assess two key performance or capability levels. Using a variation on a tool called the Capability Maturity Model, you will lead the participants through a subjective assessment of where your organization is today and where it would like to be in the future as it relates to certain capabilities. For our purposes, we will define a maturity model as "any model that shows a continuum of maturity from early, immature development all the way through advanced maturity." Carnegie Mellon University, and its sister organization, The Software Engineering Institute or SEI, together have provided an excellent example of maturity modeling as it relates to software development. In their book *The Capability Maturity Model: Guidelines for Improving the Software Process*, SEI defines the maturity continuum in terms of five distinct stages. These stages are: Initial, Repeatable, Defined, Managed, and Optimizing. The stages, as defined below, are from *The Capability Maturity Model* (pgs. 15–17) and are reproduced here by permission:

- Stage 1, Initial. This stage in the software process maturity framework is characterized as ad hoc and occasionally even chaotic. Few processes are defined, and success depends on individual effort and heroics. Outside of the software realm, this stage is largely reserved for those processes that lack uniformity across business functions and may even be manual. There is certainly no interface to an enterprise-wide system.

- Stage 2, Repeatable. This stage in the software process maturity framework is marked by basic project management processes which are established to track cost, schedule and functionality. The necessary process discipline is in place to repeat earlier successes on projects with similar applications. One simple word to describe this phase is disciplined. The process is disciplined, even if it is not automated. Outside of the software realm, one might find processes that are repeatable using Excel or Word templates but not integrated into an enterprise-wide system to ensure seamless collaboration across departments.

- Stage 3, Defined. This stage in the software process maturity framework is the first enterprise-wide step. This process holds that both management and engineering (development) activities are documented, standardized and integrated into a standard software process for the organization. All projects use an approved, tailored version of the organization's standard software process for developing and maintaining software. The key concept for this maturity level is "standard, consistent process." Outside the software realm, this phase can be seen to have uniform processes across the organization. All similar functions use the same process to accomplish their assigned tasks. This allows for basic uniform audits of compliance to company standards. An enterprise at this maturity level has processes in place to ensure that all applicable employees know the basic, uniform expectations of task execution and can be monitored to evaluate compliance of those uniform standards.

- Stage 4, Managed. Organizations that have reached this maturity level have detailed measures in place to ensure that the software development process and the resulting software product quality are collected. Both the software process and products are quantitatively understood and controlled. Enterprises that have achieved this level of maturity not only have standard processes, but have elevated their performance to have predictable processes and predictable outcomes. Outside of the software realm, organizations with this level of maturity have sophisticated KPIs defined for each process and are rigorous in measuring performance and evaluating that performance to deliver consistently higher results for the next measurement cycle. This stage represents those systems that are completely integrated across business unit boundaries and may even be stretching beyond the enterprise to integrate with customers and suppliers.

- Stage 5, Optimizing. This stage is the Holy Grail of maturity. You'll notice that each of the previous stages had verbs that indicated past tense—Repeatable, Defined, Managed. This stage is defined with an on-going verb—Optimizing. This stage is not a past-tense stage. This stage represents those organizations that are ever-striving to improve, never accepting that they have achieved perfection. CMMI defines this stage as a continuous process improvement that is enabled by quantitative feedback from the process and from piloting innovative ideas and technologies. This maturity stage represents an enterprise that is well integrated within its own enterprise and well integrated beyond the enterprise. This maturity level represents a company that integrates with suppliers to determine the supplier's ability to ship raw material on time and is integrated with customers to predict their demand even before they place orders with the company. This is a highly integrated enterprise.

Now that we have defined the five stages, we will explore how to best use this tool as a discussion starter for the final exercise in our workshop. Our need to employ a maturity model is driven by our need for credibility. As discussed previously, a sound business case will incorporate research to support the hypothesis that benefits are achievable. That research likely identified other organizations that had achieved benefits similar to those identified in your hypothesis (e.g., possibly a certain percentage reduction in costs or a certain percentage increase in sales). So far, so good. However, most of these research studies do not mention the starting and ending points for the case studies upon which their research is based. As a result, readers may assume that they can attain benefit percentages similar to those outlined in the research studies. Possibly, but not certainly.

The issue here is that no two organizations begin their projects from the same starting point. It is reasonable to suggest that some organizations began with their capabilities being more mature than others. It is also reasonable to posit that some organizations determine to achieve different levels of capability maturity in the future. For example, a company that uses Excel spreadsheets to track shop orders is less mature in manufacturing technologies than a company that uses a sophisticated integrated shop-floor order-tracking system. Yet the company that uses Excel spreadsheets is more mature than a company that might still use a manual paper-based system (if any still exist). Similarly, it cannot be assumed that your company wishes to achieve the highest level of optimization from a given project. While that might strike you as heresy, the truth is that achieving advanced levels of optimization is costly and disruptive. Many organizations are quite content to pluck the low-hanging fruit from a project and let the more advanced capabilities remain unrealized. And by starting partway up the continuum and by not reaching for the final Optimizing stage, we must conclude that we are not going to reap the same level of benefits that a company might reach if their original capabilities were less mature than ours and if their goal was to achieve full optimization (which is to say that we are planning to cover less of the continuum than the company in the research).

With that in mind, let's consider the next two diagrams. The first diagram shows the progression of the Capability Maturity Model. In the diagram below, we see a typical assumption, namely that our company has the full spectrum of benefits to achieve. It suggests that we are way behind the curve today and we desire to be a company on the leading edge of technology when this project is complete.

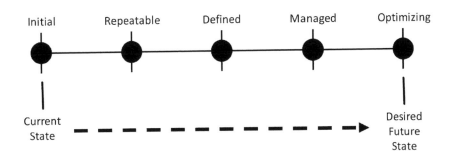

Applying some analysis to your organization's current state and desired future state might yield a diagram more in line with the image below. In that image we see a company that has made some progress already and really does not desire to achieve the fullest, most optimized state as its future state.

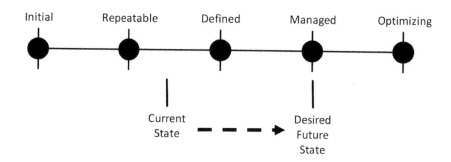

When looking at the second diagram, we conclude at least two things. First, the company has already made strides in achieving a repeatable process. This is good. And we can infer that the company has determined that striving to achieve the Optimizing state is out of reach or not cost beneficial, at least for the moment. During your workshop, you need to walk your participants through the various considerations and determine your current and desired future states of maturity.

As we employ this tool in our workshop, we are trying to determine two basic maturity levels—where is the organization today and where does it intend to be in the future. In the workshop, show these stages to your participants and ask them to evaluate where your company is today on this scale. It is best to stick with the business functions that you are discussing in your workshop, so, for our example, we'll stick with the HR scenario. Ask your participants to review the list of business processes that were presented in the SWOT exercise in chapter 33 and ask them to evaluate where your company is relative to those business processes. This will not be a scientific outcome. It is a subjective guess based on the opinions of those assembled in this workshop. And you should expect that one measurement will not apply to all of the business processes. For example, your participants might agree that your company is somewhat mature (possibly Defined) in the area of maintaining employee data, but they might also believe that the company's capabilities are immature in the areas of recruiting, onboarding, and keeping up to date with formal job descriptions (see example below). It is common to emerge from a maturity discussion with several maturity diagrams depicting the different maturity levels of various capabilities.

Likewise, the participants might not agree on the desired future state of various business processes. When that happens, work with them to reach some compromise so you can plot the answer as a single point rather than a range or several points. This murky, less-than-conclusive interaction is an expected and predictable outcome. The value for you is that you will have a much more credible picture of the current state and desired future state of the business based on this discussion because you will have captured the input (and even some interesting disagreements) from the workshop participants.

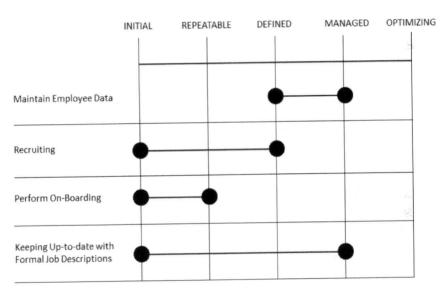

In the Analysis section, in chapter 41, we'll discuss how we translate the outcome of the Capability Maturity Modeling into values that we can use in our business case.

Chapter 35

Validating Your Evidence

Seeing is believing. From your interviews and workshops you have likely heard challenges in the processes that create benefit opportunities if solved. Hopefully, during the workshop, you explored the comments a level or two deeper to determine the size, scope, and validity of the challenge. And with your exploration, hopefully you gained some preliminary confirmation that there is a measurable financial benefit to overcoming that challenge. With that as our foundation, it is now time to visually confirm the challenge.

During your interviews and workshops you heard of challenges. Let's say you heard that the process for receiving, checking in, and putting away raw materials is cumbersome and creates problems and errors. For visual verification, request a demonstration of that challenge. For factory matters, the plant manager or work area foreman can usually schedule such an event. You, of course, would want to attend, and you may want to bring one or two others to observe the offending process.

> Be prepared to ask a lot of questions. Your goal is to integrate your workshop and interview notes with physically observable confirmation. This creates a very compelling story line for your business case.

It is possible that your host of this demonstration was not in the workshop and may be unfamiliar with your hypothesis and with your business case effort. If so, be prepared to spend a few minutes to briefly explain the hypothesis and the goals of your business case. With that background, your host will now be better able to highlight inefficiencies for you to observe. Be prepared to ask a lot of questions. Your goal is to integrate your workshop and interview notes with physically observable confirmation. This creates a very compelling story line for your business case. The story line will go like this:

During our workshops I (or we if you are building this as part of a team and not as a solo effort) heard that we have an inefficient receiving and put-away process. The workshop participants (you might choose to list their names) told me that this inefficiency is creating warehouse problems and those problems are costly. Based on those comments I went to the receiving area and met with the receiving manager and observed the process first-hand. I observed that during certain high-volume periods, material can sit in the pending area for quite some time, often days. Since it sits there and has not been accounted for or put away, purchasing buyers think the goods are not in the warehouse and therefore place another order for those same items, creating excess inventory.

A story such as this can become a compelling feature of your business case.

An opposite outcome can also occur. Imagine that you go to observe an inefficient process, and while observing it, you don't see the same difficulties as you were hoping to find. What should you do? You should work with the people that suggested this was a problem and have them explain it to you further. It is possible that someone thinks something is a big problem, when in fact it is merely an annoyance—a pebble rather than a boulder. You'll want to know that for yourself before you present that to your sponsor or review committee. It is likely that the review committee is well aware that this problem is merely an annoyance, despite all of the complaining that some workers may have voiced. Seeing is, therefore, believing.

Chapter 36

Section Three Summary

Collecting supporting evidence for your business case is a vital activity and one that requires detailed focus and discipline. In this section, we covered a lot of ground. We began with a basic discovery primer. We explored methods to validate our hypothesis, how we align our hypothesis with stated corporate goals, how we get ourselves organized for success, and an overview of common discovery methods.

We learned the value of conducting external research to validate our hypothesis; specifically, we learned several key public financial indicators that can help us compare our company with other, similar companies and also allow us to explore opportunities for improvement based on that research.

As we seek to gain supporting evidence, it is important to have a thorough one-on-one conversation with your executive sponsor. During that conversation, you should ask several critical questions so that you can gain the sponsor's perspective on this project and its value to the company.

Planning for meetings is an important activity. Attempting to conduct meetings, whether they are individual one-on-ones or group workshops, without proper planning is unprofessional and typically leads to disappointing results. Proper planning should consist of four key elements:

- A rough cost estimate for the project
- A discovery approach, including key questions and desired contributors
- Focused data collection
- A follow-up plan

You were introduced to the concept of boulders, rocks, pebbles. This concept is a helpful stratification concept to help you walk your workshop participants through the justification and explanation of proposed potential benefits. You learned that boulders—our most desirable benefit category—have several key criteria, such as materiality, reasonableness, measurability, observability, attainability, corroboration, indisputable, and line-management commitment.

Gathering evidence is often a function of asking the right questions. We explored a number of high-yield questions and techniques that can be useful for collecting sound evidence. Beyond the high-yield questions, we explored methods of collecting evidence using individual interviews and group workshops. We learned the particulars of three key workshop facilitation tools: top ten lists, SWOT diagrams, and the Capability Maturity Models.

Finally, we learned the value of adding observable evidence to our list of potential benefit considerations.

SECTION FOUR

Analyzing Your Findings

Chapter 37

Analyzing Your Initial Findings

Congratulations again! You now have a hypothesis that suggests a business pain exists, and you have some evidence that your hypothesis is valid. You have collected evidence by interviewing staff, managers, and executives; by observing certain inefficient behaviors; and, where applicable, looking outside of the company to confirm that such problems have occurred in other organizations and that other organizations have realized value from solving them.

Now it's time to sift through all of your notes and analyze just what you have collected. Consultants and project managers arrive at this stage of the development of their business case and can't wait to build a spreadsheet that impresses everyone who sees it. Don't rush into this. Credibility is always our goal. The Analysis section is much more than just putting together a spreadsheet. The power of the analysis is in actually analyzing the evidence. Sure, some of that analysis requires a sound mathematical approach, but don't get caught up in trying to build the ultimate spreadsheet.

In their book *Making Your Case: The Art of Persuading Judges*, authors Antonin Scalia and Bryan A. Garner present a concept called "Scrupulous Accuracy" which they define as "not merely in never making a statement that you know to be incorrect (that is mere honesty), but also in never making a statement that you are not certain is correct." (pg. 13). Thorough analysis will add certainty to your benefit estimates.

While you will find little benefit in manipulating the data to fit your expectations, you can coax the data and present the data in ways that both preserve your credibility and show a strong business justification for adopting your recommendation.

As you begin analyzing your notes, you should see a picture form that reveals the size and value of your potential benefits. You'll recall that I said that you should aim to find benefits whose value is roughly ten times the estimated cost of your project. What you may not know is that there are unwritten upper boundaries that should not be exceeded if you are to have a credible business case. A credible business case is one that shows sound analytical evidence and presents numbers that are achievable, reasonable, and conservative. Showing a $500 million benefit on a project that costs $2 million is often seen as too good to be true. Such impressions dilute credibility and injure the effectiveness of your business case.

In your analysis, you need to discern exactly what you have and exactly what you don't have. It is always helpful to play the role of trial attorney as she prepares to address the jury. *Webster's* defines "jury" as "a body of persons sworn to give a verdict on some matter submitted to them or as a committee for judging and awarding prizes in a contest." It is the second definition that applies here. You will be attempting to convince your jury (in your case, it would be more accurate to call them approvers) that your hypothesis is worth supporting and that your recommendation is worth funding based on the evidence you present. You have to convince your jury (or approvers) of two things. First, you must convince the jury that your entry is worth the prize. Second, you must convince the jury that your entry is the most worthy use of the limited capital funds.

Consider analyzing your evidence in two passes. With the first pass, you will evaluate the evidence from the overall project perspective. In this pass, you will consider your benefits as a total package (without dollar values at this point) to determine whether or not you think the benefit categories that you have discovered will justify the project, at least in principle (review chapter 27, "Boulders, Rocks, and Pebbles," if necessary). If you believe that certain critical benefits are missing from your business case, you must return to the discovery activity to collect the relevant data to support your hypothesis. Once you believe that you have the right framework and broad business benefit areas to justify your project, you must now evaluate the individual benefits a second time to confirm that you have, in fact, collected sufficient evidence to make your case credible and compelling. You will want to confirm that you have as many boulders as possible. You'll recall in chapter 27 that we discussed the many requirements for classifying a benefit as a boulder. You might consider building a table like the example below to help you identify the gaps in your individual benefits.

Benefit Name and description	Potential Dollar Value	Material	Reasonable	Measurable	Observable	Attainable	Corroborated	Indisputable	Commitment
Decrease Days in Inventory	$500k	Y	Y	Y	-	Y	-	-	-

Look at the example above. Here we are suggesting that the company can decrease the number of days that inventory is on the books (which is the same as saying that we're proposing that the company can increase inventory turnover). If the company can effectively achieve this goal, the company will realize a $500,000 benefit. In the scope of this example, we are saying that we already know that four of our boulder criteria have been met. Now we must gather additional evidence to confirm the other criteria. Without those other criteria, this benefit is nothing more than our speculation that this is possible. Specifically, in this example, we are missing at least two important aspects—corroboration that the benefit is plausible and commitment from the primary party responsible for achieving this benefit that this benefit is achievable in their minds and that they will step forward and commit to achieving it. Without those key criteria in place, the credibility of this specific benefit is seriously weakened.

In the chapters that follow, you will learn additional ways to enhance your business case and enhance your credibility. Not every suggestion will apply to very business case. You'll have to evaluate each suggestion and determine its relevance to your individual business cases. Before we explore additional evaluation considerations, it is important to introduce a cautionary view of elaborate financial calculations.

Chapter 38

Don't Outkick Your Coverage

Building the business case is really just a combination of five simple activities:

1. Preparing a hypothesis
2. Identifying and analyzing the benefits
3. Identifying and analyzing the costs
4. Distilling your notes into a compelling executive presentation
5. Presenting your recommendation

Beyond this, many business case practitioners try to display great prowess and build elaborate spreadsheets that show the actual impact of their proposal in discounted cash flows and earnings per share. While this is admirable, and even understandable, it is misguided if you are not a seasoned finance professional. The purpose of this chapter is to introduce you to certain advanced concepts and explain the potential pitfalls of attempting to present yourself as a finance expert if you are not one. You will learn that a compelling, credible business case does not require a command of complex finance principles. But since there are many practitioners that aimlessly wander into this trap, it is necessary to devote some time to

> One of the biggest setbacks you could suffer would be for the finance executive to expose your incompetence in financial matters, thus casting doubt about the credibility of all of your potential benefits and recommendations.

explaining things in detail. Hopefully, you will be able to sidestep this very common—and often disastrous—pitfall.

You will be presenting your business case to a jury of approvers. This jury will almost always have one senior accounting or finance executive representing the financial domain of the business. This finance executive is likely very skilled with financial calculations, especially if your company is a public company where the finance executives must interact with institutional investors and analysts. One of the biggest setbacks you could suffer would be for the finance executive to expose your incompetence in financial matters, thus casting doubt about the credibility of all of your potential benefits and recommendations.

It is understandable if you want to attempt to show your prowess with financial matters. It is understandable if you want to leverage certain advanced Excel functions and dazzle your audience. However, I must caution you using a football phrase, please don't outkick your coverage. It's true that Excel has great built-in capabilities such as net present value and internal rate of return functions. But correctly presenting discounted cash flow is much more involved than just using the Excel function. Properly and accurately presenting discounted cash flow assumes a certain competency in technical accounting and financial calculations. First, it assumes that you are well versed in common accounting and finance topics. In addition to the calculations, you must demonstrate an expert-level understanding of tax considerations related to balance sheet and income statement items (yes, there are different tax considerations for each financial statement). Those advanced topics are beyond the scope of this book. However, it is important for you to know some of these concepts and common pitfalls, and this chapter will provide an overview of them. Unless corporate finance and financial accounting are your core competencies, you run the risk of really stumbling in your presentation. The finance representative will spot accounting irregularities and errant tax calculations easily. And your trouble will cascade from there if he proceeds to publicly discredit your assumptions since he has already determined that you lack a fundamental understanding of financial principles—principles that he believes are elementary.

Discounted cash flow is a specific finance and accounting consideration. To be accurate, when computing discounted cash flows, you cannot just add up all of your estimated benefits over five years and then run an Excel equation using the NPV or IRR function. Though using Excel to compute a five-year view of your calculated benefits might seem to produce the result you desire, it will not be a technically accurate portrayal of the discounted cash flow of your benefits. The reason lies in the intricate accounting rules necessary to blend a mixture of benefits from incongruent sources. This becomes an issue when you seek to mix benefits from the balance sheet (such as optimizing inventory or reducing outstanding receivables) with benefits from the income statement (such as increasing revenue or reducing expenses). Mixing these disparate benefits is a common accounting blunder that will expose you to criticism from anyone with an accounting or finance background. You may not realize that your benefits must comply with standard accounting rules. You also may not realize that those rules require that you properly account for tax considerations on your benefits if you wish to present them as a unified set of benefit dollars over time.

Benefits that impact income statement items (specifically revenue increases and expense reductions) are computed by multiplying your estimated benefit by one minus the corporate income tax rate (Benefit*(1-Corp Income Tax Rate)). Benefits that impact the balance sheet, such as working capital and other assets, are computed at face value, but can only be presented as occurring a single time, not year over year (well, you could divide the benefit over two or three years if that's how long you expect it to take to fully realize the single improvement, but working capital benefits do not continue indefinitely like many income statement benefits). Benefits that create changes in estimated depreciation, amortization, and write-offs are computed by multiplying the benefit times the corporate income tax rate. There can be other intricate considerations that must be applied if your benefits are derived from a foreign subsidiary or when multiple currencies are used. Hopefully, you can appreciate that there are specific technical requirements that must be properly employed if you plan to present your basic and likely credible benefit projections as an estimate of cash flow over time. And only after you have accurately presented the discounted cash flow can you then attempt to compute the impact on earnings per share. Therefore, trying to present raw benefit numbers as impacting earnings per share highlights a lack of expertise in the financial considerations for capital benefit projections. Doing so will also, unfortunately, demonstrate that you have an incomplete understanding of the true financial impact. And that compromises your credibility.

Within the scope of this book, it is recommended that you forego trying to reduce your business case down to discounted cash flows and earnings per share calculations unless you are a finance professional. It is very easy to get tripped up when presenting these intricate considerations, and such missteps will undermine your credibility. Keep your benefit projections and future costs limited to just that, benefit projections and future costs. To maintain accuracy without compromising the integrity of your recommendation, consider including a notation that reads, "Benefits are presented as undiscounted, pre-tax values." That statement, as shown in the example below, alerts the readers that you are not trying to pass your calculations off as something more than they are.

Estimated Potential Benefits (by year)	Year 1	Year 2	Year 3	Year 4	Year 5	Total
Reduce Overtime in Michigan and Alabama factories	150,000	309,000	477,405	546,364	562,754	2,045,523
Reduce redundant IT spending across regional offices	127,500	262,650	405,794	464,409	478,341	1,738,694
Improve inventory turnover in North Carolina factory	275,000	275,000	0	0	0	550,000
Total Estimated Potential Benefits (by year)	552,500	846,650	883,199	1,010,772	1,041,096	4,334,217

Note: Benefits are presented as undiscounted, pre-tax values

There are times when executives do demand a sophisticated business case that presents the impact of the benefits as earnings per share. If that's your situation, ask for assistance from your finance organization. They will typically have a preferred capital request form or template that they commonly use for capital project requests. Larger organizations typically have a very specific template that they use. You can work with and rely upon that assigned finance professional to help you complete the designated form. It has been my experience that the finance person will be very competent and able to assist in every area except the dollarization of benefits. But since that's the part that you produced, you should be able to work well together as a team.

Chapter 39

Preserving Credibility through Reasonability Analysis

One mistake that will compromise your credibility is to suggest results that are simply unreasonable. In the chapters that follow, you will learn a few methods to temper excessively aggressive benefit projections. You'll review our previous topic of maturity modeling as well as learn the basics of realization timing and range bounding.

However, before we can explore those topics, it will be helpful to examine basic reasonability analysis. And within this topic, there are two primary considerations: what is reasonable within your organization and what is reasonable when comparing your organization to peer organizations. To meet the reasonability test, your benefit projections must be evaluated against the following six considerations: identify, isolate, calculate, evaluate, articulate, and corroborate. We'll explore each of these individually.

IDENTIFY YOUR BENEFIT AREA

You should have identified your benefit area as part of crafting your hypothesis. Assume, as an example, that your business case proposes a project that will cut staff overtime by 50 percent. That statement, by itself, might be viewed by some executives as unreasonable, simply because it is so broad. To make it reasonable, you'll need to isolate relevant segments of your benefit area as candidates for reduction.

ISOLATE THE BENEFIT CANDIDATES

Continuing with our overtime example, it could be possible that some over-time can be reduced or eliminated. To add reasonability to your hypothesis, you must isolate the pools of benefit within the universe of all benefits. The universe of all benefits, in this case, would be the total overtime paid by the company across all business units and departments. In any broad-based benefit assumption, not all components of that benefit universe are created equal. If we look at overtime costs across multiple departments, some over-time might be excessive, some might not qualify as excessive but might still be unnecessary, and some might be appropriate. You need to determine just how to slice up the total benefit universe into the pieces that apply to your business case. One of your first considerations is to better understand the components of your proposed benefit—in this case, overtime. Is the over-time largely from one administrative area, or is the overtime spread across dozens of departments within the company? This is significant because suggesting that you can reduce overtime in one department is easy to grasp while suggesting that your proposed project will cut overtime across the entire company might be seen as unlikely (or as unreasonable). It might, though, be reasonable to propose cuts in overtime by 50 percent in one department, 20 percent in another, and 10 percent in a third department. Isolating the relevant pools of your proposed benefit shows thoroughness. It allows you to highlight where, in our example, you have shown defer-ence to one department that may not be able to cut overtime simply by the implementation of your proposed project. For example, a new accounts payable system might be able to cut the overtime in the accounts payable department but might not have any effect on the overtime in the sales area.

CALCULATE THE VALUE OF YOUR BENEFITS

After you have isolated the appropriate pool of benefits, you would then calcu-late the value of those benefits. As you calculate these values, be aware that there may be by-product benefits that are associated with your original benefits that you can add in to your benefit calculation. For example, if you are reducing overtime hours (and corresponding costs), the company would also owe fewer dollars in payroll taxes. That is, as you reduced the overtime pay, you would correspondingly reduce the tax obligations that your company would owe to various government revenue agencies. If the reduction of overtime translates into reduced operating time for certain facilities, you might also be able to project a reduction in utility costs associated with the reduction in operating hours at that facility. Don't rush through this step. Invest the necessary time to consider the possibility and value of by-product benefits.

EVALUATE YOUR ESTIMATED BENEFITS

Evaluation can take many forms. Below are a few of the common ones. One of your evaluations should involve ascertaining if work has been done in this area before. Staying with our overtime example, it is very possible that the company has not only determined that overtime is not bad, but instead has actually determined that a certain amount of overtime is beneficial. It is possible that the company's managers have determined that it is more cost effective to have a certain amount of overtime than it is to hire more workers (and incur the learning curve, training costs, and other start-up expenses for new employees). It could be that a reduction of 50 percent of the current overtime might push the work effort below the threshold already established by the managers. So, even if the proposal is reasonable—at least from an objective point of view—it wouldn't be received as reasonable given these existing management parameters. Additionally, your organization may have conducted a vigorous overtime analysis a few years ago, and the current level of overtime may represent a significant reduction from years earlier. So, although additional reductions might cut costs, they might also cut too deep and have an adverse impact on the company's overall productivity.

A second evaluation should analyze key trends. Your business case will present a hypothesis that something will occur as a result of implementing your proposal. Analyze the trends for the past three years on those key metrics. If you are suggesting that overtime costs will shrink, explore the actual overtime expense over the past three years to understand the trend. Are you reversing an unfavorable trend or accelerating an already favorable trend? Explore the key metrics year by year for the past three years. How are they trending? Are overtime costs becoming better controlled or getting further out of control? Understanding these trends will help you add further credibility to your business case.

On the revenue side, the same considerations exist. Your proposed project might increase sales. If sales have been sluggish and the company has applied no real focus to the sales area, your suggestion might be right on target. But if the company has previously analyzed sales and has applied effort to increase it, you must carefully evaluate just how great an impact your proposal could make. For example, if the company has had a sales growth of 5 percent for each of the past five years, suggesting a 20 percent growth in a single year might seem unreasonable since there is no historical basis that such an achievement is possible. However, if your proposal boosted growth from 5 percent to 8 percent for each of the next three years, that might seem more reasonable. There is no single rule for testing reasonability. You must use your judgment and enlist your sponsor for guidance.

These examples are meant to provoke your own thinking. They are meant to help you analyze your discovery evidence and, where appropriate, rationalize your projections so that your business case is viable and your benefit projections are received as reasonable.

ARTICULATE THE ASSUMPTIONS AND RISKS

When you build the case for reasonability, you must base it on certain assumptions and certain risks. For your benefits, document the assumptions that hold the benefits together. In our overtime example, one assumption would be that productivity will not suffer materially with the reduction of overtime. Likewise we might state that we assume that employee morale will not be unfavorably impacted (you might state that while employees will see less in their weekly paychecks, they will welcome the additional off-work hours for personal activities). Whatever your assumptions are regarding your benefits, you help your case by documenting them and reviewing the assumptions with key stakeholders and your sponsor. You may have assumptions that are at two levels—the individual benefit level and the overall project level.

> Whatever your assumptions are regarding your benefits, you help your case by documenting them and reviewing the assumptions with key stakeholders and your sponsor.

Risk is another element that you must document. Like your assumptions, it is helpful to document risks at both the individual benefit and project level.

What risks might appear if your proposal is adopted? Keeping with our overtime example, what risks might be exposed if overtime was reduced?

Would there be a reduction in employee output? Would there be morale implications? These and similar evaluations should be discussed as you evaluate the reasonability of your proposed benefits. If the risks are minimal and the rewards are attractive, it is likely that your proposal would pass this reasonability test.

CORROBORATE THE BENEFITS

Finally, it is necessary to corroborate your potential benefits from both internal and external sources. We'll explore internal corroboration in more detail in chapter 44, "The Delicate Act of Gaining Commitment." For this example, we will focus on corroborating our projections with external evidence. You may have done this piece during the Hypothesis section, but it's worth revisiting again.

We'll focus on expenses for this example. One way to assess reasonability would be to look at two key measurements from your company and then compare those two measurements from similarly sized publicly traded competitors. Expenses are an easy target because, on the surface at least, most executives suspect that expenses could always be reduced. Regarding the topic of reasonability, it becomes necessary to do your homework and look at the public data of comparable companies.

The first and best choice is to analyze data about competitors as we did in the Evidence section. You'll be well served when comparing your company to its peers (not just competitors), and best served when you identify other companies that are similar in size, complexity, and market environment (for example, if you sell complex technical products, seek other companies of a similar complexity even if they are not direct competitors of yours). Analyze your company's SG&A as a percentage of sales and compare that to the same calculation of your peers or competitors. If your percentage is higher (meaning that you spend a higher percentage of your sales dollars on expenses than your peers), it would be reasonable to suggest that reductions are possible since your peers seem to perform better, at least on this metric. However, even if your peers are considerably more efficient than you on this metric, there is only so much cutting you can propose and still appear reasonable. In those cases, you'll want to negotiate with key business unit managers as part of your benefit projection calculations. Sometimes, when your company outperforms the peer group, you can still suggest incremental improvement estimates, such as 1 percent or

2 percent improvements as a starting estimate. Such a suggestion would require sound supporting evidence—for example, a quote or two from key stakeholders indicating that improvements are possible or notes from your observations identifying obvious inefficiencies.

When doing financial peer comparisons, it is important to compare your company to its closest peer group. Consider this: companies your size might have higher inventory turnover, but companies in your industry, regardless of size, may not. As an example, let's say that your employer is a specialty pharmaceutical company. For such companies, inventory levels will be higher due to the extensive testing that is required before pharmaceuticals can be introduced into the public distribution system. Even though the manufacturing process of a candy company is similar to the manufacturing process of a pharmaceutical company, comparing them will not yield the credibility that you seek because the companies operate under vastly different market and regulatory conditions. Readers of such comparisons would reject your hypothesis, and corresponding business case, because the comparisons are not relevant and therefore any conclusions you present based on this flawed comparison would be discredited and compromise the whole recommendation.

Once you can identify suitable companies for comparison, you can now select the metrics you want to evaluate. For this example, we'll look at some common metrics from the published financial reports. Below, we have figures from our target company that we introduced in chapter 21 and our three sample peers.

Reasonability Testing	Target	Peer 1	Peer 2	Peer 3
Sales Growth (one year)	-1.55%	-0.02%	-3.33%	-2.90%
Sales Growth (three years)	14.14%	25.24%	15.84%	16.08%
COGS+SG&A as a Percent of Sales	84.71%	75.69%	79.60%	61.79%
SG&A Growth (one year)	6.29%	-1.10%	-6.13%	-7.86%
SG&A Growth (three years)	18.64%	22.58%	21.42%	13.58%
COGS Growth (one year)	-6.36%	-4.91%	-1.61%	-0.35%
COGS Growth (three years)	8.83%	18.34%	17.43%	22.51%
COGS+SG&A Growth (one year)	-3.89%	-3.21%	-3.39%	-4.38%
COGS+SG&A Growth (three years)	10.81%	20.23%	18.92%	17.72%
Income from Operations (as a percent)	14.78%	23.59%	20.40%	25.45%
Revenue per Employee	$360,660	$425,750	$585,400	$542,956
Operating Income per Employee	$53,302	$100,417	$119,430	$138,202
Days In Inventory	58.45	69.83	64.56	102.49
Days Sales Outstanding	49.00	38.72	26.95	56.88
Days Payables Outstanding	55.20	60.94	56.11	109.64

We can observe several things using the external reasonability analysis. First, our target company and each of its peers all suffered reduced revenues in the past year. But if we look at the three-year horizon, we see that our company had the weakest sales growth among all companies in this list. It would be reasonable, then, to suggest that we could increase revenues a little more aggressively. Consider the term "headroom." When you have headroom, it suggests that you have room to grow without outgrowing your current environment. Because others have grown at better growth rates, it suggests that we have headroom to grow without outgrowing our market. So, if your proposal involves increasing revenue, you could reasonably make the case that your competitors have been successful doing this—even more successful than your company. That suggests that the marketplace is facilitating growth. It suggests that we have headroom on this metric. Our challenge is to propose a project that taps into that existing demand and get our share of it.

Conversely, it would be unreasonable to suggest that we could realize a 25–35 percent revenue growth over the next three years as no other company, except one, had that kind of performance. Seeing that our target company's three-year growth was 14 percent, it might be reasonable to suggest that we could see 15–20 percent growth over the next three years. Such growth would require the right products and the right pricing strategies, but if your business case is proposing solutions that favorably impact the product offerings and pricing strategies, it would seem reasonable to propose growth rates in this range.

Turning our focus to expenses, consider the line item called "COGS+SG&A as a Percent of Sales." Cost of goods sold, or COGS, refers to manufacturing costs. SG&A refers to sales, general, and administrative costs. These two costs are the largest cost categories of most manufacturing and distribution companies. Referring to our earlier example, overtime costs would be a component of one or both of these cost categories. Our target company's performance trails all of its peers. This means we have headroom to reduce costs. (I know that sounds backwards, but stick with me on this.) Our peers have found better ways than we have to control these costs. Therefore, referring to the performance of our peers, it would be reasonable to suggest that we target a lower percentage for these two categories. However, it would unreasonable to suggest that we could achieve a performance of 55 percent (meaning that 55 percent of our sales dollars would be spent on COGS and SG&A). Such a performance is unreasonable simply because we see that none of our peers achieves a performance of that level. So, while we can structure our benefit projections to suggest that better control of expenses might be possible, we must apply some reasonability analysis to make sure we don't overshoot the boundaries that contribute to a reasonable recommendation.

All of the reasonability tests are meant to guide you to thinking properly about your business case. When you present your case, someone from the finance area will typically attend the meeting. Any doubts regarding the reasonability of your proposal will be fair game for this person to poke at and unravel. Doing your due diligence beforehand will work greatly in your favor when it is your time to present your recommendation.

Chapter 40

Anticipate the Impact of Fine-Tuning Your Benefits

Potential benefits are, by their nature, estimates. Using a variety of tools and techniques, we strive to make our estimates reasonable and credible. You will strive to convey that the methodology that you used to calculate these potential benefits is sound and objective. With that in mind, it is very common that your efforts may involve several iterations of a benefit topic. Experience reveals that each iteration causes a reduction in benefits. It is very rare that the benefits will increase with additional focus.

Many of the benefits that you will suggest will be derived by multiplying a baseline number against some improvement percentage. Whether your baseline number involves payroll costs or marketing expenses or the purchase of raw materials for factory use, the approach is very similar. You start with today's value of a baseline number and then suggest that the number can be improved by a percentage. The math is easy, but there's more to this than just math.

Let's consider a common example from the procurement area. Assume, for this example, that your organization wants to improve the purchasing process in such a way as to reduce the cost of purchased raw materials. As part of this effort, they plan to consolidate their purchase requisitions across their many facilities so that they can maximize their volume discounts and gain improved leverage in price negotiation. A number of studies have been conducted that state that companies that consolidate their purchases across geographic and divisional lines and employ measures to ensure purchasing is only done through approved channels result in improved price leverage with their suppliers, which saves them a significant amount of money. Let's assume that you are working on a proposal for a project that will improve purchasing efficiency through improved information sharing and that you hypothesize that your organization can trim 3 percent from its current spending by implementing your project. That's a good starting point. You need to know how much your organization spent last year, so you ask one of the financial or procurement managers for last year's spending figures. You learn that the organization spent $200 million on raw materials. You then calculate that 3 percent of $200 million is $6 million. This is a big number. And over a three-year period, this is $18 million. You might begin to get excited because you suspect that this will easily offset the cost of your project. Not so fast. You may recall our earlier discussion of the benefit filter and Benefit Myth number five (The more we investigate the more benefits we'll find). You should anticipate the trimming and filtering that will inevitably occur before sharing your original $6 million benefit number with the project sponsor. Some project sponsors have a tendency to broadcast benefit projections prematurely to their managers. Such premature declarations may undermine your project, as it might set unnecessarily high expectations for your final benefit numbers.

It's true that you have computed a value that, on the surface, is reasonable and probably quite supportable. Here's where the real need for credibility enters into the picture. You will need to gain agreement from one or more purchasing managers that such an improvement is reasonable and possible. During those conversations, you will likely learn that certain purchased items are already well negotiated or nonnegotiable, and those items will need to be identified and excluded from your calculation.

There are certain purchasing categories that only get renegotiated at the expiration of existing buying contracts. The purchasing leader may also state that much work has already been done on the big-ticket raw materials and that no additional improvement is likely. (That would be code for "I am not willing to agree to further improvements since I've already done a good job in that area.") There will also be areas where your main contact will ask you to exclude certain items from your consideration. Your initial estimate, if taken as a broad generalization, will likely be refined by the people most knowledgeable about the area. You may learn about certain contractual obligations that extend for several years and are not due for renegotiation for several years. In the end, you'll end up with a very credible but much smaller number.

> Due diligence produces two by-products—one favorable and one less favorable. The favorable by-product will be a business case that has a high level of credibility. The unfavorable by-product will be a smaller pool of confirmed benefits.

The example we've just examined was unique to projects in the purchasing or procurement area. But this consideration happens in every topic area. The rule to understand is this: you must perform due diligence. The due diligence produces two by-products—one favorable and one less favorable. The favorable by-product of your thoroughness will be a business case that has a high level of credibility. The unfavorable by-product of that thoroughness will be a smaller pool of confirmed benefits.

In the next three chapters we will explore three advanced benefit considerations. You'll see how these simple (but frequently omitted) techniques can add additional credibility to your business cases.

Chapter 41

Advanced Benefit Consideration #1—Maturity Modeling

Executives are wary of business cases that project benefits with unrealistically high return. Trying to determine what qualifies as unrealistically high is a bit of a challenge, as it differs from company to company. The best way to determine what is reasonable for your company is to discuss the issue with one of the managers in the finance organization. You might learn that the finance department typically considers a 30–50 percent return to be reasonable but that a return of 500 percent or more would be considered over the top and therefore unrealistic.

When your benefits are overly ambitious, there are several techniques you can use to tame them. We are going to explore three of those techniques. These advanced benefit considerations are used to apply an additional level of due diligence and thoroughness. The three advanced benefit considerations covered in this book are:

1. Maturity modeling
2. Realization timing
3. Accounting for business growth

Capability Maturity Modeling—introduced in chapter 34—is a helpful tool to gauge how mature your processes are today and to project how mature you'd like them to be in the future. Understanding the starting and ending points will be necessary so that you can present your benefit projections with credibility. Below is the diagram that we'll use for our next example.

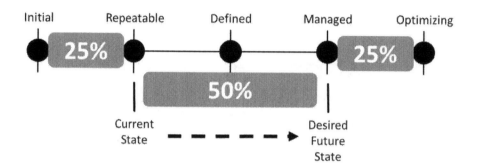

Let's assume that your earlier research suggested that a benefit of 30 percent reduction in certain costs was possible, as documented by other companies that had attained this percentage of savings doing a project similar to your proposed project. Here's where you must analyze and be rational. It is likely that you'll not know where the researched company was on the maturity scale when they began. Were they at Initial or Repeatable? And you'll likely not know where, on this scale, they ended up. So, you'll have to adjust the original benefit numbers down based on the assumption that the 30 percent indicates that the researched company started at Initial and progressed all the way to Optimizing. The adjustment is warranted because the diagram above clearly shows that your company is only seeking a portion of the benefit. On the left side, your company has already made progress, thereby eliminating the benefits that would be possible in moving from Initial to Repeatable. Likewise, the diagram shows that your company is willing to forego the benefits that might be attained when progressing from Managed to Optimizing. This leaves us with a subset of total benefits. The artful exercise for you, the business case developer, is to determine what that subset is. Are benefits linear across the continuum? If so, then each stage represents an equal 25 percent of the total benefit (as in the example above). Or are the benefits more heavily weighted in the middle stages? It could be possible that, of the total benefit potential for this benefit, 10 percent is achieved between

Initial and Repeatable, 40 percent more is achieved between Repeatable and Defined, another 40 percent between Defined and Managed, and the final 10 percent between Managed and Optimizing. Just how might the benefits be segmented in your case? That's for you to decide. The trick in using this tool is to consider it like a sliding scale. You, as the business case developer, are charged with determining and presenting this detail. Through negotiations—which we'll cover in chapter 44—you'll work with your sponsor or the executive stakeholders and determine just where on the continuum of total potential benefits this particular approach will fall.

With the boundaries of your own capability maturity now established, you may need to retreat from the full measure of benefits that were introduced in your original hypothesis. Again, this is where the art comes in to play. Consider the left side of our scale in the preceding diagram. How much of the total benefit has already been realized? Would that be 10 percent, 20 percent or maybe 25 percent? In our example, we're saying that 25 percent of the benefit had already been realized by your company. Furthermore, how much of the benefit is forfeited by stopping your project at the Managed stage and not marching fully on to Optimizing? Is that another 20 percent (or 25 percent or 30 percent)? Again, we're saying that an additional 25 percent of the potential benefit will be forfeited. Using these numbers, you might now estimate that the benefit pool is not the original 30 percent of the administrative costs but is now only 50 percent of the total benefit pool, or yielding 15 percent (30 percent times 0.50). It is important to remember that you are not seeking an answer with four-decimal precision. These are guesses. The goal is to apply some reasonable analysis so that your guess is within credible boundaries.

This is a valuable exercise and typically adds additional credibility to your business case. By including the results of this exercise in your business case, you are showing that you understand the value that the company has already realized with existing improvement efforts. You further demonstrate that you are not just mindlessly applying research statistics to financial numbers. This exercise shows that you have applied some thoughtful analysis of the variables and that you are attempting to be objective and rational in your approach to computing potential benefits.

Using maturity modeling in this way is a good way to dial back some overly aggressive initial benefit projections.

Chapter 42

Advanced Benefit Consideration #2—Realization Timing

Realization timing is another technique that is very helpful in adding credibility to your business case, especially when the initial calculations suggest unreasonably high benefits. This technique is also helpful for boosting existing credibility even if the benefits are not excessively high. Realization timing can be defined as fine-tuning the benefit projections to reflect a gradual or staircase approach to realizing benefits.

Consider the following scenario. Assume that you compute benefits for a new human resources (HR)/payroll system and that those benefits are largely derived from the adoption of a self-service capability for employees. Assume that you have computed this benefit to be $1 million per year, indefinitely. That $1 million is the gross annual benefit number when everything is working as proposed. But everything will not be operating at peak performance from day one. So, since you're not going to be 100 percent efficient on the first day that you roll this out, it is reasonable to assume that you will also not realize 100 percent of those benefits on the first day, either. Benefits are realized as new technology is adopted. Benefits are realized as internal processes are improved and implemented.

At this point, the calculation becomes another example of art over science. What is the right ramp-up timing? Some metrics are simple, such as our example of an HR system. It's simple to determine the realization timing of such a benefit because it can be easily tied to the employee base. As 10 percent of the employee base adopts the new technology, 10 percent of the benefits will be realized. Should you assume 10 percent the first year or 25 percent? Will the adoption and efficiency move to 50 percent or 80 percent in year two? One effective way to work this out is to consider the rollout schedule and the number of employees that might benefit during each year. If your rollout schedule assumes that 25 percent of the employee population will be able to utilize this technology in the first year, then you'd show a benefit equal to 25 percent of your projected annual benefit in year one (see the example below). If another 50 percent of the employee population will be enabled in the second year, then you'd show a 75 percent benefit in year two (the first year's 25 percent plus the second year's 50 percent). From there you might show a 100 percent benefit in years three and beyond. In our example, we see our benefits listed as $1 million per year. Then, showing the realization rate, we see the timing of those benefits—with year one yielding a 25 percent benefit, year two a 75 percent benefit, and years three and beyond showing the full benefit.

	YEAR 1	YEAR 2	YEAR 3	YEAR 4	YEAR 5	TOTAL
Benefit	$1,000,000	$1,000,000	$1,000,000	$1,000,000	$1,000,000	
Realization Rate	25.0%	75.0%	100.0%	100.0%	100.0%	
Value of Benefit	$250,000	$750,000	$1,000,000	$1,000,000	$1,000,000	$4,000,000

Chapter 43

Advanced Benefit Consideration #3—Accounting for Business Growth

Our third advanced consideration should be applied to all benefit projections, regardless if they are conservative or ambitious. Businesses grow. That's the hope and the expectation. As the business grows, so too grows the revenue, the employee count, the overhead expenses, and so on. It is reasonable, then, to reflect this anticipated growth in our business case.

Presenting business growth is important because it adds another layer of credibility and thoroughness to your business case. Consider the benefit projections from the previous chapter. Without accounting for business growth, that benefit looks like $4 million over five years (see below). If, however, you factor in a 5 percent annual growth factor, the five-year benefit is $4,155,127. It's the same $1 million per year benefit, but with the added kicker of a 5 percent annual growth factor.

	YEAR 1	YEAR 2	YEAR 3	YEAR 4	YEAR 5	TOTAL
Benefit	$1,000,000	$1,000,000	$1,000,000	$1,000,000	$1,000,000	
Realization Rate	25.0%	75.0%	100.0%	100.0%	100.0%	
Value of Benefit	$250,000	$750,000	$1,000,000	$1,000,000	$1,000,000	$4,000,000
Growth Projections	5.0%	5.0%	5.0%	5.0%	5.0%	
Value of Growth	n/a	$12,500	$38,125	$51,906	$52,595	
Projected Benefit	$250,000	$762,500	$1,038,125	$1,051,906	$1,052,595	$4,155,127

There are several ways to represent a growth factor. The example above is a simplified method of incorporating a growth factor. In this example, we are estimating a sustainable growth trend of 5 percent per year. At 5 percent per year, the calculations yield the results shown. In year one, there is no growth projection, as we are using year one as the baseline. In year two, the 5 percent growth factor is computed against the prior year's benefit. Thus, $250,000 times 5 percent yields $12,500. That $12,500 is then added to the computed benefit. This pattern continues for the length of your business case horizon, typically 3–5 years. It must be restated, though, that using this calculation adds another layer of apparent scientific accuracy to what many approvers will view merely as a wild guess. You'll have to determine if and how you incorporate such a calculation in your business case.

There is also an approach that compounds the value of benefits year over year. Regardless of your preferred method—and depending on your audience—factoring in business growth can add credibility to your business case.

Chapter 44

The Delicate Act of Gaining Commitment

All of this data collection and analysis can only take you so far. Benefit estimates lack credibility until they have been corroborated with key functional managers and executives. While this idea of corroboration was introduced in chapter 27, "Boulders, Rocks, and Pebbles," it merits further explanation here. To obtain such corroboration, you will need to meet with each manager whose area stands to benefit from your proposal and review your benefit estimates with them. You will need to gain their approval and support for your claims that these benefits are realistically achievable—and that your proposal will make it possible for the company to achieve them. This will frequently require negotiation on your part.

Imagine the following scenario, using our target company's data: your hypothesis suggests that the accounts receivable (AR) function can collect cash from customers sooner. Currently, the company collects its cash in an average of 49 days from the date of the invoice. Based on your discovery activities, you believe that the company can collect its cash two full days sooner, producing a one-time working capital improvement of roughly $104 million. You have come to this conclusion based on three pieces of evidence:

1. Internal evidence: You are aware that the AR department has increasingly been granting credit extensions to a growing number of customers.

2. Internal evidence: Just last year the company's days sales outstanding (DSO) performance was better than your hypothesis.

3. External evidence: Of the three peers against which you compared your company, two peers have significantly better DSO performance (one is at 38 days and one is a remarkable 26 days).

Even though this potential benefit is valuable, suggesting that this potential benefit is achievable might trigger an adversarial response from the manager responsible for that performance. The manager might fear that the executives will interpret your benefit presentation as a negative reflection on his current performance. Why would there be a $104 million opportunity to improve unless the current manager is ineffective? While this is not a common executive response, I have seen numerous managers raise it as a concern. This is particularly evident when discussing boulders. Suggesting that the AR function has an opportunity for a $104 million improvement could cause the manager to fear that he'll be viewed as lacking focus on his department, since he allowed such a large opportunity to even exist. You must anticipate this and prepare to soften the fear while simultaneously gaining the necessary commitment that such improvements are reasonable and possible.

You may also find that a manager will withdraw support for an apparently accepted benefit. Previously, the manager may have expressed his support for your proposed improvement. Unfortunately, the passage of time will occasionally interfere with your benefit projections. After an initial, and enthusiastic, show of support for your benefit projections, a manager may get cold feet and decide to reconsider his initial commitment. You need to revisit each manager before you make your presentation to ensure that each manager still strongly supports your benefit projections. I have experienced "benefit remorse" on more than one occasion. Benefit remorse works like this. The manager agrees with your initial projections that certain improvements or benefits are possible in his area. You move on to the next manager, believing that this benefit is well supported and documented. Without your knowledge, the manager thinks through the benefit and begins to realize that he will be held accountable for that number. Possibly he fears that his compensation plan will be amended and linked to achieving this benefit that you are so eager to present. That's when the remorse sets in. This is why it is essential that you must re-verify each manager's commitment to your benefit projections before your final presentation. The stakeholders are the only ones who can stand by that number. For that reason, they must buy in to the number that you present. If you have a manager showing signs of benefit remorse, work with him and negotiate with him, and then adjust your numbers to fit his comfort level. A smaller benefit number that is supported by the stakeholder is much more credible than a larger number that gets publicly refuted. Work together, rather than as adversaries, to reach an acceptable, supportable number.

And one more thing. There have been times when I believed that a certain benefit was achievable, but the area manager would not agree. There have been a few rare times when the area manager strongly disagreed and would not support my projections. In those rare cases, I have presented my projections and calmly stated that though I believed the benefit projections were reasonable, the area manager did not agree. In most cases my projections were accepted as reasonable and credible. Not all cases, certainly, but in most. I believe this is due, in part, to the manner in which the numbers were presented. It is best not to be timid about your numbers, and it is best not to try to hide the fact that disagreements exist. State your case with calm professionalism and let the approvers decide on their own if your business case has merit.

Chapter 45

Using Ranges to Add Credibility

All of your approvers know that your estimates are just that—estimates. To add credibility to your estimates, you may find it helpful to present your business case with a range of benefits, rather than as a single number. There are many ways to incorporate ranges into your business case calculations. There is, however, one cautionary note you should consider. When using ranges, it is preferred—when possible—that your project achieves justification from the smallest number in the range. If you state that your business case shows a range of benefits from $1 million to $4 million over three years, it is best if your project can be justified for less than $1 million during those three years. If your project requires more than your most conservative estimate, at least one of the approvers will point out that a scenario exists where your project does not pay for itself. It is best if you can avoid this stumbling block.

Below are some different considerations for adding ranges to your projections. These are not the only different ways that you can do this. These are presented as examples to provoke your thinking about ways that might work in your individual case. When using ranges, it is helpful to categorize them in ways that make sense to your readers. One categorization approach is to name your categories as follows: conservative, pragmatic, and ambitious.

BASIC RANGE CONSIDERATIONS

Consider that your earlier research suggested that other companies that had successfully completed projects similar to the one you propose had realized a 10–15 percent reduction in certain expenses. That simple reference can provide the basis for your range calculations. Using those numbers, you might calculate your conservative value at 10 percent savings, the pragmatic value at 12.5 percent savings (the midpoint between 10 and 15), and the ambitious value at 15 percent savings. Or you could apply some logic or other method to have your values compute at 10 percent, 11 percent, and 15 percent if you choose. This would be another art versus science consideration in which your own judgment is applied to producing the numbers for your ranges.

SOPHISTICATED RANGE CONSIDERATIONS

Beyond the basic range example, you can employ a number of variables to show the range of values of your proposal. You can tinker with the projected business growth (from x percent to y percent). You can tweak the maturity evaluation such that you suggest that your company is more or less mature today and seeks a more modest or more ambitious maturity level for the future state. Likewise, you can manipulate the timing of the realization of benefits such that your conservative estimate shows a longer timeline to realization and your ambitious estimate shows a shorter timeline to realization.

EXPLAINING YOUR RANGES

There is no limit to the number of variables that you can consider when presenting ranges. The biggest concern, though, should be that you fully understand the implications of each range criterion and that you can competently explain and defend each one. If you find yourself tripping over the words or variables or equations, retreat to a simpler range approach so that you can confidently make and defend your presentation.

It requires more than just math to incorporate ranges into your business case projections. For each consideration—conservative, pragmatic, and ambitious—you must provide a narrative that explains the underlying assumptions and variables. To the readers of your business case, whether you intend this to be true or not, it will appear that you are suggesting that the least possible benefit pool described in your conservative calculation is the worst-case scenario. In other words, your business case will appear as though you are stating that your project cannot return less than the conservative estimate. By stating all of your assumptions associated with each alternative, you enable your readers to see your thought processes and help them to develop confidence in your proposal.

Chapter 46

The "What" and the "How"

Thus far you've been exposed to methods for collecting and analyzing evidence for your business case. Beyond collecting and analyzing, you must also prepare to present *how* these benefits are to be realized. This is a frequently overlooked aspect of business cases.

The foundation for explaining benefit realization is built on two key pillars—sound discovery evidence and corroboration from the key managers in the affected business area.

For every benefit that you propose, you should anticipate being asked how the organization will achieve that benefit. Having a prepared answer for this question is vital. And one answer does not address every benefit because different benefits often deliver value to the organization through different means.

> It is not sufficient to simply state that the acquisition of a new technology will, by itself, produce the proposed benefits. You must invest the time to prepare a compelling and thoughtful explanation for how each business function will realize its benefit as a direct result of your proposal.

As you prepare your explanation for the realization of each benefit, keep in mind that each explanation must be thoughtful and reasonable. It is not sufficient to simply state that the acquisition of a new technology will, by itself, produce the proposed benefits. You must invest the time to prepare a compelling and thoughtful explanation for how each business function will realize its benefit as a direct result of your proposal. Typically, an IT-driven benefit is realized by some combination of new technology and improved business processes. One of the best sources for articulating the business benefits from any project is the business area stakeholder—or advocate—for the project. Sit with this advocate and ask specifically how they envision the project delivering benefits to their area, or to the business overall. Ask how it differs from the current environment and why such a project is necessary. You should also prepare a thoughtful response to the most expected of questions, namely, "If changing our procedures and methods are necessary to achieve this benefit, can we not achieve this benefit simply by changing the procedures, as you recommend, without the investment in your proposed new technology?" Documenting the stakeholder's perspective on this question will be valuable to you when you present and defend the business case.

To help you determine how your benefits will be realized, consider the following questions as you analyze your data:

- What value is placed on the potential benefit (annually or over a certain number of years)?
- Whose department or business area will reap these proposed benefits?
- What policies, procedures, methods, or behaviors must change in order for the benefit to be realized?
- Can the benefits be realized without an investment? Specifically, can the benefits be realized by simply changing the necessary procedures, methods, or behaviors?
- What changes in personnel, if any, are required to achieve the proposed benefits?
- How long will it be before the full benefit is realized?

When explaining how the benefits will be realized, you must factor in many variables. First, what specific evidence exists that a problem requires attention? This answer should have been discovered during your evidence-gathering sessions. Second, what changes in business process are necessary for the benefits to be realized? Or put differently, how will the business processes or workflow change in order for this benefit to be realized? Third, what specific capabilities of your proposed solution actually address this issue? For this answer, you may need to work with your vendor (if you have one) for specific details. And if you are working with a vendor, press them very strongly to be specific about how their solution actually delivers this benefit. You should also ask them to refer you to specific customers who have faced your situation and who have realized the benefits that you are proposing so that you can use them as references in support of your proposed benefits.

Can we get these benefits without purchasing the expensive technology you propose? As this question is frequently asked, I offer the following answer as a guide. "The proposed solution enables these benefits and enables the business process changes. While business process changes alone could deliver some of the benefits, your current environment does not enable you to sustain these benefits over time. The proposed solution provides the necessary technological underpinning that makes these benefits both achievable and sustainable." Naturally, that statement must be true in your case for you to use it with credibility.

Chapter 47

Don't Forget the Soft Benefits

At this point you've evaluated the numbers and determined the monetary value of your prospective benefits. Hopefully, your numbers present a favorable picture— that your proposed project delivers a higher value than it is projected to cost. But even after you've put together all of your numbers, you likely have a stack of interview and workshop notes left over that could also tell a compelling story, if only you could compute benefits for these items. Some call these unquantified benefits soft benefits. Some call them qualitative benefits. Whatever term you use, these benefits were identified during your discovery sessions and should be presented as part of your business case. Since you have not calculated benefit estimates for these items, their value is largely for discussion purposes more than as part of your financial benefits analysis. But don't discard those old notes. There is a great and powerful use for them. These leftover nuggets, or non-financial benefits, can be presented effectively as a stand-alone PowerPoint slide called "Benefits beyond the Math."

Even though you have not prepared credible calculations that present the value of these leftovers, there is still value you can mine. Imagine that you had the following leftover benefits:

- *Enriched up-sell and cross-sell opportunities* from better information and analysis
- *Reduced time to market and accelerated return on investment on new projects* realized from improved integration capabilities

- *Improved reliability of travel-related tax deductions* with more complete data
- *Tighter travel policy enforcement*, which will promote expense recording in the proper accounting period
- *Improved internal auditing capability*, which will reduce external auditor fees
- *Recovery of lost revenues* as fewer fee-based services are provided free under expired warranties
- *Improved project evaluation capabilities*, which will provide better information—allowing the organization to cancel struggling projects earlier rather than later
- *Reduced sources of common data.* The organization can move to a "single source of truth." One system of record for inventory, sales, order management, distribution and customer service provides an improved customer experience
- *Improved user interface* that attracts and holds customers longer on our website

Take these non-financial benefits and organize them into a separate PowerPoint slide—or chapter if you're presenting your business case as a Word document. The value from all of these bullets can be presented in a simple one-or-two-slide table. Below are two effective ways that you can present these values that have not been quantified. You will find that these benefits, when presented as shown below, often evoke as much positive feedback and support as the previously presented financial benefits. There are many different ways to present these non-financial benefits. You could just list the benefits, in bulleted form, on a PowerPoint slide. By investing some time to organize your bullet points, you can not only create a tidy benefit list, but you can help the readers to categorize the benefits in their own minds. Below are two common organizational approaches—by financial statement category and by business category.

The simplest example is to map your leftover benefits against the common financial statements—the income statement and the balance sheet. In the first example, you see a simple two-column table that has been excerpted from a PowerPoint presentation. In the PowerPoint presentation, the presenter has already shown the quantified benefits, totaling $8 million. In this example, the presenter is listing the benefits (from his left-over notes) that also represent a benefit, just without any calculated value. The nine bulleted benefits are arranged to match against the financial statements. This is done to help the reader align the benefits with common business terminology.

Benefits beyond $8 million

Financial Statement	Business Benefit
Income Statement (Revenue Increases)	• Recover lost revenues as fewer fee-based services provided free under expired warranties. • Improved user interface attracts and holds customers longer on website. • Enriched up-sell and cross-sell opportunities from better information and analysis.
Income Statement (Expense Reductions)	• Reduced time-to-market and accelerated return on investment on new projects realized from improved integration capabilities. • Tighter travel policy enforcement will promote recording expenses in proper period. • Improved reliability of travel-related tax deductions with more complete data. • Reduced sources of common data. Move to a "single source of truth." One system of record for inventory, sales, order management, distribution, customer returns provides improved customer experience. • Improved internal auditing capability reduces external auditor fees.
Balance Sheet (Asset Optimization)	• Improved project evaluation capabilities, which will provide better information – allowing the organization to cancel struggling projects earlier rather than later.

There are numerous other ways you can organize these non-financial benefits. Instead of organizing by financial statement, as shown above, you could elect to align the benefits along the lines set forth by Ram Charan in his book *What the CEO Wants You to Know*. Charan states that there are five primary presentations of value that CEOs recognize: "Cash generation, margin, velocity, growth and customers: Everything else about a business emanates from this nucleus" (pg. 29). Each of these topics, with the possible exception of velocity, should be easy to grasp. Charan defines velocity as "the idea of speed, turnover and movement." He continues: "Think of raw materials moving through a factory and becoming finished products, and think of those finished products moving off the shelf to the customer. That's velocity" (pg. 37). The example below shows how you might align these same unquantified benefits using Charan's categories.

Benefits beyond $8 million

Business Category	Business Benefit
Growth	• Enriched up-sell and cross-sell opportunities from better information and analysis.
Velocity	• Reduced time-to-market and accelerated return on investment on new projects realized from improved integration capabilities.
Margin	• Improved reliability of travel-related tax deductions with more complete data. • Improved project evaluation capabilities, which will provide better information – allowing the organization to cancel struggling projects earlier rather than later. • Tighter travel policy enforcement will promote recording expenses in proper period. • Improved internal auditing capability reduces external auditor fees.
Cash Generation	• Recover lost revenues as fewer fee-based services are provided free under expired warranties.
Customers	• Reduced sources of common data. Move to a "single source of truth." One system of record for inventory, sales, order management, distribution, customer returns provides improved customer experience. • Improved user interface attracts and holds customers longer on website.

Regardless of which presentation style you choose—or even if you choose something completely different—packaging your soft benefits like this helps you put those leftover items to good and productive use in your business case.

Chapter 48

Packaging Your Benefits into Spreadsheets

Now that you've discovered and calculated all these benefits, it's time to organize them into spreadsheets. The goal is to identify, calculate, and communicate the value of your proposal. But more than just filling a few cells with calculations, you will find it beneficial to build your spreadsheets in such a way that they tell a full and compelling story. From an organization perspective, you'll also find it helpful to keep all of your calculations in a single spreadsheet file, thus making it easier to share the full calculation story with others. Organizing your calculations in this way is necessary, as you will have several approvers that may have little or no background on your funding request. By collecting and organizing all of your calculations in one place, you'll make it much easier for executives and others to gain a thorough understanding of just how you reached your conclusions. You might ask why such organization and extra effort is necessary. It is necessary because you will not always be present to explain or defend your business case. This document may get passed from person to person, especially via broadcast email. The more detail and organization that you include, the more credibility you will accrue. This method, while somewhat time-consuming, is exceptional for selling your business case in your absence. And since you can't always be present, this is exactly what you'll need.

Before you build any spreadsheets, take a moment to plan your approach. You will need to build two separate story lines. The first story line will be to explain each individual benefit in some detail. Later in this chapter you'll be introduced to a powerful presentation template that helps you organize your benefit presentation succinctly. The second story line will be to organize an executive summary that will include all of the totals from your individual benefit estimates. For our purposes, we will build the individual benefit story line first, and then, once it is complete, we will build the summary story line.

As you begin organizing your benefits, consider devoting an individual tab in your spreadsheet file to each benefit. These individual tabs will represent the detailed story line for your overall spreadsheet. For this chapter, we'll review excerpts from an actual spreadsheet from one of my previous business cases.

In the two images below you'll see an example of a nine-tab spreadsheet—four summary tabs (one for the executive summary, one by value, one by financial statement, and one that displays charts) and five detailed benefit tabs. This is the preferred order of tabs. You want the organization to flow the way a typical, uninformed reviewer might read the file. You want to direct your readers to first read the executive summary to familiarize themselves with the project. After the executive summary you would want the readers to view the summary tabs as this will give them a concise overview of the financial aspects of the project. Following the summary tabs, you will then present the individual benefit spreadsheets as a means of providing sufficient detail to explain and promote your position on these benefits.

First four tabs:

Executive Summary	Summary by Value	Summary by Finl Statement	Charts

The remaining five tabs of our example:

Reduce Direct Material Costs	Increase Revenue	Improve Productivity	Reduce Days in Inventory	Reduce IT Costs

In your case, you might end up with fifteen or twenty tabs. Regardless of how many you have, this approach allows you to keep each of the benefits compartmentalized. We're going to examine one of these benefits in detail—"Reduce Direct Material Costs"—for this hands-on example. Appendices C, D, and E contain examples of other benefit calculations.

After you've created the tabs for your individual benefits, consider investing the time to really build out benefit worksheets that can stand alone and tell a compelling story. Having designed and experimented with numerous spreadsheet templates, the most concise and useful format is the model detailed by Jack Keen in his book *Making Technology Investments Profitable.* Keen has named his presentation method "PayoffCard" (one word) and describes it as follows: "A PayoffCard is typically a one-page, structured document designed to collect and communicate succinctly the essence of what senior decision makers need to know regarding the value-based implications of a single decision criterion" (pg. 134; see also pages 134–140). PayoffCards clearly present all of the variables and all of the calculations in an effort to minimize confusion. Using Keen's PayoffCard approach, we eliminate the oft-derided "trust me" math (those calculations where very little is disclosed to the reader and the reader is asked to trust the presenter's assertion that all of the assumptions and calculations are reasonable and valid). Keen's example takes us back to early math classes where we show all of our work. This allows the reader to understand and evaluate all variables, assumptions, and other factors. And presenting the math in a transparent and open way eliminates many of the questions that skeptical or uninformed approvers raise during the formal presentation. Below is a diagram that shows the different aspects of Keen's PayoffCard. For our purposes, we will focus on the first two— "Explanation" and "Calculation."

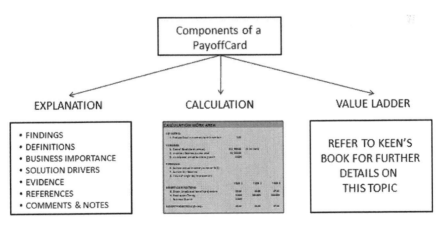

Source: *Making Technology Investments Profitable: ROI Roadmap from Business Case to Value Realization, by Jack M. Keen,* (John Wiley & Sons, New Jersey, 2011, 2nd Edition), 135.

Over time, I have determined that a subset of those items in the "Explanation" section (noted above) are most relevant for me. Specifically, I use "Definition," "Business Importance," and "Evidence." In lieu of a section called "Comments & Notes" I have substituted a section called "Calculation Overview." You may choose to include additional items in your spreadsheet.

In the example below, you'll see that the entire story regarding the benefit entitled "Reduce Direct Material Costs" is presented. First, the reader is introduced to the definition of the benefit. This helps place all readers on the same footing. Next there is the "Business Importance" section. This is intended to confirm your understanding that this benefit is important; it also introduces the potential value of your benefit. Next we have the "Evidence" section. This section is intended to highlight a high-level summary of the evidence that you believe supports your hypothesis that this benefit is achievable and realistic. The fourth section is the "Calculation Overview." This section is meant to be a narrative that explains your calculation in plain English. Finally, there is the "Calculation Work Area," where your full benefit calculation is presented. The completed PayoffCard performs a very valuable function. It attempts to address most of the questions and most of the assumptions on a single page. This is very beneficial as there will be times when you will be asked to send your findings to one of the approvers in advance of your meeting. Providing your reviewers with the benefit information in this concise and easy-to-follow format enables them to discern your conclusions without difficulty. An example of my adaptation of Keen's PayOffCard is shown below.

REDUCE DIRECT MATERIAL COSTS

DEFINITION

One of the largest costs of production is the cost of the material necessary to make the company's finished products. That material is referred to as Direct Material. Direct Material is different from Indirect Material (which is not the object of this benefit). Indirect Material refers to those items which are not directly used in production, such as cleaning supplies, office supplies and so on. This benefit will address the value of improving our methods and procedures for acquiring direct production material.

BUSINESS IMPORTANCE

Last year, our company spent over $7.62 billion on Direct Materials. Any measures that can be utilized to reduce that cost are beneficial to our Operating Income. Most of those materials are covered under well-negotiated, long-term contracts. However, there exists an opportunity to do more to bring our costs of certain materials down. We believe the annual savings will exceed $6.09 million.

EVIDENCE

We have evaluated our purchasing processes for the purchase of Direct Materials. We have generally found that our Purchasing department does an outstanding job in negotiating favorable contracts for our company. There are, however, a few opportunities for further improvements that have been brought on by our recent acquisitions. Our company has not yet made the acquired companies comply with our purchasing methods and we have not fully replaced their individual systems with our corporate purchasing system. Doing so should save our company in excess of $6.09 million per year in additional cost savings.

CALCULATION OVERVIEW

This benefit is computed using the following variables. First, we determine the amount of annual Direct Material Spend. In our case, we spend roughly $7.62 billion annually on Direct Material. Then we determine how much is subject to the proposed improvement. Our evaluation has determined that 4% of the total spend is subject to further negotiation and cost reduction. That 4% represents $304.68 million in annual spend. We believe that implementing our corporate Procurement system in the newly-acquired companies will enable us to negotiate another 2% price reduction on the cost of purchased materials. That 2% represents an annual savings of $6.09 million. We believe that the implementation will take one year and full adoption will take two years. During the first year, we expect 25% of the purchasing functions to pilot, adopt and begin realizing benefits. In the second year, we expect another 25% of the sites to implement and adopt this capability and by year three all of the company's purchasing facilities will be integrated and benefiting from these rich capabilities.

CALCULATION WORK AREA

KEY METRIC:

A. Reduce Direct Material purchasing costs by:	2.00%

VARIABLES:

B. Total Annual Direct Material Spend	$7,617.00	(in millions)
C. Percent of total spend eligible for improvement	4.00%	
D. Anticipated annual business growth	3.00%	

FORMULAS:

E. Direct Material eligible for improvements (B * C)	$304.68	(in millions)
F. Projected annual savings (E * A)	$6.09	(in millions)

	YEAR 1	YEAR 2	YEAR 3	YEAR 4	YEAR 5	TOTAL
BENEFIT CLARIFICATIONS:						
G. Gross, Unadjusted benefit projections	$6.09	$6.14	$6.32	$6.51	$6.71	
H. Realization Timing	25.00%	50.00%	100.00%	100.00%	100.00%	
I. Business Growth	3.00%	3.00%	3.00%	3.00%	3.00%	
BENEFIT PROJECTIONS (G * H + Business Growth)	$1.52	$3.07	$6.32	$6.51	$6.71	$24.14

Source: *Making Technology Investments Profitable: ROI Roadmap from Business Case to Value Realization, by Jack M. Keen,* (John Wiley & Sons, New Jersey, 2011, 2nd Edition), 134-140.

To take your understanding a little deeper, let's explore each of these sections in detail, beginning with the "Definition." The definition for our benefit is shown below.

One of the largest costs of production is the cost of the material necessary to make the company's finished products. That material is referred to as Direct Material. Direct Material is different from Indirect Material (which is not the object of this benefit). Indirect Material refers to those items which are not directly used in production, such as cleaning supplies, office supplies and so on. This benefit will address the value of improving our methods and procedures for acquiring direct production material.

The definition should be written in such a way that an uninformed reviewer can easily understand your benefit, including the boundaries of your benefit. The definition should answer the following question: "What is the basis for this benefit?" You might consider this statement to be similar to a scoping statement for a project, explaining what is and what is not considered part of the benefit. The objective of the definition is to provide an understanding of your basic foundation of this benefit. Reading the last sentence in our definition presents this foundation: "This benefit will address the value of improving our methods and procedures for acquiring direct production material." Everyone who reads this PayoffCard will understand what you mean by "Direct Material." In our example above, Direct Material is explained in rather simple terms.

The "Business Importance" section, shown below, should answer the following question: "Why is this important for the business?" Typically, the "Business Importance" section will introduce the financial value of this benefit. In this example, this section states that this benefit, once fully realized, will produce annual savings in excess of $6.09 million. This section also introduces necessary baseline variables, such as the total annual amount spent on direct materials ($7.62 billion, in this case).

BUSINESS IMPORTANCE

Last year, our company spent over $7.62 billion on Direct Materials. Any measures that can be utilized to reduce that cost are beneficial to our operating income. Most of those materials are covered under well-negotiated, long-term contracts. However, there exists an opportunity to do more to bring our costs of certain materials down. We believe the annual savings will exceed $6.09 million.

In the next section, "Evidence," you would present a subset of your discovery findings. You will want to present the most powerful and compelling segments, as this section provides limited space for extensive narratives. Notice in this example that the business case author did not jump directly to the conclusion that all purchased materials were applicable for this benefit. Rather, the author states that most of the purchased items are *not* applicable for this benefit. However, there remains a large enough pool of purchased items that are not currently well-negotiated that reviewing those items produces this particular benefit.

EVIDENCE
We have evaluated our purchasing processes for the purchase of Direct Materials. We have generally found that our purchasing department does an outstanding job in negotiating favorable contracts for our company. There are, however, a few opportunities for further improvements that have been brought on by our recent acquisitions. Our company has not yet made the acquired companies comply with our purchasing methods and we have not fully replaced their individual systems with our corporate purchasing system. Doing so should save our company in excess of $6.09 million per year in additional cost savings.

The last narrative section of my version of the PayoffCard provides a written explanation of the calculation which will appear below this narrative. This is an important section for two reasons. First, you may have certain approvers that are not typically mathematical in their daily jobs. As an example, executives in human resources and legal may not be involved with mundane operational data on a daily basis. It could compromise your presentation to assume that they know statistics outside of their domain. The second reason that this is an important section is that you can use it to demonstrate your own competency. As you prepare to formally present your recommendation to the approval committee, you will need to rehearse and prepare for the defense of your business case. Much of your effort will be defending the calculations—and corresponding assumptions—that can be easily explained in this narrative section.

CALCULATION OVERVIEW

This benefit is computed using the following variables. First, we determine the amount of annual Direct Material Spend. In our case, we spend roughly $7.62 billion annually on Direct Material. Then we determine how much is subject to the proposed improvement. Our evaluation has determined that 4% of the total spend is subject to further negotiation and cost reduction. That 4% represents $304.68 million in annual spend. We believe that implementing our corporate Procurement system in the newly-acquired companies will enable us to negotiate another 2% price reduction on the cost of purchased materials. That 2% represents an annual savings of $6.09 million. We believe that the implementation will take one year and full adoption will take two years. During the first year, we expect 25% of the purchasing functions to pilot, adopt and begin realizing benefits. In the second year, we expect another 25% of the sites to implement and adopt this capability and by year three all of the company's purchasing facilities will be integrated and benefiting from these rich capabilities.

Most benefit calculations require a fair amount of explanation. In this example, the "Calculation Overview" starts with the basic information that the company spends $7.62 billion on direct materials every year. Next, the reader is informed that only a certain percentage of that number is applicable to the benefit calculation—in this case 4 percent, or $304.68 million. This first step-down of the base variable is critical, as it informs the reader that you are not assuming that 100 percent of the direct material spend is up for discussion. You are, in essence, conceding that 96 percent of the purchased materials are properly negotiated, thereby leaving no additional wiggle room for additional price reductions. There is no magic formula for determining this percentage. This would have been determined during the discovery sessions and follow-up negotiations with key procurement managers.

The final section of the PayoffCard is shown below. It is the "Calculation Work Area." Using Keen's PayoffCard style transparently shows the reader just exactly how you arrived at your benefit calculation. This area shows your calculations, including all variables and all supporting calculations. To ensure that you could see the important aspects of this area, I have truncated the image of the full five-year projection and shown only the first three years of benefits.

Notice how the variables are presented, followed by the supporting calculations (under the heading "Formulas") This calculation work area, combined with the narrative that you provided in the calculation overview section should enable any reader to follow your logic and validate your results.

CALCULATION WORK AREA

KEY METRIC:

A. Reduce Direct Material purchasing costs by:	2.00%	

VARIABLES:

B. Total Annual Direct Material Spend	$7,617.00	(in millions)
C. Percent of total spend eligible for improvement	4.00%	
D. Anticipated annual business growth	3.00%	

FORMULAS:

E. Direct Material eligble for improvements (B * C)	$304.68	(in millions)
F. Projected annual savings (E * A)	$6.09	(in millions)

	YEAR 1	YEAR 2	YEAR 3
BENEFIT CLARIFICATIONS:			
G. Gross, Unadjusted benefit projections	$6.09	$6.14	$6.32
H. Realization Timing	25.00%	50.00%	100.00%
I. Business Growth	3.00%	3.00%	3.00%
BENEFIT PROJECTIONS (G * H + Business Growth)	$1.52	$3.07	$6.32

In the above calculation, you can see that the benefit is computed to be $6.09 million per year. However, due to the realization timing variable (and noted in the calculation overview) the first year does not qualify for a full year's benefit but instead qualifies for only a 25 percent benefit. Accordingly, the first-year benefit is not $6.09 million but $1.52 million. This particular benefit ramps up to 50 percent in year two and then 100 percent for years three and beyond. The anticipated business growth (Variable "I") is also factored into the calculations. In the image below, you can see that the five-year valuation of this benefit is $24.14 million.

These annual numbers will be transferred to the summary tabs, which are presented later in this chapter.

YEAR 1	YEAR 2	YEAR 3	YEAR 4	YEAR 5	TOTAL
$6.09	$6.14	$6.32	$6.51	$6.71	
25.00%	50.00%	100.00%	100.00%	100.00%	
3.00%	3.00%	3.00%	3.00%	3.00%	
$1.52	$3.07	$6.32	$6.51	$6.71	$24.14

You should expect your reviewers and approvers to raise two very common questions as they evaluate your PayoffCards. The two questions arise from examining the calculation work area. Those questions are:

1. How did you determine that a 2 percent savings was reasonable and possible? (Variable "A")
2. How did you determine that 4 percent of the total spend was reasonably eligible for this potential savings? (Variable "C")

Both of these percentages would have been determined during the discovery phase of your business case efforts. When asked those questions during your upcoming presentation, you should be prepared to name the individual who provided you with those numbers and how you arrived at their value (commonly these numbers are agreed upon during some negotiation of benefits). Identifying the source of your information and being able to state that this individual has reviewed and agreed with your recommendation will add additional heft to your position. If you are not comfortable with the process of gaining agreement through negotiation, return to the Evidence section of this book and review those chapters.

It is important to note that most of your PayoffCards will *not* contain project cost information but will only contain the value of a prospective benefit. The costs are presented as a bundle (shown later in this chapter) and are balanced against the total bundle of benefits in the summary spreadsheets. The one common exception to this approach is when you are performing a Total Cost of Ownership (TCO) calculation. Those occur frequently in business cases where a new technical environment is largely replacing an older technical environment and the cost of operating the new environment is substantially less than the existing one. In those cases, you would have a different Calculation Work Area. For TCO benefits, you would show the current costs, the projected future costs, and the anticipated benefit of the new system or environment (which would be the difference between the two). If your business case calls for TCO benefits, be careful not to double-count the costs (once in the PayoffCard and then again in the summary tab) as that would incorrectly suggest a lower return on your project. A detailed example of a TCO benefit can be found in Appendix D, under the benefit titled "Reduce Costs Due to System Consolidation."

Once the individual PayoffCards have been created and once the five-year benefit estimates have been computed, it is time to move those totals to your summary tabs. You'll recall earlier in this chapter I recommended that you create several tabs to hold your calculations. One of those tabs would be called "Summary by Value." In that worksheet you would build a spreadsheet similar to the example below.

COST/BENEFIT SUMMARY

PROJECTED ANNUAL BENEFITS	YR 1	YR 2	YR 3	YR 4	YR 5	TOTAL
Note: All figures in millions USD						
Reduce Direct Material Costs	$1.52	$3.07	$6.32	$6.51	$6.71	$24.14
Increase Revenue	$0.00	$3.66	$6.33	$6.52	$6.72	$23.23
Improve Staff Productivity	$0.16	$2.80	$4.70	$4.84	$4.99	$17.49
Reduce Days in Inventory	$4.35	$4.35	$0.00	$0.00	$0.00	$8.70
Reduce IT Costs	$0.19	$0.39	$0.80	$0.83	$0.85	$3.06
Benefit Estimates by Year	$6.22	$14.27	$18.16	$18.70	$19.26	$76.61
NOTE: Benefits are presented as undiscounted, pre-tax values						

In the above example, you can see the benefit named "Reduce Direct Material Costs" and the other four benefits in our business case. In this summary tab, the benefits are arranged from highest to lowest value based on the five-year estimate of each benefit (hence the name "Summary by Value.") Notice that all benefits do not ramp up at the same pace. The "Increase Revenue" benefit shows zero benefit for the first year. And the "Improve Staff Productivity" benefit shows only a very small benefit in the first year. This shows the attention to detail that you should incorporate in your business case. Each benefit is realized at its own pace and based on its own considerations. A closer look at these benefits implies a relative priority or sequencing for implementation. The "Reducing Days in Inventory" line shows that one-half of the benefit is realized in the first year and the remainder is realized in the second year. That indicates that the inventory aspects of this project will likely get implemented first in order to realize that benefit the earliest.

In the second summary spreadsheet ("Summary by Finl Statement," shown below), you can see that the benefits are arranged by financial area. You will observe that we are still presenting the same total value for the project over five years, namely $76.61 million. They are the same benefits, just ordered and presented in a different view. This view is helpful for the controller and CFO, as they are often the ones who bristle when income statement items are combined with balance sheet items. By highlighting these benefits in this manner, you are acknowledging that you are combining benefits from different financial statements in order to make your point. Even if the CFO pushes back on your decision to present these different categories of benefits as having equal financial treatment, this view allows a reasonable discussion of the benefits.

COST / BENEFIT SUMMARY

PROJECTED ANNUAL BENEFITS	YR 1	YR 2	YR 3	YR 4	YR 5	TOTAL
Note: All figures in millions USD						
BALANCE SHEET ITEMS						
WORKING CAPITAL ITEMS						
Reduce Days in Inventory	$4.35	$4.35	$0.00	$0.00	$0.00	$8.70
Subtotal - Balance Sheet Items	$4.35	$4.35	$0.00	$0.00	$0.00	$8.70
INCOME STATEMENT ITEMS						
REVENUE ITEMS						
Increase Revenue	$0.00	$3.66	$6.33	$6.52	$6.72	$23.23
EXPENSE ITEMS						
Reduce Direct Material Costs	$1.52	$3.07	$6.32	$6.51	$6.71	$24.14
Improve Staff Productivity	$0.16	$2.80	$4.70	$4.84	$4.99	$17.49
Reduce IT Costs	$0.19	$0.39	$0.80	$0.83	$0.85	$3.06
Subtotal - Income Statement Items	$1.87	$9.92	$18.16	$18.70	$19.26	$67.92

NOTE: Benefits are presented as undiscounted, pre-tax values

ACCOUNTING FOR COSTS

In order for your project to generate your estimated benefits, you will need certain tools. Those tools (e.g., hardware, software, consulting services) all cost money and must be acquired as part of your project. It is not sufficient for a business case only to present the benefits of a proposed project.

The corresponding costs must be presented along with the benefits so that the approvers can gain a reasonable understanding of the overall value of the project. To show that value, you must present the costs necessary to obtain the benefits and you must show the anticipated timing of those costs. Below is the cost summary from this business case. In the spreadsheet below, you can see that there are several cost categories where the company must spend money as part of this project. You can also see that the company will be spending money for many years into the future due to the maintenance contracts that will be executed.

PROJECTED ANNUAL COSTS	YR 1	YR 2	YR 3	YR 4	YR 5	TOTAL
New Hardware	$2.20	$0.60				$2.80
Recurring Hardware Maintenance		$0.11	$0.11	$0.11	$0.11	$0.44
New Software Licenses	$6.10					$6.10
Recurring Software Maintenance		$1.22	$1.22	$1.22	$1.22	$4.88
Consulting and Implementation Services	$14.25	$1.50				$15.75
Improvements to Physical Facilities	$1.25	$1.25				$2.50
Temporary Labor Costs (backfill for initial phases)	$0.75	$0.75				$1.50
Project Cost Estimates by Year	$24.55	$5.43	$1.33	$1.33	$1.33	$33.97

Additionally, as shown in the following spreadsheet, in the last row, "Benefits Minus Costs," you can observe that the first-year expenses far exceed the first-year benefits. This is a very common scenario. It takes time to implement software and to train people how to use it properly. But the company has to buy the software and supporting hardware upfront in order to install it in their environment (or with their hosting provider).

COST/BENEFIT SUMMARY

PROJECTED ANNUAL BENEFITS	YR 1	YR 2	YR 3	YR 4	YR 5	TOTAL
Note: All figures in millions USD						
Reduce Direct Material Costs	$1.52	$3.07	$6.32	$6.51	$6.71	$24.14
Increase Revenue	$0.00	$3.66	$6.33	$6.52	$6.72	$23.23
Improve Staff Productivity	$0.16	$2.80	$4.70	$4.84	$4.99	$17.49
Reduce Days in Inventory	$4.35	$4.35	$0.00	$0.00	$0.00	$8.70
Reduce IT Costs	$0.19	$0.39	$0.80	$0.83	$0.85	$3.06
Benefit Estimates by Year	$6.22	$14.27	$18.16	$18.70	$19.26	$76.61
NOTE: Benefits are presented as undiscounted, pre-tax values						

PROJECTED ANNUAL COSTS	YR 1	YR 2	YR 3	YR 4	YR 5	TOTAL
New Hardware	$2.20	$0.60				$2.80
Recurring Hardware Maintenance		$0.11	$0.11	$0.11	$0.11	$0.44
New Software Licenses	$6.10					$6.10
Recurring Software Maintenance		$1.22	$1.22	$1.22	$1.22	$4.88
Consulting and Implementation Services	$14.25	$1.50				$15.75
Improvements to Physical Facilities	$1.25	$1.25				$2.50
Temporary Labor Costs (backfill for initial phases)	$0.75	$0.75				$1.50
Project Cost Estimates by Year	$24.55	$5.43	$1.33	$1.33	$1.33	$33.97
Benefits Minus Costs	($18.33)	$8.84	$16.83	$17.37	$17.93	$42.64

In the above example, it may appear as though the project begins to show a positive return in the second year, as we are projecting a surplus of $8.84 million. Many reviewers, however, will evaluate the cumulative value of the benefits against the costs to determine where on your timeline the project shows a positive return. To aid those reviewers, consider adding the following small table.

Cumulative Benefits minus Cumulative Costs				
YEAR 1	YEAR 2	YEAR 3	YEAR 4	YEAR 5
($18.33)	($9.49)	$7.34	$24.71	$42.64

In the table above we are presenting the cumulative benefits against the cumulative costs. In this table, year 2 still shows the project spending more than it yields. The math for this table is as follows: In year 1 we showed a deficit of $18.33 million. In year 2, the project actually yielded more than it cost (by $8.84 million), but the combined benefits of years 1 and 2 still do not exceed the combined costs of years 1 and 2. In fact, as the table shows, the combined benefits minus the combined costs of those two years still yields a $9.49 million deficit. It is not until the end of the third year that the combined benefits are projected to exceed the combined costs.

Moving on to our charts summary tab, below you can see two basic charts that commonly accompany a business case. These two charts present the same message in different ways. The chart below titled "Benefits vs Costs," shows cash outlays against projected benefits, by year. This graphically presents the fact that much more is spent in the first year than is gained. But it also shows how the project begins to produce substantial results in years 2 and beyond. The other chart, titled "Cumulative Benefits," shows when the project is projected to break even. In this example, the project will break even sometime before the end of the third year. Beyond the third year, the project delivers impressive benefits.

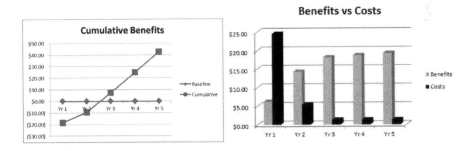

Then there is this sanity checkpoint. You will recall the detailed discussion in chapter 38, "Don't Outkick Your Coverage", how benefits from different financial categories are subject to specific and different tax treatments. This accounting fact often arises during the formal presentation. To prepare yourself for that interaction, consider preparing one additional small spreadsheet, as shown below.

ASSUMES BENEFITS CUT IN HALF TO ACCOUNT FOR TAX IMPACT					
	YEAR 1	YEAR 2	YEAR 3	YEAR 4	YEAR 5
BENEFITS AT 50%	$3.11	$7.13	$9.08	$9.35	$9.63
BENEFITS MINUS COSTS	($21.44)	$1.70	$7.75	$8.02	$8.30
CUMULATIVE YIELD	($21.44)	($19.74)	($11.99)	($3.97)	$4.34

The above table is an oversimplification of the tax treatment topic that was presented in chapter 38. Creating this simple spreadsheet shows you the impact if you revalue your benefits at half of their PayoffCard value. Admittedly, the tax treatments will not cut every benefit in half. Doing your sanity check in this way gives you an overly conservative estimate of the tax implications (the true tax implications would not cut this deeply into your benefits). This spreadsheet can be presented in the event that one of your approvers (or critics) suggests that you have overstated your benefits. Using this spreadsheet, you can see that the project is projected to break even sometime in the fifth year. I would not commonly present this spreadsheet, as I tend to use it just for my own sanity checking. I present it here as a means of nudging you to do something similar to confirm the reasonability of your own estimates.

Finally, in your spreadsheet file, you should create an executive summary tab. The value of creating such a tab is that it helps all those who review your spreadsheet understand the overall message that you are conveying and may help them navigate your spreadsheet. Below is the example executive summary from this business case.

EXECUTIVE SUMMARY

This spreadsheet presents the potential benefits of the proposed IT Transformation project. The estimates presented in this spreadsheet show that the proposed project has a favorable five-year yield in excess of $42 million, with the project showing a positive ROI at the end of year three. The benefits for years three and beyond exceed $16 million per year.

This file contains both detailed and summary project projections. The project benefits fall into five specific topic areas, which are: Reduce Days in Inventory, Increase Revenue, Reduce IT Costs, Reduce Direct Material Costs and Improve Productivity. Specific details regarding the definition, business importance and supporting evidence for each benefit can be found on the individual tabs. Additionally, each benefit is presented with a full breakdown of the calculations and assumptions used in the calculations to ensure a full presentation of the math used to arrived at each benefit estimate.

There are three summary tabs for your review. The first summary shows the five year project projections with the benefits shown in order of value, from highest to lowest over a five-year horizon. The second summary tab shows the same benefits, but aligns the benefits by financial statement. The third summary tab is a work area for the creation of the various charts and graphs that will be used in the presentation.

This example shows three simple paragraphs. The first paragraph succinctly states the value of the project and the projected breakeven horizon.

The second paragraph introduces the five detailed PayoffCards, and the final paragraph introduces the three summary tabs. Hopefully, this simple summary will enable any reviewer to make sense of the full spreadsheet in your absence.

Chapter 49

Accelerating Your Returns

Due diligence is one of the hallmarks of a thorough business case. While you have invested a substantial amount of time to get this far, you must step back from the details and take an executive view of your recommendation. Put yourself through an exercise in reflection and analysis to explore ways to improve your chances that your business case will receive approval. In *Making Your Case*, Scalia and Garner quote the following observation from Aristotle: "In court one must begin by giving one's own proofs, and then meet those of the opposition by dissolving them and tearing them up before they are made" (pg. 16). You are preparing to present your case to a jury of approvers. Anticipating their objections in advance and having carefully thought-out responses to these anticipated objections will help you carry the day. If history is any guide, you should anticipate that at least one of your reviewers will pose the following question: "What can be done to raise the ROI for this project?" That question has been asked in every business case presentation that I have ever delivered. You will show yourself to be a forward-thinking professional if you present your business case with that question in mind.

Marty Schmidt of The Solution Matrix (www.solutionmatrix.com) has created a wonderful graphic, reproduced below, that presents the four drivers that can influence the timing of the ROI of your proposal.

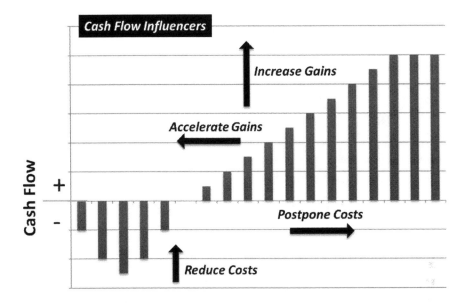

Image reproduced by permission from Dr. Marty Schmidt,
www.solutionmatrix.com.

The business case chart ("Cumulative Benefits") from the previous chapter looks quite similar to Schmidt's template. In this graphic, we see that the early periods of the project presented here have a negative cash flow. As stated in the previous chapter, this is a common scenario, as components must be acquired before you can begin implementing them. And implementing solutions often takes months or years, especially when rolling out the new capability to multiple facilities or multiple countries.

As shown, there are four influencers that can favorably influence your yield. Those four influencers are: "Postpone Costs," "Reduce Costs," "Increase Gains," and "Accelerate Gains." We'll explore each in more detail below.

POSTPONE COSTS

There are only two ways to pay for large-scale projects: use the company's own money or use someone else's money. A company could choose to write a single check to pay for the project out of its current cash reserves at the start of the project. Such an action absorbs all of the project's costs very early and makes the first year's project value deeply negative. The advantage of this approach is that the company does not incur debt to execute the project. The downside of this approach is that the company has depleted cash reserves on a project that could have been financed in ways that stretch the payments out over time.

Alternatively, the company could enlist a financial services firm to pay the initial costs, with the company agreeing to repay the financial services firm over time. The financial services firm could structure the deal like a mortgage, where the company would own the assets and pay them off over time. Or the financial services firm could structure the deal such that it would own the assets and the company would simply rent (or more accurately, lease) the equipment and services from them over time. At the end of the leasing agreement, the equipment and software would revert back to the financial services firm and the company would acquire newer, more up-to-date equipment and services.

To determine which option makes the most sense in your situation, you must determine—either on your own or with the assistance from your finance organization—which method is the most appropriate for your company at this time. You will specifically want to determine whether your proposed project should be funded out of capital expenditures—often called CapEx—or whether the project should be funded out of operating expenditures—often called OpEx. While there is no universal right answer to this question, there are common considerations. The quarterly financial statements of many publicly traded companies today are heavily scrutinized by investors and financial analysts that work for investment firms. Investors frequently examine the expense-to-sales ratios of companies to get a sense of quarterly profitability and cash flow performance. In these cases, companies often choose to fund these projects out of their capital budgets, thus keeping the project costs separate from routine monthly expenses, as debt retirement is viewed differently than other, more routine operating costs. Conversely, companies may prefer not to incur debt or tie up their lines of credit for such projects, as they may see future needs for capital funding (such as new factory construction) and might instead prefer to structure the funding out of existing operating budgets.

From an accounting perspective, either way is acceptable. The decision, however, may influence how the appropriated funds are accounted for and whether the project is viewed as a CapEx (balance sheet) item or an OpEx (income statement) item. This decision can also influence the timing and size of cash outlays and, therefore, can influence how and when your project actually shows a positive ROI. Other than paying for the project upfront, there exist many alternatives that stretch the payments over time and postpone those payments until benefits can be realized.

In many projects, especially IT projects, it may be possible to fund your project in segments, rather than all at once. Many IT projects begin with a carefully controlled pre-project. This pre-project can have many names, such as proof-of-concept or conference room pilot. When such an approach is employed, it may be possible to negotiate with the various vendors and only pay for the pieces that you need as you need them. In these pre-project scenarios, often only a small investment in hardware and only a few seats of software need to be acquired. Once the pre-project phase is over and the test issues have been addressed, then the company can place the order for the full hardware and software bundle that is called for in the business case. This allows the company to soften the initial cash outlay and defer much of the expenditure until some benefits have been validated and many of the hurdles have been overcome.

REDUCE COSTS

Sticker shock is common for large-scale projects. Even if the projected benefits are substantial, the actual amount of funding needed to execute large projects catches many executives by surprise. You should anticipate this and, before preparing your final presentation, review each cost component and ask yourself (or your business case team) several probing questions. Below is the reprint of the cost section of our spreadsheet from the previous chapter.

PROJECTED ANNUAL COSTS	YR 1	YR 2	YR 3	YR 4	YR 5	TOTAL
New Hardware	$2.20	$0.60				$2.80
Recurring Hardware Maintenance		$0.11	$0.11	$0.11	$0.11	$0.44
New Software Licenses	$6.10					$6.10
Recurring Software Maintenance		$1.22	$1.22	$1.22	$1.22	$4.88
Consulting and Implementation Services	$14.25	$1.50				$15.75
Improvements to Physical Facilities	$1.25	$1.25				$2.50
Temporary Labor Costs (backfill for initial phases)	$0.75	$0.75				$1.50
Project Cost Estimates by Year	$24.55	$5.43	$1.33	$1.33	$1.33	$33.97

Review each line item. For example, let's look at the "New Hardware" entry. Do you need all of that hardware for this project? Do you need to buy it at all? What are the trade-offs between owning (and maintaining) the hardware yourself or outsourcing that capability to a reliable hosting partner? These are common questions that you should anticipate. And since you are anticipating them, you should prepare thoughtful responses to these questions in advance. If we further explore the "Consulting and Implementation Services" entry, we can ask similar questions. Is there a way for you to shrink the scope of services without compromising the overall implementation? What can you do to reduce travel costs that are inherent in all consulting agreements? Might you be able to find capable local contractors for certain pieces of your project, thus reducing both the travel costs and possibly the hourly rate? Again, these questions are presented merely as examples for you to consider and resolve before you make your final presentation. As you explore ways to reduce the costs of the project, you must be mindful of the potential consequences that are introduced by your various alternatives. Build a simple table for yourself, like the example below. In the table you would list the cost reduction alternative along with its pros and cons.

ALTERNATIVE	PROS	CONS
Rather than purchase the hardware we can use a local hosting firm to host the equipment.	• Lower upfront cost (maybe zero upfront cost) • Possibly lower operating cost	• Hardware not on our site secured by our security protocols
Utilizing local contractors for certain tasks rather than using as many consultants from the system integrator.	• Likely lower cost per hour • Little or no travel expense for local contractors	• May not be as knowledgeable on the specific hardware or software configurations that we seek to implement.

INCREASE GAINS

When looking to increase gains, you will want to revisit each of your projected benefits with the responsible business area. Looking at our image below, and considering the entry "Reduce Direct Material Costs," go back to the head of procurement and confirm your estimates. Ask the business area manager/executive if there are any variables that you might have overlooked that could enable bigger benefits than you originally projected. Admittedly, there is a small risk that the business owner of the benefit might seek to further reduce the benefits rather than cheerfully accept an increase in the projection, but the risk is worth taking, as you may be able to further negotiate additional value for your project. You will want to do this for each benefit so that you can confidently present benefits at their best.

PROJECTED ANNUAL BENEFITS	YR 1	YR 2	YR 3	YR 4	YR 5	TOTAL
Note: All figures in millions USD						
Reduce Direct Material Costs	$1.52	$3.07	$6.32	$6.51	$6.71	$24.14
Increase Revenue	$0.00	$3.66	$6.33	$6.52	$6.72	$23.23
Improve Staff Productivity	$0.16	$2.80	$4.70	$4.84	$4.99	$17.49
Reduce Days in Inventory	$4.35	$4.35	$0.00	$0.00	$0.00	$8.70
Reduce IT Costs	$0.19	$0.39	$0.80	$0.83	$0.85	$3.06
Benefit Estimates by Year	$6.22	$14.27	$18.16	$18.70	$19.26	$76.61

ACCELERATE GAINS

Finally, you should consider what recommendations you can make that will accelerate the benefits. Is it possible and reasonable to re-sequence the implementation schedule such that the business areas that stand to benefit the most are rolled out first? Does it make sense to roll out one capability, say inventory management, across the numerous facilities of the company before addressing the sales and order management areas? Or does it make more sense to roll out all of the capabilities at one location before moving on to another location and rolling out all of the capabilities there? Are there ways to accelerate the realization of benefits that have not been considered? For example, there are times when the implementation can be shortened by employing additional contractors and part-time employees. That might cost a little more in the early stages of the project, but if the benefits are rich enough, those costs may easily be offset by the faster achievement of benefits.

By taking the time to evaluate your options regarding these four cash-flow influencers, you enhance the credibility of your business case. The added benefit is that you are much more prepared for your upcoming executive presentation. And as Aristotle recommended, you may elect to be proactive and anticipate some of these considerations by including them in your prepared presentation, rather than waiting for the questions to arise.

Chapter 50

Section Four Summary

Collecting evidence is important to your business case, but analyzing the evidence that you have collected may be even more important. It is important to analyze your evidence from a number of perspectives, specifically:

- Do you have the right evidence to support your recommendations?
- What evidence is still missing that you must collect to support your recommendations?
- Has your evidence passed the boulder, rocks, and pebbles test for completeness, especially for boulders?

When building your presentation, exercise care to not wander too deeply into intricate financial calculations if you are not a seasoned finance professional. It is much better to present basic benefit and cost numbers and be able to confidently defend them than it is to attempt to show skills that you may not actually have and that may compromise your credibility.

Reasonability analysis is a valuable exercise to ensure that your benefit projections are reasonable and corroborated. Comparing your company's key financial metrics to those same metrics of peer companies can add an additional layer of thoroughness and credibility to your recommendation. If you make recommendations that are outside the bounds of observable achievements of peer companies, your business case runs the risk of being evaluated as unreasonable (and therefore less than credible).

Additional discovery and fine-tuning of benefits presents both a favorable and unfavorable outcome. The favorable outcome is additional credibility. The more you clarify and corroborate your benefit estimates, the more believable they become. However, it is also common that the more you explore for further details, the more you discover exclusions and exceptions to your general benefit numbers, thus reducing the previous pool of benefits.

We explored three advanced benefit considerations that, when applied properly, can enhance the credibility of your benefit estimates. Those three considerations are maturity modeling, realization timing, and accounting for business growth.

Benefits are most credible when they have been corroborated by the managers and executives responsible for the areas projected to realize those benefits. Gaining their corroboration and commitment requires an artful approach to facilitation and negotiation.

Another analysis tool is to employ ranges in your benefit estimates. Most benefits are guesses. The goal is to make the guesses based on as much logic as possible. Sometimes, adding ranges helps with the credibility of your projections. Rather than simply stating that an area might be able to reduce costs by 15 percent, it might be more effective to state that the area could reduce costs from 10–20 percent and then show multiple calculations—10 percent, 15 percent, and 20 percent cost reductions as a means of adding further credibility to your projections.

Every business case states the value of a proposed project. Executives also want to know how the benefits will be realized. It is valuable for you to invest the time to articulate the policies, processes, personnel, and other changes that must be implemented in order for those benefits to become reality.

After all of these considerations, don't forget to articulate the less-than-measurable soft benefits. Oftentimes the soft benefits carry a lot of weight with the project approvers. While your business case will not likely succeed solely on the weight of soft benefits, including them adds an additional statement of benefit, even if you do not calculate the value of those soft benefits mathematically.

Jack Keen's PayoffCards are the single best method for packaging and presenting your potential benefits. They are concise, easy-to-follow, one-page executive documents that explain your benefits in plain English. Using PayoffCards makes your assumptions and calculations transparent to the executives and gives them additional confidence that you are not simply asking them to blindly trust that your math and assumptions are reasonable and valid.

Finally, as you wrap up your analysis of your discovery evidence, take a step back and ask yourself how the business case could provide a faster return on the investment. The four cash flow influencers—postpone costs, reduce costs, increase gains, and accelerate gains—are excellent tools for giving your business case a final sanity check.

SECTION FIVE

Delivering Your Recommendation

Chapter 51

Packaging Your Recommendation

Just last week I was on a Web conference with a Tier I software and consulting provider. The topic of the Web conference was social media and enabling user access on mobile devices. One of the speakers introduced a slide that described the ways the audience should consider justifying investments in these new and emerging technologies. The speaker stated that there are just three ways that he believed such projects receive funding: the project increases revenue, it reduces expenses, or it improves productivity. These, you may recall, are three of the same justification criteria that were introduced in chapter 16, called "Determine the Project Drivers" in the Hypothesis section. In that chapter, I introduced the concept of the DuPont Model, which stated that all justifications must link back to the primary financial statements (the balance sheet and the income statement). These justification parameters are universal regardless of the technology or project that you are proposing.

With that in mind, it is now time to put all of your discovery pieces together and present your recommendation to your approval board. There are three distinct stages in this phase: packaging, practicing, and present-ing. We'll explore each thoroughly to ensure your success, beginning with packaging.

There are many ways to package your recommendation and many of these ways can deliver a successful result. At its core, success—in business case terms—comes from the thoroughness of your previous evidence gathering and analysis work, combined with your effectiveness in delivering a compelling executive presentation. Your company might already have a preferred template in place for such presentations. Whether a standard template exists or not, there are certain near-universal considerations for successful business case presentations. The successful presentation tells a story and it leads the audience to a predetermined conclusion. It is not just a collection of PowerPoint slides or text pages or spreadsheets. Those things might be used to tell the story, but the story is king. And you must build the whole story.

> Never lose sight of the fact that your business case must present the value of your proposal in business terms, which is to say that your proposal must always link your benefits back to the primary financial statements—the income statement and the balance sheet.

Remember that business cases are about business. Never lose sight of the fact that your business case must present the value of your proposal in business terms, which is to say that your proposal must always link your benefits back to the primary financial statements—the income statement and the balance sheet. As you begin to prepare your document, allocate some time to reflect back on all of the notes that you took during your discovery sessions. For planning purposes, it is best to begin this activity at least one week prior to your scheduled presentation date. This week of preparation will give you time to edit your content and even revisit previous contributors to gain additional clarification. Some items that support your recommendation may be outside of the scope of the business case, such as a product demonstration. For those items, you'll want to make a list of items to hand off to other team members to ensure that those concerns are addressed; you will also want to make sure that outside contributors are scheduled to your satisfaction. Review your discovery notes to identify all of the known objections and concerns, and from this list begin to prepare your presentation so that you can check off each item as it's completed. For example, if you heard a concern about your own company's ability to successfully implement the project within the time and budget parameters that you present, you will need to address that in advance in your presentation, rather than naively hope that it does not come up during the presentation.

Consider the following passage from *Making Your Case*:

> The most difficult element of the oral argument is the unexpected—the argument for your adversary or the question from the court that has not been anticipated. It's the supreme talent of the expert oral advocate (a talent that few possess) to be able to respond immediately and accurately to these surprises. But it is a basic skill of the competent oral advocate—and a skill we can all master—to ensure to the maximum extent possible that surprises don't occur.
>
> This means thinking a lot about the case, turning it over in your mind, looking at it from various perspectives, racking your brain not only for the flaws in your adversary's case but also for the weaknesses of your own. It means preparing a defense for each of those weaknesses, even if it can be no more than an acknowledgement of its existence and the assertion that it's outweighed by other considerations. It means preparing for hundreds of different questions even though you may be asked only 20. (Scalia & Garner, pg. 150)

Using that quotation as guidance, approach the presentation of your business case as you would a court case. As such, you should anticipate that there will be an opposing counsel, an adversary who will cross-examine your evidence to poke holes in it and discredit your case. During your discovery sessions, you would have met with people who disagreed with your hypothesis or resisted your conclusions regarding benefit projections. You would have heard their comments and the reasons for their disagreements.

For many experienced business case developers, one initial and vital step in preparing to tell the story is listing the questions that you can anticipate, either on a notepad or on a whiteboard in a group brainstorming session. The objective is to have a story that flows smoothly but that at the same time answers the anticipated questions. You won't be able to anticipate every question that will arise during your presentation, but there are many that seem somewhat universal. Here are some that you might consider (the source of your answers is in parentheses):

- On which business area are we focusing, and what is the current state of that business area? (Restating your hypothesis)
- How is this current environment inadequate for helping the company meet its goals? (Evidence that a shortcoming or opportunity exists)
- Who was included and participated in your discovery conversations? How do we know that your work was thorough? (List of participants)
- What methods did you use to collect this data upon which you have built your case? How do we know that your methods were reasonable and thorough? (Describe how you collected the information—using workshops, individual interviews—and what methods you used to elicit input, such as maturity modeling and SWOT exercises)
- Why must the company act upon this now, rather than wait weeks, months, or years? (Several sources—research articles, PayoffCards, quotations from participants)
- Which, if any, alternatives were considered? (Analysis that your recommendations are not just pandering to the lure of contemporary technology hype—e.g., "We have to have this capability if we intend to survive!")
- How does this recommendation benefit the company? (Analysis showing that your financial benefits are projected to exceed projected costs)
- What do you recommend, and why?
- If we approve your proposal, how should we proceed?

After creating this preliminary list, sit down with your executive sponsor and get his or her thoughts on this list of anticipated questions. In about fifteen minutes, a thoughtful sponsor can provide you with a quick list of "Have you thought of…" questions that will supplement and enrich the initial list shown above.

One likely outcome of brainstorming a list of potential questions is that it will expose gaps in your evidence. It is possible that reasonable questions will be introduced for which you have no—or very little—compelling evidence to support an answer. This is part of this preparation phase. When such gaps are uncovered, you must invest the time to re-interview certain people or re-analyze certain evidence so that you can effectively provide crisp and compelling answers to these anticipated questions. Your goal is to have everyone (or nearly everyone) on the approval committee reach the same conclusion, namely that your proposal has value to the company, that its value exceeds the cost, and that the company should act now rather than later.

To accomplish this goal, it is necessary to take a step back and retrace all of the work you have done over the past weeks or months to reach this conclusion. You must anticipate that there will be those members of the approval committee who are only vaguely familiar with your initiative and who may not have been exposed to more than just a few anecdotal comments. It is therefore incumbent upon you to tell the complete story from beginning to end leaving nothing to the imagination. Do not assume that all of your approvers have been kept abreast by their downstream managers. Also, do not assume that all communication regarding your proposed initiative has been positive. You should assume that you have work to do to convince the approval board that your proposal is worth funding and is worth funding now.

As you reflect, you will realize that you have a large collection of notes from meetings, workshops, research from internal sources, and conversations with vendors. Within those pages of notes you also likely have something else—key expectations. In the course of your discovery work, you will have heard others list their expectations and their concerns. Among the elements of your business case should be a section where you explicitly lay out those questions and provide your best answers. If you don't give those questions proper forethought, your lack of such planning may weaken your overall presentation.

During your presentation you should expect to get many questions from the approval committee. An inquiry may take the form of a direct statement, such as, "You are aware that I am concerned about the cost of this project." Or it could be something indirect, such as when a manager states, "I heard from my team that your recommendation does not fully explore the impact of overtime in our workforce." I don't know what questions you will be asked during your business case development, but I am certain that there will be many.

For the remainder of this section, we will assume that your presentation will be created in PowerPoint.

PREPARING YOUR POWERPOINT DECK

Prepare your PowerPoint deck with three basic sections, or levels of detail— an executive summary, the main body (high-level talking points), and a detailed appendix. You should build your presentation this way because, in simple sales terms, you should present enough information to get the sale and not so much information that you lose the sale. It is possible to present too much information and lose the momentum that you might have gained by spoon-feeding the information to your audience. This is not to suggest that you are concealing information. On the contrary, this approach discloses everything that is necessary to enable the executives to make an informed decision. It is also an approach that has proven effective when presenting to very busy, very intelligent senior executives. They typically do not need every minute detail in order to feel sufficiently informed and capable of rendering a decision. Yet it has been observed time and time again that first-time business case developers (and presenters) feel some regrettable urge to share every piece of information that they have collected during their business case discovery efforts. This three-tiered presentation approach protects you from yourself in that regard. It conveys both the minimum necessary information and provides supplemental information should the need arise to dig into specific details.

Creating the most effective PowerPoint deck is equal parts art and science. One artful aspect that contributes to a slide's effectiveness is aesthetic composition. A slide with a fair amount of white space is easier on the eyes than a slide that is crammed full of graphics and text and multiple colors. But how do you convey complex topics and still preserve the aesthetics of a slide? Striking the balance between sufficient content to make your point and ample white space to maintain aesthetics is a challenge. Build your slides to appeal to the eyes. If you use graphics, use them sparingly and at a reasonably high level. When you use text, strive for brevity and impact over trying to write every salient point on the slide. Strive to use only one font throughout your presentation deck. You can fiddle with the font sizes and the attributes (bold, italic, and underline if used sparingly), but endeavor to maintain a uniform font style throughout the presentation deck.

To ensure that you and your fellow presenters remember the points of impact that you wish to make, consider using the Notes Pages function within PowerPoint. This handy feature will allow you to capture all of your brilliant ideas without respect to white space. You and your colleagues can refer to these notes when you present your slides. Your audience will see visually appealing slides while you narrate the specific details that you believe supplement your slide and amplify the impact of your presentation.

Before building the body of your presentation, begin by making a handy checklist, like the table below. This will keep you on track as you build the presentation that will become your formal business case. Here is a typical example. This example has seventeen items. Within these seventeen items you might have one or two or ten individual slides on a given topic. This format will suffice for a large percentage of business cases.

Requirement	Percent Complete	Comments
Executive Summary		
Agenda		
Statement of Business Issue(s)		
Approach Employed		
Participants		
Key Quotes		
Evidence Supporting Your Hypothesis		
External Comparative Evidence		
Assumptions		
Risks		
Cost and Benefit Considerations		
Alternatives Considered		
Implementation Timeline		
Resource Requirements		
Recommendation		
Immediate Next Steps		
Appendices		

Your goal is to have twenty or fewer slides in the main body of your presentation deck. At this point, you might be asking yourself, "So where do I put all of those great slides that I want to present that represent all of the hard work that I did to get this business case prepared?" If your content doesn't fit nicely and neatly within this format, you'll likely move the remaining content to the appendix. It is very common for me to have fewer than twenty slides in the main body of the presentation, yet as many as one hundred available in the appendix. How this all fits together to make your compelling and powerful business case is explained below. Let's begin exploring each of the listed slides, beginning with the executive summary.

THE EXECUTIVE SUMMARY

The executive summary is the single most important slide that you will create for your presentation. It is the most important because it contains the complete summary of your proposal on a single slide. It is strongly recommended that you create this slide last. That's right, last. It should be positioned as the first content slide in your PowerPoint deck, but you should not create it until you have built all of the other content. You will then summarize and reduce that rich content onto this one slide. With that in mind, the detailed explanation of the executive summary slide in this chapter has been moved to the bottom of the list.

AGENDA

This is a very simple slide. Add bullets to this slide to give the attendees a sense of where the meeting is headed and what topics you plan to cover. Using the example from the table above, this agenda slide would be as follows:

- Executive Summary
- Statement of Business Issues
- Approach Employed
- Participants
- Key Quotes
- Internal Evidence
- External Evidence
- Assumptions
- Risks
- Resource Requirements

- Cost and Benefit Considerations
- Alternatives Considered
- Implementation Timeline
- Recommendation
- Immediate Next Steps
- Appendices

For the sake of brevity—and to adhere to our requirement of more white space—you could combine a number of these bullet points on your agenda slide. For example, you could combine internal and external evidence into a single bullet point and call it "Evidence." You would still have multiple slides under that agenda heading, but you would not need to have each individual slide called out on this agenda slide.

A consolidated agenda slide might look more like this:

- Executive Summary
- Statement of Business Issues
- Approach Employed
- Participants (which would include Key Quotes)
- Evidence (which would include both Internal Evidence and External Evidence)
- Assumptions and Risks
- Cost and Benefit Considerations (which would include Alternatives Considered)
- Implementation Timeline (which would include Resource Requirements)
- Recommendation (which would include Immediate Next Steps)
- ** Using an abbreviated agenda, it would be unnecessary to call out the existence of the appendices. You would still have them, but you would not need to call them out on the agenda slide.

Using the abbreviated approach for this example, we have compressed our bullets from seventeen to nine.

Each of us builds presentations in different ways. I prefer to write out, in long form without respect to brevity, everything that I wish to say on each slide. Once I can see all that I intend to say, it is then quite easy to organize and bulletize key points necessary to create my PowerPoint slides.

I would typically move that written content to the Notes Pages of the corresponding PowerPoint slides to keep things within easy reach for review and practice later on.

STATEMENT OF BUSINESS ISSUES

As stated in previous chapters, you may find that several of your approvers are less than familiar with your proposal. Never assume that everyone is up to speed when you start. That knowledge makes this slide very important. This slide introduces your hypothesis and sets the scope of your work. Furthermore, it conveys your basic purpose and tees up your forthcoming proposal. This slide might contain very few bullet points. It might state your hypothesis, as in the following example:

- Concern was voiced that our purchasing functions are not optimized to squeeze the maximum cost out of the buying process.
- Our company would benefit from consolidating purchasing departments across the country into one centralized purchasing group.
- This consolidation will enable us to gain economies of scale and leverage our overall buying power for purchasing raw materials and can drive our costs down by $2.6 million annually,

For brevity, your bullets might be much more concise, as follows:

- Observation: Current purchasing processes are not optimal.
- Objective: Consolidate purchasing into one national, centralized function.
- Result: Cost savings will exceed $2.6 million annually.

This whets the appetite of the audience and typically gets them engaged to learn more about your hypothesis, your approach, and your recommendation. Using this concise approach also achieves a great white-space-to-overall-content balance on your slide, thus making it aesthetically appealing.

APPROACH EMPLOYED

The executives will want to understand the approach you used to validate your hypothesis. They will also want to understand your methods in order to gain confidence that your approach is not simply a cleverly disguised pathway designed to help you buy some fad-of-the-moment technology.

They will evaluate your approach as they will seek assurances that you were thorough and comprehensive. In business parlance, they will want to confirm that you have done the necessary due diligence. You should explain, in straightforward terms, just how you determined your hypothesis and how you validated it using interviews, workshops, research, and so on. It would be expected that your executive sponsor has been fully apprised each step of the way. Invoking his or her name and explaining how you conducted checkpoint meetings and status updates with your sponsor will help to assure the other approvers that your methods were thorough and that your recommendations are consistent with other similar projects that the company has undertaken.

PARTICIPANTS

During your business case discovery activities, you met with and interviewed many people. This slide should list all of the people with whom you have met. You would include those that were interviewed individually, those that participated in group workshops, and those that may have participated only by phone or Web conference. Showing such a list further demonstrates your thoroughness. You are presenting facts and opinions about the current state of the business and the value of moving to a future state. In each functional area, there are people who are viewed as knowledgeable experts. Your approvers will be evaluating your list of participants to ensure that the experts they count on have been included on specific topics.

There are some common ways to arrange this slide. Arranging the names alphabetically by last name is the most common. Alternatively, you could choose to list the participants by job function or other common grouping. Even within this grouping, you should still list the names in alphabetical order. And please, please don't overlook this—make sure that everyone's name is properly spelled, including hyphenated names.

KEY QUOTES

As you conducted your discovery activities, you likely heard some great and memorable quotes. Where applicable, it will benefit your business case to include quotes from key people whose opinions or perspectives bolster your position. It is important to include the name and title of the person to whom this quote is attributed. You won't need many quotes, but if you choose to include some, you should have more than just one. Here are some examples:

- One of your interview candidates may have come from another company where things were done differently. Possibly this interviewee said, "In my previous company, we consolidated our purchasing functions, asserted our buying leverage, and achieved a 6 percent reduction in the cost of common raw materials."
- Another interviewee may simply state, "I am aware that there is much inefficiency in purchasing, and this is compounded by the fact that the different regional offices all use different purchasing systems."

You will want to include quotes that support your hypothesis and make your case. You will also want to use quotes from those employees that are most highly regarded. But most importantly, before you include the quote in your presentation, you must return to the specific person and obtain his or her informed consent to use the quote in this context. Their informed consent is necessary because one of the approvers may seek out that individual during or after your presentation to validate that this person made and supports this statement. Your credibility would be injured if that person is not prepared to confidently support the quote that you have included.

EVIDENCE SUPPORTING YOUR HYPOTHESIS

This slide seeks to demonstrate that you have validated your hypothesis during your discovery activities. Here you will want to present any evidence that confirms your hypothesis. Review your discovery notes and extract as much supporting evidence as you can find. Did you observe processes that were inefficient? If so, include a diagram or reference to the process that you observed. Did someone state that improvements could be made but not want to go on the record and be quoted by name? Such statements can comfortably go here. You can mention that you heard certain things during your group interviews and that these comments or concerns were voiced by several people (assuming that this is the case) without calling them out by name.

Be aware that without good supporting evidence from internal sources, you risk having your hypothesis discredited. Without such evidence, the approvers may conclude that there really isn't a problem sufficiently troubling to justify this level of investment.

EXTERNAL COMPARATIVE EVIDENCE

Reflect back on your external research. What pieces of data from that activity can be included here to supplement your business case? Did you find articles that suggest that companies that initiated projects similar to your proposed project were able to realize benefits? Did you examine your company's financial statements and compare them to your competitors and peers? If so, are there relevant elements of data that can further support your hypothesis?

If your proposal includes the purchase of products or services from another company, very possibly that vendor can provide you with good supporting evidence, possibly a few reference customers who have succeeded at projects similar to the one you are proposing. Such references make your potential benefits seem even more plausible and realistic. External references add additional credibility to your presentation.

ASSUMPTIONS

Listing the assumptions for project success is one of the two common oversights in business cases. The other common oversight is omitting known risks (which we'll address in the next slide). The concept of documenting your assumptions was first introduced in Chapter 39, "Preserving Credibility through Reasonability Analysis." It is important to list all of your assumptions, because it is upon these assumptions that you are committing to succeed. If the assumptions prove false, you may be in a position to renegotiate completion dates or project costs. If you omit this list, you are—knowingly or unknowingly—committing to execute a successful project without respect to any hindering or disruptive factors.

Common assumptions are that no significant business disruptions will occur, such as acts of nature (e.g., floods, tornadoes, earthquakes), acts of terror, and so on. Spend some time working with your colleagues and executive sponsor to brainstorm several other assumptions. You will likely produce a list of a dozen or so. List them in some prioritized order. The criteria for prioritization are up to you. Other common assumptions that you might consider are:

- The benefits that are presented are believed to be reasonable and achievable.

- The project will receive full support by all business areas involved in the project.
- No business disruptions will occur due to labor disputes during the course of the project.
- Any software will be implemented as is, without modifications.
- Lead times associated with shipment of hardware and other project assets will be reliable.
- We have thoroughly identified every business process and have assurances from each business unit that the proposed software successfully meets their needs.

This list will create a lively discussion in your presentation. You can expect at least one approver to state, "We can't assume that. We don't know that to be true." That's the very reason that you present these assumptions. If such a comment is raised (and it usually is) you will have a great opportunity to discuss the considerations necessary to adjust the project expectations should those assumptions prove false.

RISKS

Every project faces risks. Many of the previously mentioned assumptions create risks. There are at least two good sources for risks in your notes. First, review your list of assumptions. Which of those assumptions, if they prove false, would introduce risks to your project? The second rich source for risks is to review your notes from your SWOT exercise, especially the notes regarding the threats introduced by the proposed future project. Those threats might also be candidates for inclusion in your risk assessment.

One effective way to present risks is to present them in a two-column table, as shown below. The first column would list the risk, and the second column would elaborate the implications of that risk. Management will appreciate that you have taken the time to present both the risks and your perspective on the implications of those risks. You may wish to add another column that offers your comments on possible actions to take in advance to mitigate those risks. You should expect that your assembled approvers will introduce a number of alternative mitigation approaches, but don't let that diminish your enthusiasm. This simply means that they are engaged with you on the risks and seek to introduce better mitigation approaches than you might have considered.

RISK	IMPLICATION
Business areas will not provide enthusiastic support	Adoption may be slow or even undermined.
Software not implemented as-is	Modifications will take time, be costly and may compromise our ability to upgrade in the future

RESOURCE REQUIREMENTS

The purpose of this slide is to identify all of the anticipated resources (and their respective costs) that your project will require. Every project needs resources. People are the most common resource that you should consider, but also consider other resources such as training facilities, temporary office space for consultants and temporary workers, available hardware and software, and special tools that may need to be rented for the duration of the project. You will want to highlight the number of internal resources that are required for your project and the number of external ones that are required. Can you find external consultants locally, or will you have to bring them in from other cities, thus incurring travel, lodging, rental car, and meal costs?

It is common to wrestle with the following conundrum: you want the best internal people for your project, but they are vital in their current job and do not have additional discretionary blocks of time to allocate to your project. Do you ask them to work overtime, allocating time to both their regular job and your project? Such an increased workload, especially for extended periods of time, might contribute to burnout, job dissatisfaction, and turnover. Or do you attempt to backfill those people with temporary workers so that their current jobs get completed by others, thus allowing them to allocate more of their time to your project? What about consultants? How many would you need? What skill sets are required? When do you need them and for how long will you need them? You must think through the likely resource questions so that you have good answers handy in case such questions arise during your presentation.

You can present this information in a variety of formats. You could choose to list names or roles and list their anticipated starting and ending dates on the project. Or you could choose instead to represent this information graphically along a timeline, showing the times that various participants will roll on and off of the project.

The point of this slide is to help the approvers understand the level of effort that is required and the various times that additional resources are required. It helps the approvers visualize that all of these resources are not required at full utilization for the entirety of the project. Once they grasp the effort required, there may be some discussion as to whether it is preferable to demand more or less from internal resources or more or less from external resources. By presenting this slide, you position yourself to have a productive discussion and receive some beneficial guidance from the executive team as to how best to allocate the planned workload between internal and external resources.

COST AND BENEFIT CONSIDERATIONS

This slide (or collection of slides) will be the focus of much discussion. Invest the time to have these slides tell a compelling story. The story flows best when you introduce the summary slide (shown below) first, and then follow that slide with individual slides showing select PayoffCards detailing how each benefit was determined.

COST/BENEFIT SUMMARY

PROJECTED ANNUAL BENEFITS	YR 1	YR 2	YR 3	YR 4	YR 5	TOTAL
Note: All figures in millions USD						
Reduce Direct Material Costs	$1.52	$3.07	$6.32	$6.51	$6.71	$24.14
Increase Revenue	$0.00	$3.66	$6.33	$6.52	$6.72	$23.23
Improve Staff Productivity	$0.16	$2.80	$4.70	$4.84	$4.99	$17.49
Reduce Days in Inventory	$4.35	$4.35	$0.00	$0.00	$0.00	$8.70
Reduce IT Costs	$0.19	$0.39	$0.80	$0.83	$0.85	$3.06
Benefit Estimates by Year	$6.22	$14.27	$18.16	$18.70	$19.26	$76.61

NOTE: Benefits are presented as undiscounted, pre-tax values

PROJECTED ANNUAL COSTS	YR 1	YR 2	YR 3	YR 4	YR 5	TOTAL
New Hardware	$2.20	$0.60				$2.80
Recurring Hardware Maintenance		$0.11	$0.11	$0.11	$0.11	$0.44
New Software Licenses	$6.10					$6.10
Recurring Software Maintenance		$1.22	$1.22	$1.22	$1.22	$4.88
Consulting and Implementation Services	$14.25	$1.50				$15.75
Improvements to Physical Facilities	$1.25	$1.25				$2.50
Temporary Labor Costs (backfill for initial phases)	$0.75	$0.75				$1.50
Project Cost Estimates by Year	$24.55	$5.43	$1.33	$1.33	$1.33	$33.97
Benefits Minus Costs	($18.33)	$8.84	$16.83	$17.37	$17.93	$42.64

You may also choose to include some of the charts from your spreadsheet, such as the two examples shown below:

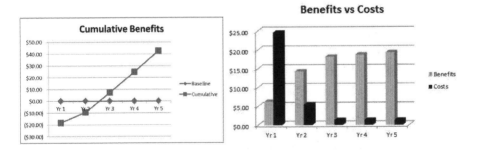

The final slide in this section might be a slide on the soft benefits as depicted in the example below:

Benefits beyond $8 million

Financial Statement	Business Benefit
Income Statement (Revenue Increases)	• Recover lost revenues as fewer fee-based services provided free under expired warranties. • Improved user interface attracts and holds customers longer on website. • Enriched up-sell and cross-sell opportunities from better information and analysis.
Income Statement (Expense Reductions)	• Reduced time-to-market and accelerated return on investment on new projects realized from improved integration capabilities. • Tighter travel policy enforcement will promote recording expenses in proper period. • Improved reliability of travel-related tax deductions with more complete data. • Reduced sources of common data. Move to a "single source of truth." One system of record for inventory, sales, order management, distribution, customer returns provides improved customer experience. • Improved internal auditing capability reduces external auditor fees.
Balance Sheet (Asset Optimization)	• Improved project evaluation capabilities, which will provide better information – allowing the organization to cancel struggling projects earlier rather than later.

ALTERNATIVES CONSIDERED

Napoleon is credited with placing a very specific expectation on his junior officers with respect to their reporting of problems or issues. His approach involved three specific directives: First, state the problem. Second, present a list of the top three alternatives. And finally, state which of those three you recommend and why.

Your business case has already addressed the first and last of these three directives—state the problem and recommend a solution. On this slide, list the alternatives that you have also considered but have rejected. This is necessary, as at least one of your approvers will ask you, "What other approaches or solutions have you considered?" Be mindful that "do nothing" is a valid alternative and should be listed. You will recall from chapter 7 that anytime large capital investments are being discussed, someone will commonly suggest that the best course of action is to conserve the capital and not spend it on the proposed project.

You were introduced to the concept of the anti-sponsor in chapter 11 entitled "The Role of the Executive Sponsor." You should invest a reasonable amount of preparation time to address those issues that you anticipate the anti-sponsor will attempt to champion. You should also anticipate that this opponent has whispered to his designated representative on the approval committee and presented his view of the flaws in your business case and the perils of approving your proposal. If you've been paying attention to the interviews and reading between the lines during conversations, you know if an undercurrent exists, what the main objections are from that camp, and what course of action they prefer. If their objections have merit, or if they can derail your presentation, you should work with your executive sponsor to plan an articulate explanation during your presentation. Rather than ignore the issue and hope that it is not raised during the presentation, the better course of action is to address the rejected alternative head on. When doing so, address the issue matter-of-factly, state why it was not the preferred alternative, and move on to the next aspect of your presentation.

IMPLEMENTATION TIMELINE

Providing guidance on creating detailed project plans is beyond the scope of this book. Nevertheless, your approvers will expect to see some sort of project plan or timeline in order to grant you approval to move forward. The approvers will want to know several things relative to timing. They will want to understand how long your project will take, how you determined the sequencing of project stages, how long before tangible results are realized, and they will also want to know about all of the numerous, intricate tasks that must be performed in order to ensure a successful project. Well, actually, they may not want to hear all of that. What they really want to know is that *you* know all of that and *you* have thought through every possible task.

To determine sequencing, there are many methods you can employ. One method is to determine which project phases must be implemented as prerequisites for other phases. In the example below, it is possible that the benefit titled "Reduce IT Costs" involves replacing old, obsolete, and expensive-to-maintain equipment with newer, state-of-the-art systems. Replacing the old equipment might best be done before the other phases are attempted so that all new software solutions are installed on the newest, most efficient systems. Even though this benefit is neither the easiest to perform nor the most lucrative, you might have determined that it provides a strong foundation for the implementation of the other phases.

When you have several phases that can be implemented without respect to dependencies, you should determine which ones provide the greatest benefit for the least effort, and then prioritize so that you can show realized value soonest from your project. One way to visualize this prioritization method is to map the various project phases (or individual benefit categories) against a two-axis grid and then to plot the project benefits in the grid. In the example below we have the vertical axis indicating level of difficulty (or effort) or level of complexity and the horizontal axis indicating the estimated perceived value of the benefit.

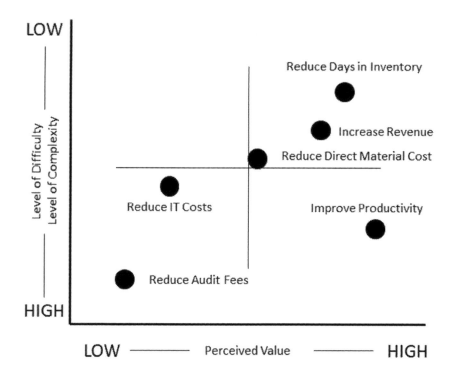

To determine the project phases, you would then need to determine the specific tasks necessary to achieve the individual benefit items. The above grid can be presented to the approval committee so that they can observe and evaluate your criteria for selecting the implementation sequence of your project elements. This grid can then lead you to sequence your project phases and their individual subordinate tasks in the order that suggests the most valuable items are addressed first. For example, to reduce days in inventory might require that the company implement an order management system and an inventory management system. It would be expected that you would determine all of the necessary tasks, showing task duration, resource assignments, and task dependencies (using a tool like Oracle's Primavera or Microsoft Project). Your project plan might have hundreds or even thousands of individual, interdependent tasks.

Having presented numerous timelines to approval committees, I have learned that the most effective method for presenting detailed project and implementation plans is to spoon-feed the executives the plan in three specific levels (much the way this recommended business case deck is presented). The three levels can best be described as overview, high level, and detailed. I recommend that you plan to present the first two levels in your presentation and move the third, detailed level to the appendix.

Below is a sample project plan for our project. The overview can be as direct as a single statement: "The project will require eighteen months from the start date until the full rollout has been done across the company." That's it. This overview statement is perfect for inclusion on your executive summary slide. The second level—the high-level view, shown below—shows the project divided into easy-to-understand phases.

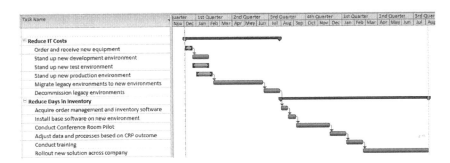

This view shows the major project phases for achieving our benefits. This summarized task view will suffice for most of your presentations. In the case of this project plan, you may have identified hundreds of individual tasks. But showing hundreds of individual tasks is typically unnecessary and can introduce unnecessary distractions. This view shows a summarized view of the phases of the project. There will be those approvers who will want to dig into the minutiae of your project plan and review each of the many, many tasks for themselves. For those individuals, you can easily flip to the appendix to provide the complete, detailed project plan. For those individuals that desire a thorough discussion of each task, you might consider convening a separate meeting just for that purpose so that you don't lose track of your primary goal—presenting your formal business case—and risk losing the attention and support of the assembled executives.

As it relates to your business case presentation, showing a list of hundreds of tasks invites unproductive discussions about whether this task or that task should precede or succeed another task and whether its duration should be estimated to be five days or ten days. Placing the full project plan in the appendix allows you to quickly turn to those pages should specific questions arise, while allowing you to keep your prepared presentation at a high level—as appropriate for this discussion.

RECOMMENDATION

Too many business cases omit a recommendation slide, assuming that the approvers know just what is being recommended. Leave nothing to chance. Include this slide and state directly what you want the approvers to approve. And consider this carefully. You only get one chance to state your recommendation. Do you want the project to be started tomorrow? Then state that. Do you want a specific vendor to be chosen to do the work? Then state that, too. Do you have a specific project manager in mind? State that, as well. You want your approvers to all know exactly what they are being asked to approve. The more clearly you state this, the better.

IMMEDIATE NEXT STEPS

Once you have made your recommendation, the approval board needs to know what you plan to do (or what you plan to direct others to do). This slide should list the tasks and activities that you believe must be completed within the next thirty days, including items such items as the following:

- Begin vendor negotiations.
- Begin selection of internal project team.
- Begin site evaluation for new facility.
- Secure financing from capital markets.

Organizing your task list in table form will help your approvers to see the tasks, the assigned parties, and their respective projected completion dates. The example below shows a four-column table with just such information.

TASK	RESPONSIBLE PARTY	START DATE	END DATE
Begin vendor negotiations	Steve H.	Oct 5	Oct 12
Begin selection of internal project team	Ashley T.	Oct 5	Oct 19
Begin site evaluation for new facility	Mike R.	Oct 5	Nov 5
Secure financing from capital markets	Michael E.	Oct 5	Nov 5

APPENDICES

As you reflect on the content that has been created within these seventeen topics, you may be asking yourself, "But what about all of the other collateral that I've collected and created to help state my case? Where does all of that go? Do I just discard it and forget about it?" The answer is that all of that supporting information goes into the appendix. You may have one appendix for each of the slides above, and each of those appendices might contain one or two or two dozen detailed slides with graphs and diagrams and schematics and other great collateral.

The appendix approach helps you achieve three objectives. First, it provides a logical place within your PowerPoint deck for all of those slides that might be needed but are not appropriate or are simply too detailed to be included in the main body of the presentation. Second, it allows you to manage the size of the body of the document without losing the impact of the detailed slides. And finally, it enables you to quickly flip to certain slides in the event that the discussion turns in that direction and requires more detail than you had originally determined to provide in the body of your presentation.

EXECUTIVE SUMMARY (revisited)

The executive summary is the most important slide in your business case presentation. If you create it following these guidelines, you will have summarized your entire business case on one slide. One piece of guidance that I must put right upfront is that you should include the cost of your proposal on this slide. There is an old adage among professional journalists—"Don't bury the lead." It means that the writer (or in our case the business case creator) should not make people read deep into the story to uncover the lead item. Rather, it should be out front and not concealed. Executives will want to know the cost at the outset. If you do not include it on this slide, many of your assembled approvers will begin thumbing through your presentation to find the cost. That is very disruptive to the flow of your presentation. We're all adults here. No need to play games and bury the cost numbers deep in the presentation hoping that your sheer cleverness will make a weak business case somehow acceptable. At this stage of your business case development, you must be confident that your business case is sound and that the costs are offset by credible benefits that justify the project.

I have conducted scores of successful business case presentations where the discussion never moved beyond the executive summary. It is a vital communication vehicle in your overall presentation. This slide is to be built with careful thought and deliberation. The best executive summaries are limited to a single slide and contain one bullet point that summarizes the main points of the subsequent slides. For example, if you have twenty slides in the main body of your presentation, you might have fewer than ten bullet points on the executive summary slide. By building this slide last, you can evaluate the content from your other slides to pick and choose the most relevant items to include on this slide. Furthermore, building this slide last ensures that your executive summary will accurately summarize the slides that follow. If you attempt to build this summary first, you may find that your subsequent slides don't align well with the body of your presentation.

At its basic, most concise level, the Executive Summary should address six issues:

- What is the problem you believe needs to be solved? (Answer: your hypothesis)
- How did you determine that this problem was more than just a mere annoyance? (Answer: your approach and the people with whom you met)
- What is the monetary value (or benefit) to solving that problem? (Answer: the benefit summary)
- How long will it take to begin realizing value (or benefits) from the project? (Answer: your project timeline)
- How much will it cost? (Answer: your cost-benefit spreadsheet)

- What do you want the approvers to do? (Answer: your recommendation and next steps slides)

Answering those questions upfront on the executive summary slide will accelerate and focus the discussion on the most important points of your business case. If time permits and if interest exists, you can then march through the other slides in the body of your presentation.

Executives have countless things competing for their time. Even if they agree to a two-hour meeting, it is unlikely that you will be able to hold their undivided, rapt attention for two solid hours. They will be checking their smartphones, possibly handling email, and mentally checking out as they ponder other upcoming issues. To hold their attention, you need to state your case and make your most compelling argument early in the presentation. You should be prepared for a thorough question-and-answer session, and that session might consume the bulk of the allocated time. Your complete presentation might consist of twenty or more PowerPoint slides. But the executives are not going to be willing to sit through twenty slides to get to the meat of your business case and your recommendation. The executive summary distills the body of your presentation down to a single slide so that they can get a concise view of the issues and the considerations within a few short minutes (while their attention and focus are highest). When I introduce the executive summary, I typically tell the assembled executives that we have all of the supporting evidence, complete with an assessment of risk, and I am prepared to walk through all of that detail with them if they are interested. But rather than bury the lead, I present the executive summary to hit them directly and get things out in the open. No surprises. Here's an example:

- We have identified several challenges in our purchasing, receiving, and IT functions.
- We have a recommendation to solve those issues, and the recommendation includes the purchase of hardware, software, and consulting services, as well as select changes in our internal business processes.
- We have determined that addressing those challenges as proposed here will result in a five-year benefit of $76.61 million.

- The cost of the proposed project is $33.97 million over five years.
- Our plans include rolling this out over the next six months to all locations.
- With your approval, we'd like to get started as soon as possible.

That is a crisp, concise executive summary. There is enough content on that slide to spark vigorous debate for hours. Yet the whole project is summarized on a single slide.

REVIEWING WHAT YOU'VE CREATED

You're striving to present a compelling argument explaining the value of your proposal and why it should be approved and adopted. If your proposal cannot obtain approval on the strongest points, even if there are just three very strong points, it is unlikely that you will obtain approval by including another fifteen points that are weaker. A few well-articulated, strongly substantiated points are much better than dozens of weak, unsubstantiated points.

Once you've built your first draft of your presentation, it is time to begin the challenging task of streamlining and refining your presentation. As a guide, attempt to keep your primary presentation to twenty or fewer slides. A common planning benchmark states that you should allow an average of three to five minutes for each slide that you present. If you have been given an hour to present, it is therefore unlikely that you will be able to effectively discuss more than twenty slides (and that's cutting it real close). While trimming your content may not seem feasible, remember what Shakespeare wrote: "Brevity is the soul of wit." Less is always more when planning for executive presentations.

You may have created hundreds of slides based on your thorough discovery notes. You might wonder how you could possibly cut them down to twenty or fewer. Simply put, you must edit ruthlessly. This is frequently a tough consideration for inexperienced business case developers. You've worked hard to collect reams of data. You've interviewed many people. You may be tempted to try to include all of your data in your presentation to validate just how hard you have worked on this business case. Resist that temptation. The main body of your presentation needs to be crisp and concise. No unnecessary content. None.

As mentioned previously, get comfortable placing many of your slides at the back of your PowerPoint deck in the appendix. This section contains all of the slides that you might need as backup to a discussion but that are not crisp or powerful enough to make it into the main body of your PowerPoint deck. By placing them in the appendix, they are readily available in case they are needed to support or explain an answer, but they won't be distracting to the audience. Another recommendation is to not include the appendix in any materials that you hand out for the actual presentation meeting. You don't want the attendees to be distracted by the number of pages or to get themselves all tangled up with slides that may or may not ever get presented.

Now that you've built a working draft of your business case, it's time to invite others in to evaluate your work before you deliver your final presentation.

Chapter 52

Practice, Practice, Practice

You have assembled, edited, and fine-tuned your presentation deck. It is now necessary to conduct a couple of dry runs with a critical yet supportive and safe audience. It will be up to you to determine who you will include in your dry run rehearsals. You are seeking to include people who will offer honest, helpful feedback. Conducting a rehearsal with those who would only praise your work and readily accept your recommendations is not a real-world practice scenario. You need to engage trustworthy colleagues who will provide honest commentary, even if that commentary is critical of your findings and conclusions. Their candid comments can help you uncover weaknesses in your presentation. It is better to discover and address these weaknesses during a practice session than when you are before your approval board.

In conducting the rehearsal, it is always beneficial to ask your audience to be mindful of the following questions as you present your business case:

1. Does your presentation lead the listener from hypothesis to recommendation in a logical and sensible way?
2. After hearing your presentation, was there something in your presentation that the listener was expecting to hear but did not?
3. Was there something in your presentation that your listener heard that seemed detrimental to your cause?
4. How did the listener find the overall presentation? Was it well organized? Did you make your case in a compelling and credible manner?

5. Did the listener think that you placed too much or too little emphasis on certain topics?

6. What comments would most improve the presentation?

When conducting your practice sessions, appoint someone to routinely ask two specific questions. These two questions are: "So what?" and "Who cares?" These questions are on everyone's mind. You will do yourself a favor by having someone ask them directly during your practice sessions. Too often business case developers make the mistake of believing that because they built a business case, others will accept it at face value. You should, in fact, do just the opposite and assume that nobody will accept anything that you present without sufficient convincing evidence to support your claims. Keep in mind that great quote from the movie *A Few Good Men*, when Tom Cruise's character Lt. Daniel Caffey states, "It doesn't matter what I believe. It only matters what I can prove." And so it is with your business case.

In preparing for and practicing your presentation there is a third question that you must ask yourself honestly. That question is, "Is there some aspect of my business case that is weak and that I really hope no one asks about or discovers its weakness?" If you have such a question lingering in your mind, you must invest the necessary time and energy to eliminate that weakness. I've been a musician most of my life. As a musician, the goal of practice is to be ready to play as flawlessly and genuinely as possible when performance time comes. In music, some passages are technically more challenging than other passages. To get those passages right, musicians might spend hours working to gain mastery over them. Complicated sections of a symphony might only last thirty seconds when performed, but those thirty seconds might have required hours and hours of practice due to their intricate musicality. Some music passages require intensity and power. Others are soft and flowing. The dynamics of a piece are, in many ways, just as important as hitting the right notes at the right time. So it is with your business case. To project mastery of the topic, you might need to spend hours gaining a deeper and more comprehensive understanding of a specific topic in order to explain it thoroughly and defend it confidently when you are cross-examined during your presentation. Practice will also help you produce the right ebb and flow of emphasis in ways that add more punch and credibility to your overall message. Not every bullet point on every slide carries the same weight. Some must be made more emphatically, while others may be presented in simple, matter-of-fact tones. Practicing what to say is important. Equally important is practicing how to say it. Your practice sessions will expose areas where your presentation needs to be refined and strengthened. It will also reveal areas where you are lingering too long on a topic. Be prepared to make a final round— or two—of refinements to your presentation before planning to present it live to your approval board.

You should always expect that seasoned executives have endured many, many wide-eyed capital project requests and that they have heard every hypothesis and listened to every "trust me" story about potential future benefits. You will not pull the wool over their eyes. Therefore don't deceive yourself into thinking that you can tiptoe around such a weakness. Furthermore, you must anticipate that they will assume you have missed key points. This statement is not meant to be pejorative. It is meant to prepare you for this meeting. If the executives are going to agree to spend a large sum of money, they will cross-examine you to ensure that you have thought through the important and the uncommon considerations.

It is also important to anticipate dissenting opinions and to provide for them in your·presentation. Doing so shows two things. One, it shows the executives that you are not just narrowly presenting one perspective but that you have carefully considered other alternatives—and that you have sound reasons for not recommending those alternatives. Maybe more importantly, anticipating dissenting opinions well in advance gives you time to prepare well-crafted responses to objections the executives might raise. This can prove quite helpful as presentations in front of executives can be intimidating, and having to defend your positions on the fly can be uncomfortable. And if you're uncomfortable in answering some hard questions, it naturally makes the executives skeptical of your proposal. In preparing your responses to anticipated objections, spend some time with your executive sponsor. He should be able to provide some insight into many of the objections and personalities that you will encounter in your presentation. Understanding how the executives pick apart a business case and what criteria they use to evaluate proposals will help you prepare for a successful presentation.

As a final part of your planning activities, you need to evaluate the invitee list of the formal presentation. It is important that the assembled audience has the jurisdiction and authority to advance your recommendation.

It could be that this audience is neither empowered nor willing to approve your proposal on the spot, but they should be able to advance your proposal to the next stage. Don't be disappointed if your audience has to take your proposal and business case to a final, higher authority. If your proposal represents a significant investment, it may require approval from the board of directors, which may only meet once a month or even once a quarter. Nevertheless, plan to invite those who have the authority to recommend your proposal to the next level.

Chapter 53

Delivering the Formal Presentation

The time has come to finally present your business case to your approval committee. There are eight "P's of Presentation" that ensure your presentation is the best it can be:

- Prepared
- Props
- Polished
- Punctual
- Professional
- Perceptive
- Purposeful
- Performance

BE PREPARED

Assuming you have read and applied the guidelines in the past two chapters, you should be well prepared by now. Thorough preparation, by itself, goes a long way toward removing the butterflies and anxieties associated with presenting before a panel of directors and executives.

HAVE PROPS READY

Every successful presentation requires more than just your brilliant self standing before executives. You will likely need various props, or supplemental accessories, to aid in your delivery. Consider what you need in advance of the presentation and ensure that those tools are available and in good working order. If your company has a shortage of conference rooms, book your conference well in advance of your meeting. And, when possible, book the room thirty minutes earlier than your start time. You will need time to set up your laptop and projector and perform various other housekeeping activities to ensure that the room is presentation-ready when your executives arrive. You may need a projector to connect to your laptop. If so, make sure you have the necessary connectors. You may plan to use a whiteboard or paper flipcharts. If so, verify that the room has working, reliable markers before you begin your presentation. You may intend to hand out printed copies or excerpts of your presentation. You'll want to have those prepared a day in advance so that they are ready to go. And if you are making handouts, make more than you think you need. You don't want last-minute guests to have to sit in the meeting empty-handed.

BE POLISHED

While it may seem superficial, you will be judged by your appearance. To this end, make sure that your clothing is freshly pressed and that your shoes are clean and polished. A good rule of thumb for your attire is to dress one level above your normal working attire. For example, if your work environment is casual, men should consider wearing a crisp, freshly laundered and starched business shirt and a freshly pressed sport coat. If sport coats are common in your workplace, then upping the attire to a suit might be most appropriate, at least for this presentation. For women, the same guidelines apply. Dress for success. The better your appearance, the more easily you command respect in your presentation. Remember, you are asking these executives to approve your proposal to invest a large sum of money. They must feel comfortable that you will be a responsible steward of those funds. When asking for money, dress like a banker. It may be superficial, but it is a reality in business.

BE PUNCTUAL

Commanding an executive audience demands respect for their time. You may not be able to control when the executives arrive, but you are in complete control of your arrival and the arrival of your team members. Part of your punctuality is also ending on time. As you will need time to resolve any open issues and clearly establish the next steps, prepare to conclude your remarks at least fifteen minutes before your published ending time. This will give you time to conclude your recommendation and elicit feedback on both your recommendation and your suggested next steps.

BE PROFESSIONAL

In our current culture, attempts at stand-up comedy and sarcasm seem to pervade all forms of communication. These styles have no place in your professional business case presentation. When presenting your business case, be mindful that you are making a professional presentation, and keep your style and tone professional. This is especially true if your audience includes executives from other cultures. The old standby approach of presenting your case in a matter-of-fact style is typically the most successful. It is certainly the least likely to offend or be misinterpreted.

BE PERCEPTIVE

As you present your business case, pay attention to body language and signs of confusion or disagreement. If you notice such signs, it is best to address these issues as they arise. Be prepared during your presentation for unexpected interruptions and interrogations about your presentation. You may get questioned on your discovery methods. You may receive resistance to your hypothesis. Any number of questions can arise and any number of interruptions can occur. If these interruptions cause you to get flustered, the executives' perception of you might weaken. As mentioned earlier, the executives have limited time to absorb your recommendation and render an opinion. Allow them to interrupt and explore as they need to. I am assuming that these interruptions are professional and not blatantly rude. Encountering rudeness in these presentations is rare.

If you happen to notice signs that your presentation is not meeting with approval, it may be best to stop your presentation periodically and ask if there are any questions. You should not expect to march through your presentation from start to finish without questions and interactions from the approvers in the room.

PRESENT WITH PURPOSE

The nineteenth-century French author and philosopher Henri Bergson is credited with saying, "Think like a man of action, act like a man of thought." This is good for amplifying your points on credibility.

Executives expect that you know what motivates them and what inspires them. There are five things that we have reviewed multiple times—increase revenue, reduce expenses, improve productivity, optimize assets, and mitigate risks.

It is very important to clearly state what you want them to do. Do not assume that they know what you want. For example, you might state, "If you approve this business case, I am asking you to approve this expenditure and authorize me to begin executing the steps that are listed in the business case including ordering all necessary software and hardware and selecting an implementation partner to help us implement this solution."

You want your presentation to inspire people to action, not just inform them with sound evidence. But once you've inspired them, once you've sold them, stop selling. You've invested a lot of time building the business case. You've invested additional time preparing and practicing to deliver a top-notch presentation. If the executives are predisposed to approve your business case and if they move quickly to reach a decision in your favor, do not feel cheated or disappointed if you don't get to present all of your presentation. I have had business cases approved on the strength of the executive summary alone. It's not common, but executives are busy and many have done their own homework before the presentation to educate themselves on the issues. Many will arrive at your meeting having already determined whether or not they will support your business case before you introduce the executive summary. So, if you find yourself obtaining their approval to your recommendation, thank them and consider yourself victorious. After all, the goal is not to make them sit through all of your slides. The goal is for them to approve your recommendation. Once you get the approval, you've won.

EVALUATE YOUR PERFORMANCE

Two levels of evaluation will be beneficial to you for future business cases. First, you should have a formal debriefing session with your sponsor to evaluate how well you performed. This evaluation will likely occur a day or two after your presentation. Even if you have received approval to move your project forward, you should spend an hour or so reflecting on areas where you might have done better. This will help you perform even better when you need to create and present future business cases.

The other evaluation should come sometime in the future. The reality of most projects is that they cost more than the original projections and they take longer to fully implement than originally projected. These two data points will be commonly tracked and remembered by astute executives. Your project may only run over by a few dollars or it might run over by millions. Likewise, you might miss your originally published target completion date by one week, or you might miss it by several years. There will be a number of factors that contribute to project budget and timeline overruns. If that's the only thing that gets tracked, it can easily paint a negative picture on your project's overall performance. Therefore, it is incumbent upon you to take the initiative to also track the very metrics by which you proposed this project in the first place. Did you suggest that inventory turnover would improve? If so, invest the time in the future to re-evaluate your company's performance on that key metric. If the inventory turnover improvement was greater than your original estimate, a case can be made that while the project suffered overruns, it also returned more than originally projected, thus making the project successful. Such an evidence-based observation can turn the perception of your project from one of failure to success—the very perception that you wish to have attached to any work that you do.

So there you have it. A successful method to identify, calculate, and communicate the value of capital projects. Each business case that you create in the future should be easier than the previous one. Here's hoping your business cases are well received and strongly supported.

Chapter 54

Section Five Summary

Package, practice, and present. Having done all of the necessary evidence gathering and data analysis, it's time to put your presentation together and make your formal recommendation to your approval board.

It is important to package your business case in the form of a story. Not everyone on the approval board knows the complete story. This is your opportunity to provide a uniform perspective on your proposal, from hypothesis to recommendation. Use this opportunity to be thorough and compelling.

A complete business case presentation contains various elements. The most common elements are:

- Executive Summary
- Statement of Business Issues
- Approach Employed
- Participants
- Key Quotes
- Evidence Supporting Your Hypothesis
- External Comparative Evidence
- Assumptions
- Risks
- Cost and Benefit Considerations
- Alternatives Considered
- Implementation Timeline
- Resource Requirements

- Recommendation and
- Immediate Next Steps

Your presentation deck may also include numerous additional supporting slides that you would place in the appendix for possible future use or discussions.

It is vital to review and edit the initial draft of your business case to make it as crisp and concise as possible. Busy executives do not frequently sit through long, protracted presentations of seemingly endless slides (which some have humorously titled "Death by PowerPoint"). Your presentation must be focused and succinct. A general rule of thumb is that you should allow three to five minutes for each slide. Using that rule, if you are allotted sixty minutes, you should have no more than twenty slides in the main body of your presentation.

After you've created and edited your presentation deck, you must invest the time to conduct simulated presentations with a competent yet friendly audience. You'll benefit greatly by having colleagues pretend to be the approval board, especially if they do not accept your assumptions or glowingly agree with your recommendation. Such tension in a practice setting can truly prepare you for your presentation to an executive approval committee. After you've conducted a mock presentation, allocate sufficient time to refine your presentation materials based on feedback from your practice rounds.

Finally, approach the formal presentation with the eight P's of Presentation in mind. Those eight elements are:

- Prepared
- Props
- Polished
- Punctual
- Professional
- Perceptive
- Purposeful and
- Performance

In the end, you should be able to reflect on your business case and be confident that you have identified, calculated, and communicated the value of your proposed capital project.

APPENDIX A

INTRODUCTION

TEMPLATE

There will be those readers who will create business cases as part of a sales proposal. When providing a business case for a company or organization other than your employer, you might consider having some standard boilerplate introduction information. Below is a starting point for your boilerplate information. It is advisable for you to submit this to your internal legal department, as they will likely have specific wording that they will prefer you use when conveying such information to a potential customer. You need to review the bracketed phrases and change them to fit your company and your customer situation. In this template, "seller" is used to identify the company authoring this document, whether it is a software company or consulting firm.

Purpose

The purpose of this document is to identify potential benefits that may be attainable through the [acquisition and implementation of seller's] products and services. The benefits that are presented herein were estimated by collecting various performance indicators from [client] personnel and then comparing those measurements against various industry benchmarks and publicly available research statistics.

Overview

[Client] stands to realize measurable and value-added benefits from [acquiring and implementing seller's] recommendations.

This business case was constructed using a structured methodology for assigning estimated benefit values to various initiatives. The proposed benefits in this document are estimates only and may require a combination of new technologies and changes in business practices to be fully realized. The benefits presented here may represent a combination of currently unrealized benefits and benefits from projects already under way. A review by [client management and staff] is therefore recommended to determine the applicability of these potential benefits. [Seller] can also assist in constructing an additional, comprehensive business case analysis including a more detailed analysis of specific benefit opportunities and drafting a time-to-benefits analysis that applies uniquely to your company.

Use of Third-Party Research Statistics

This document contains references to selected third-party research and reference materials. The inclusion of such data in this document is solely to provide independent, comparison data for this benefits assessment. However, the inclusion of this data neither constitutes the third party's acceptance of the assumptions nor their endorsement of [seller's] products or services. Further, [seller] presents these data "as is" and does not express any opinion as to the accuracy or the relevance of the assumptions used by any third party in the presentation of their data.

Forward-Looking Statements

Some of the statements in this document constitute forward-looking statements. In some cases, you can identify forward-looking statements by terms such as may, will, should, expect, plan, intend, forecast, anticipate, believe, estimate, predict, potential, continue, or the negative of these terms or other comparable terminology. The forward-looking statements in this document are subject to known and unknown risks, uncertainties, and other factors that may cause the actual project results, performance, or achievements to be materially different from any projected results, performance, or achievements expressed or implied in this document. These forward-looking statements were based on various factors and were derived utilizing numerous important assumptions and other important factors that could cause actual results to differ materially from those set forth in this document. Forward-looking statements include information concerning future financial performance, business strategy, operational performance, levels of activity, projected plans, and objectives. Significant changes in current business practices and operating procedures may be required to realize the benefits presented in this document.

These provisions apply to any figures presented throughout this assessment (e.g., dollars, percentages, days, working capital, and human resources).

Safe Harbor Statement

The following is intended to outline our general product direction. It is intended for information purposes only, and may not be incorporated into any contract. It is not a commitment to deliver any material, code, or functionality, and should not be relied upon in making purchasing decisions.

The development, release, and timing of any features or functionality described for [seller's] products remains at the sole discretion of [seller].

APPENDIX B
Common Financial Metrics

There are a number of common financial metrics used for commercial businesses. Many business cases benefit from evaluating these metrics and comparing the performance of one company against another company on these very metrics. These metrics are not benefits, at least not by themselves. They are simply barometers that we use to compare one company against itself (in year-over-year comparisons) or against other companies in its industry or market segment. No one metric is inherently better than another metric. Different companies consider different metrics to be the most important in their individual situation and industry and market environment.

One clarifying note: for consistency, where currency is discussed, the term "in dollars" could be interpreted to mean "in local currency" as not every reader of the book will report their financial performance in US dollars.

Many of the following metrics will refer to the example case study of our target company, first introduced in chapter 21, Creating Your Sandbox.

The metrics that will be explained below are as follows:

- Days sales outstanding (often called DSO)
- Days in inventory (often called DII)
- Inventory turnover (or simply inventory turns)
- Days payable outstanding (often called DPO)

- Cash conversion cycle (also called cash-to-cash cycle)
- SG&A as a percent of sales
- Cost of goods sold as a percent of sales
- Operating income
- Operating margin
- Quick ratio
- Debt to equity
- Return on equity
- Return on sales
- Return on assets

Days Sales Outstanding

Days sales outstanding, often called DSO, is the measure of days from the day an invoice is created until the company receives payment for the invoice. When considering performance, fewer days are better than more days. DSO is one of the three elements of the cash conversion cycle. To compute the current DSO, use the tables below.

DSO is an important measurement because it shows how efficiently and quickly the company collects cash from its customers. The ability to collect cash a single day earlier means that the cash is available one day earlier. The benefit, then, is the value of a single day's collection. For example, in our case study example (found beginning in the Hypothesis section), a single-day improvement in DSO would be worth $52 million. As this is a short-term asset, this benefit would only get recognized one time. This benefit does not recur year-over-year, although there are situations where this benefit can be split. In such a split, a portion of the computed benefit will occur in the first year and the remaining benefit will occur in the second year.

Variable Section		
ID	Variable	Comments
A	Accounts receivable balance	Pulled directly from the balance sheet. Determine whether you are using the year-end value or quarter-end value.
B	Sales revenue	Pulled directly from the income statement. Use the same period as the accounts receivable number above (annual or quarterly)
C	Days in period	If you are using the annual numbers for sales and AR, then this number will be 365. If you are using the quarterly numbers for sales and AR, this number will be 91.

Intermediate Calculations	
No intermediate calculations	

Metric Calculation		
ID	Metric Definition	Calculation
D	The current days sales outstanding (DSO)	(A/B)*C

The DSO, from our case study example, is 49.00 days. To compute the value of incremental benefits, as in the value of a single day's improvement, you would compute the value of a day's sales (annual sales divided by 365). A one-day improvement in this metric is the value of one day's sales. One day's sales in our example is $52.3 million.

($19,115,000,000 / 365 = $52,369,863)

Days in Inventory

Days in inventory, often called DII, is the measure of days it takes a company to convert purchased raw materials into finished product and ultimately into sales. When considering performance, fewer days are better than more days. DII is one of the three elements of the cash conversion cycle.

DII is an important measurement because it shows how efficiently and quickly the company converts its inventory into sales. The ability to sell inventory faster means that the cash is available one or more days earlier. The benefit, then, is the value of a single day's inventory. For example, in our case study example (found beginning in chapter 21, Creating Your Sandbox), a single-day improvement in DII would be worth $34.7 million. As this is a short-term asset, this benefit would only get recognized one time. This benefit does not recur year over year, although there are situations where this benefit can be split. In such a split, a portion of the computed benefit will occur in the first year and the remaining benefit will occur in the second year.

To compute the value of incremental benefits, as in the value of a single day's improvement, is a bit more complicated than our DSO example. First, you must determine the number of days in inventory. In our example that would be 58.45.

(($2,033,000,000 / 12,695,000,000) * 365 = 58.45).

To compute days in inventory, use the tables below.

Variable Section		
ID	Variable	Comments
A	Combined inventory balance	Pulled directly from the balance sheet. Combined inventory refers to all stages of inventory: raw material, work in process, and finished goods. Determine whether you are using the annual balance or quarterly balance.
B	Cost of goods sold	Pulled directly from the income statement. Use the same period as the combined inventory number above (annual or quarterly).
C	Days in period	If you are using the annual numbers for inventory and COGS, then this number will be 365. If you are using the quarterly numbers for sales and AR, this number will be 91.

Intermediate Calculations	
No intermediate calculations	

Metric Calculation		
ID	Metric Definition	Calculation
D	The current days in inventory (DII)	(A/B)*C

Once determined, the value of improving by one day is calculated by computing the value of one day's inventory, which is computed by dividing the combined inventory balance by the newly computed DII, as follows:

$$(\$2,033,000,000 \: / \: 58.45 = \$34,780,000).$$

Inventory Turnover

Inventory turnover, sometimes simply called inventory turns or just turns, measures the number of times that inventory is turned over during a year. For example, a turnover value of 12 means that the company sells enough inventory that it must refresh its finished goods stock 12 times per year. The greater number of turns the better. More turns means better performance since you don't want unsold inventory sitting around in the warehouse. Inventory turnover is not one of the three elements of the cash conversion cycle.

Inventory turnover is an important measurement because it shows how frequently the company turns its inventory over. Higher inventory turnover means several things. First, it means that the company is effective at converting raw material into product that has been sold. Second, it means that the customers are getting fresher products. While this is an obvious concern in the food industry, it is just as much of a concern in the technology industry where product obsolescence is an expensive fact of life. The more the company turns over its products, the fewer products that will remain when a new model is released. In our example, inventory turnover is 6.24. That is determined by using the following equation:

($12,695,000,000 / 2,033,000,000) = 6.24.

As far as computing a benefit, the benefit is computed using the days in inventory example shown in the previous metric.

To compute inventory turnover, use the tables below.

Variable Section		
ID	Variable	Comments
A	Combined inventory balance	Pulled directly from the balance sheet. Combined inventory refers to all stages of inventory: raw material, work in process, and finished goods. Determine whether you are using the annual balance or quarterly balance.
B	Cost of goods sold	Pulled directly from the income statement. Use the same period as the combined inventory number above (annual or quarterly).

Intermediate Calculations	
No intermediate calculations	

Metric Calculation		
ID	Metric Definition	Calculation
C	Inventory turnover	B / A

Days Payable Outstanding

Days payable outstanding, often called DPO, measures the number of days it takes a company to pay its creditors. When considering performance, more days are better than fewer days because it means that the company is holding onto its cash longer. DPO is one of the three elements of the cash conversion cycle.

DPO is an important measurement because it shows how well the company manages its vendors. Extending the time before it pays a vendor is a two-edged sword. A longer payment cycle benefits the company but can irritate the vendor. There is point at which the vendor will no longer consider the relationship beneficial. The company needs to balance this effectively. In general, then, the benefit is the value of prolonging payment one or more days. For example, in our case study example (found beginning in chapter 21, Creating Your Sandbox), a single-day extension in DPO would be worth $34 million. As this is a short-term asset, this benefit would only get recognized one time. This benefit does not recur year over year, although there are situations where this benefit can be split. In such a split, a portion of the computed benefit will occur in the first year and the remaining benefit will occur in the second year.

The DPO for our case study example is 55.20 days. To compute the value of incremental benefits, as in the value of a single day's improvement, you would compute the value of a day's payables (annual cost of goods sold divided by 365). A one-day improvement in this metric is the value of one day's cost of sales. One day's cost of sales, in our example is $34.78 million ($12,695,000,000 / 365 = $34,780,822)

To compute days payable outstanding, use the tables below.

Variable Section		
ID	**Variable**	**Comments**
A	Accounts payable balance	Pulled directly from the balance sheet. Determine whether you are using the annual balance or quarterly balance.
B	Cost of goods sold	Pulled directly from the income statement. Use the same period as the accounts payable number above (annual or quarterly).
C	Days in period	If you are using the annual numbers for AP and COGS, then this number will be 365. If you are using the quarterly numbers for AP and COGS, this number will be 91.

Intermediate Calculations	
No intermediate calculations	

Metric Calculation		
ID	**Metric Definition**	**Calculation**
D	The current days payable outstanding	(A/B)*C

Cash Conversion Cycle

The cash conversion cycle, also called the cash-to-cash cycle, is a measure of how long it takes, in days, for a manufacturer or distributor to convert its purchases into cash. The logic is as follows: A company buys raw material on credit. The company then takes that raw material and converts into sellable product. The company sells the product to its customers on credit. So the math is pretty simple. You add the number of days it takes to convert raw material to sold inventory (DII) to the number of days it takes the company to collect cash from its credit customers (DSO). From that sum, you subtract the number of days it takes to pay its vendors. Generally, the goal is to have this around 30 days with each component of the equation being 30 days (30+30−30). This is not always practical, but it is a common target. In our example, our case study company has a cash conversion cycle of 52 days. To compute the cash conversion cycle, in days, use the tables below.

Variable Section		
ID	Variable	Comments
A	Days sales outstanding	Compute this value using the example from earlier in this section.
B	Days in inventory	Compute this value using the example from earlier in this section.

| C | Days payables outstanding | Compute this value using the example from earlier in this section. |

Intermediate Calculations		
	No intermediate calculations	

Metric Calculation		
ID	**Metric Definition**	**Calculation**
D	The current cash conversion cycle	A + B − C

The cash conversion cycle is an important measurement because all companies need to manage their cash effectively. There is no single benefit calculation for the cash conversion cycle as any benefits are derived by improving the individual components (DII, DSO, and DPO). This metric is presented here because many CFOs manage their businesses by staying on top of this vital metric.

SG&A as a Percent of Sales

Among the many expense categories, SG&A is typically the one with the most discretionary spending. SG&A stands for sales, general, and administrative. Commonly, this category will contain all expenses that are not directly related to the production of finished product. Those expenses related to the cost of producing product are called costs of goods sold, or COGS, or cost of revenue (see next metric). As a rule, a company strives to keep costs as low as possible so that they can drive more profit. When considering performance, a smaller percentage of sales dollars spent on this category is preferred. Our case study company spent 18.30 percent of their sales dollars on this category. There is no direct metric to say that a 1 percent lower SG&A spend would yield a certain benefit. Even though the math can be calculated, the variables don't align nicely. For example, in this category a company would typically have rent and utilities for various sales offices. Additionally, this category probably contains such things as office supplies and employees' salaries. While a solution that you recommend might help reduce certain aspects of SG&A, it would be unlikely to reduce SG&A across the board given the diverse nature of the items in this category. The two best uses for this metric are:

- Comparing the company against itself in year-over-year comparisons
- As a comparison to similar companies

If your company performs unfavorably against itself or unfavorably to peer companies, a case could be made that an increased focus on these expenses is warranted to keep the company competitive with its peers. To compute SG&A as a percent of sales, use the tables below.

Variable Section		
ID	Variable	Comments
A	Annual or quarterly SG&A value	Pulled directly from the income statement. Determine whether you are using the annual value or quarterly value.
B	Sales revenue	Pulled directly from the income statement. Use the same period as the SG&A number above (annual or quarterly).

Intermediate Calculations	
No intermediate calculations	

Metric Calculation		
ID	Metric Definition	Calculation
C	SG&A as a percent of sales	A / B

Cost of Goods Sold as a Percent of Sales

In manufacturing companies, the company has to convert various raw materials into a finished product. The costs associated with this conversion are called costs of goods sold (or sometimes cost of revenue). This measurement is also commonly abbreviated as COGS. Commonly, this category will contain all expenses that are directly related to the production of finished product. Just as they do with SG&A expenses, companies strive to keep costs as low as possible, without compromising product quality or employee safety, so that they can drive more profit. When considering performance, a smaller percentage of sales dollars spent on this category is preferred. Our case study company spent 66.47 percent of their sales dollars on this category. Like our SG&A example above, there is no direct metric to say that a 1 percent lower COGS spend would yield a certain benefit. Even though the math can be calculated, the variables don't align nicely here either. For example, in this category a company would typically have rent and utilities for various factories plus the cost of all of the materials and labor used in manufacturing. While a solution that you recommend might help reduce certain aspects of cost of goods sold, it would be unlikely to reduce it across the board given the diverse nature of the items in this category. The two best uses for this metric are:

- Comparing the company against itself in year-over-year comparisons
- As a comparison to similar companies

If your company performs unfavorably against itself or unfavorably to peer companies, a case could be made that an increased focus on these expenses is warranted to keep the company competitive with its peers. To compute cost of goods sold as a percent of sales, use the tables below.

Variable Section		
ID	**Variable**	**Comments**
A	Annual or quarterly cost of goods sold value	Pulled directly from the income statement. Determine whether you are using the annual value or quarterly value.
B	Sales revenue	Pulled directly from the income statement. Use the same period as the COGS number above (annual or quarterly).

Intermediate Calculations	
No intermediate calculations	

Metric Calculation		
ID	**Metric Definition**	**Calculation**
C	COGS as a percent of sales	A / B

Operating Income

Operating income is the amount of profit, in dollars, that the company makes from routine business activities. The equation, detailed below, subtracts routine expenses and depreciation from revenue. Operating income differs from net income in that net income also factors in the impact of extraordinary items and interest—both interest income and interest expense (in most cases). Operating income is not, by itself a particularly helpful metric, but it is helpful for two other purposes. Operating income is helpful as it is a key component of operating margin, which is defined in our next metric. Operating income is also helpful when you evaluate it year over year to determine if it is growing or shrinking. For example, is operating income growing at a faster or slower rate than sales, when compared against that sales revenue year over year? Such knowledge can provide the basis for other benefit discussions and for comparisons between your company and your peers. To compute operating income, use the tables below.

Variable Section		
ID	Variable	Comments
A	Total revenue	Pulled directly from the annual income statement.
B	Total costs	While total costs is not a common category, you should include all costs for this component including cost of goods gold and SG&A expenses. Taxes and interest expense are excluded from this calculation.
C	Depreciation	Pulled directly from the annual income statement.

Intermediate Calculations	
No intermediate calculations	

Metric Calculation		
ID	Metric Definition	Calculation
D	Operating Income	$A-(B-C)$

Operating Margin

Operating margin is a percentage and tells the reader how much of each sales dollar is left over after routine expenses (COGS and SG&A). This is also commonly called return on sales. Interest on debt and taxes are not included in the operating margin calculation. Operating margin shows how much profit is created from each sales dollar and is very helpful when used to compare similar companies in similar industries. Such comparison can highlight whether the company outperforms or underperforms against its peers. How effectively a company controls its expenses has a direct impact on this measurement. To compute operating margin, use the tables below.

Variable Section		
ID	Variable	Comments
A	Operating income, in dollars	Compute this value using the example from earlier in this section.
B	Sales revenue, in dollars	Pulled directly from the income statement. Use the same period as the operating income number above (annual or quarterly).

Intermediate Calculations		
	No intermediate calculations	

Metric Calculation		
ID	Metric Definition	Calculation
C	Operating Margin	A / B

Quick Ratio

The quick ratio is a percentage and shows how able a company is to pay its short-term debts with ready—or liquid—assets. A higher number is better. The equation, as shown in the tables below, considers current assets and current liabilities. To compute the quick ratio, the value of inventory is subtracted from the current assets total because inventory, while an asset, cannot be reliably converted quickly into cash to pay current obligations. The quick ratio is very helpful when used to compare similar companies in similar industries. Such comparison can highlight whether the company outperforms or underperforms against its peers. How effectively a company manages its cash and controls its credit lines has a direct impact on this measurement. To compute the quick ratio, use the tables below.

Variable Section		
ID	Variable	Comments
A	Combined inventory balance	Pulled directly from the balance sheet. Combined Inventory refers to all stages of inventory: raw material, work in process, and finished goods. Determine whether you are using the annual balance or quarterly balance.

| B | Current assets | Pulled directly from the balance sheet. Current assets are commonly defined as those assets that the company can expect to convert to cash within the current year. Such assets as accounts receivable, combined inventory value, stocks and bonds (often called marketable securities), and, of course, cash. Use the same period as the inventory number above (annual or quarterly). |
| C | Current liabilities | Pulled directly from the balance sheet. Current liabilities are commonly defined as those obligations that are due in the short term. Such obligations include accounts payable and accrued liabilities (debts that are accumulating but have not actually become due, such as taxes that employers withhold from employees until the payments are sent to the government—not to be confused with past-due obligations, these are just debts that are accumulating and will be paid on their assigned due date). Use the same period as the inventory number above (annual or quarterly). |

Intermediate Calculations		
ID	**Calculation Description**	**Calculation**
D	Current assets less inventory	B – A

Metric Calculation		
ID	**Metric Definition**	**Calculation**
E	Quick ratio	D / C

Debt to Equity

The debt-to-equity ratio is a percentage and shows how much the company has used debt to finance its growth. It's tough to say that higher or lower is better. This is an individual corporate board decision. If debt helps the company grow and flourish, then it is assumed that the future growth will easily fund the debt service without much risk. But if the company doesn't grow as robustly as anticipated, the debt service becomes a real burden and can threaten the sustainability of the company.

The equation has two possibilities. Most analysts consider the total liability value as the numerator for this equation. Some, however, only consider long-term debt as the numerator as they do not consider short-term debt (such as trade accounts payable) as a proper representation of the definition—financing growth with debt. For our purposes, we will use the traditional definition, which includes total liabilities. To compute the debt-to-equity ratio, divide the current equity value (from a recent balance sheet) by the total liabilities (from the same balance sheet). The debt-to-equity ratio is very helpful when used to compare a company's performance year over year. It can also be helpful when comparing similar companies in similar industries. To compute the debt-to-equity ratio, use the tables below.

Variable Section		
ID	Variable	Comments
A	Total liabilities	Pulled directly from the balance sheet.
B	Total shareholder equity	Pulled directly from the balance sheet.

Intermediate Calculations	
No intermediate calculations	

Metric Calculation		
ID	Metric Definition	Calculation
C	Debt-to-equity ratio	A / B

Return on Equity

The return-on-equity ratio is a percentage and shows the percentage of profit produced from the money invested by the shareholders. To compute the return-on-equity ratio, divide the current equity value (from a recent balance sheet) by the annual net income (from the recent annual income statement). The return-on-equity ratio is very helpful when used to compare a company's performance year over year. It can also be helpful when comparing similar companies in similar industries. To compute the return-on-equity ratio, use the tables below.

Variable Section		
ID	Variable	Comments
A	Net income	Pulled directly from the annual income statement. Net income is commonly known as "the bottom line" as it reflects that amount left over after all expenses, depreciation, taxes, and other charges are deducted from total revenues.
B	Total shareholder equity	Pulled directly from the year-end balance sheet.

Intermediate Calculations		
	No intermediate calculations	

Metric Calculation		
ID	Metric Definition	Calculation
C	Return-on-equity ratio	A / B

Return on Sales

Return on sales is a percentage and tells the reader how much of each sales dollar is left over after routine expenses (COGS and SG&A). This is also commonly called operating margin. Interest on debt and taxes are not included in the operating margin calculation. Return on sales shows how much profit is created from each sales dollar and is very helpful when used to compare similar companies in similar industries. Such comparison can highlight whether the company outperforms or underperforms against its peers. How effectively a company controls its expenses has a direct impact on this measurement. To compute return on sales, use the tables below.

Variable Section		
ID	Variable	Comments
A	Operating income, in dollars	Compute this value using the example from earlier in this section.
B	Sales revenue, in dollars	Pulled directly from the income statement. Use the same period as the operating income number above (annual or quarterly).

Intermediate Calculations		
	No intermediate calculations	

Metric Calculation		
ID	Metric Definition	Calculation
C	Return on sales	A / B

Return on Assets

Return on assets is a percentage and tells the reader how much profit is returned from its asset investment. Return on assets is very helpful when used to compare similar companies in similar industries. Such comparison can highlight whether the company outperforms or underperforms against its peers. To compute return on assets, use the tables below.

Variable Section		
ID	**Variable**	**Comments**
A	Net income	Pulled directly from the Annual income statement. Net income is commonly known as "the bottom line" as it reflects that amount left over after all expenses, depreciation, taxes, and other charges are deducted from total revenues.
B	Total assets	Pulled directly from the year-end balance sheet.

Intermediate Calculations	
No intermediate calculations	

Metric Calculation		
ID	Metric Definition	Calculation
C	Return on assets	A / B

APPENDIX C

REVENUE IMPROVEMENT BENEFITS

An Overview of Revenue Improvements

Revenue improvements (often called uplift) are those benefits that increase the revenue line of a business. Increasing sales for a product company, or increasing tax revenues for a city government, or increasing charitable contributions for a local or national charity are all examples of this benefit—increasing revenue.

There is a calculation warning that must be provided for this benefit. Many inexperienced business case developers will look at this benefit and compute the results incorrectly. The only benefit that a company can use is a benefit that occurs in the profit area. Simply increasing revenue does not by itself create a benefit. The benefit is created when you calculate the profit on that additional revenue. For example, if a company increases its revenue by $100 this month, did it really gain a $100 benefit? Typically, the answer is "No!" The reason is because it cost the company some amount of money to generate that extra $100. By looking at your company's current income statement you can determine the current profit percentage. Let's say that your company is operating at a 12 percent profit percentage. This means that for every $100 of revenue that it generates, it costs the company $88 in various operating expenses. Therefore your company's benefit in this example would be $12, not the $100 of increased revenue. Keep that in mind for all of the following calculations unless otherwise noted.

For this section, there are four benefit examples that represent common revenue-improvement scenarios. Dozens more benefits are possible in this realm, but these are presented as a representative set of benefits. These four benefits provide a starting point to discuss within your company. Not every company will see value in every benefit. Additionally, most companies will also have other benefits in this area (revenue improvement) that you will likely discover during your evidence-gathering activities. The four revenue benefit examples are:

- Develop new sales channels
- Improve revenue through cross-selling and up-selling
- Billing for previously unbilled services
- One percent revenue increase

Develop New Sales Channels

WHAT DOES THIS MEAN?

Companies use a number of selling channels to sell their products. They might use direct sales (where sales representatives call on customers face-to-face), indirect sales (where sales reps call on recommenders of products, such as in the pharmaceutical field where reps call on doctors but do not actually make the sale to doctors), outbound telemarketing (where call center personnel dial prospective customers and solicit goods and services), Internet sales channels (where a sophisticated website collects customer orders and prepares picking and shipping information), and so on.

WHY IS IT IMPORTANT?

Additional sales channels mean additional ways that customers can buy from your company. For example, if your company has a direct sales force and a static Web page, how might they increase sales if they could receive orders over the web? An interactive website is available twenty-four hours a day, seven days a week, and in every country. A website can reach where traditional sales forces might not. Certainly, there are other channels that could be considered.

HOW DOES THE COMPANY REALIZE THIS BENEFIT?

A company determines that it can increase revenue by adding one or more new sales channels to its sales arsenal. It must consider how much, if any, of its current sales would be cannibalized by a new sales channel and incorporate that consideration into the calculation. Once these factors have been considered, the company begins realizing benefits in the new channel.

HOW IS THIS BENEFIT COMPUTED?

This benefit is a negotiated number. The negotiation is between you and the owner of this business function. Start with your company's current annual sales revenue. If you have reference material from a competitor you might be able to use that as a growth point. For example, if your company is looking to add a Latin American channel to its sales approach, you might seek to find what percentage of a competitor's sales come from their Latin American sales arm. Let's say that the competitor achieves 10 percent of their sales from Latin America. Your company might be able to reach 10 percent in a few years but probably not at first. You negotiate with your business function owner and determine what they will accept in year 1 of the new approach, then year 2, and so on. Remember to factor in their current cost of sales percentage before arriving at a benefit number (revenue minus the costs to generate that revenue yields the benefit number).

WHAT IS A REASONABLE RANGE?

A reasonable starting range for this benefit would be less than 5 percent of total revenue in the early years with growth to 10 percent or more in later years.

DETAILED BENEFIT CALCULATION EXAMPLE

Variables:
a. Current annual sales revenue, in dollars
b. Net profit margin, as a percentage
c. Anticipated growth in revenue from new channel (% of total revenue)

Formulas:
d. Annual profit, in dollars (A*B)
e. Estimated benefit, per year (C*D)

BENEFIT OCCURRENCE
This benefit occurs annually and in perpetuity.

DUPONT MODEL ALIGNMENT
This benefit, like all revenue enhancement benefits, aligns to the income statement.

Increase Revenue through Cross-selling and Up-selling

WHAT DOES THIS MEAN?

Cross-selling is the practice of selling complementary products or services. Think of Amazon.com. Typically, when you buy a book from Amazon, the book selection page also displays other books that other readers placed in their shopping carts when buying the same book. This practice, called cross-selling, enables a seller to sell more than just the single item that the buyer originally intended to purchase. Cross-selling increases the number of products sold during a single transaction. Likewise, up-selling is the practice of getting the buyer to buy an upgraded product instead of his or her originally intended purchase. This also increases the size of the sale. Either method, or both when possible, increases the size of the sale at the moment you have a buyer ready to buy something.

WHY IS IT IMPORTANT?

It is quite expensive to get a potential customer to the buying decision point. Once you get a customer to that point, it is much less expensive to get him to either buy more or buy something more expensive or upgraded. It is, therefore, worth the effort to attempt to cross-sell or up-sell when the customer is at the point of purchase.

HOW DOES THE COMPANY REALIZE THIS BENEFIT?

Some combination of technology and processes enable a company to achieve this benefit. Frequently the implementation and deployment of self-service ordering systems is a contributor to this benefit. For companies that use inside sales teams, powerful cross-sell and up-sell systems can provide call center reps with the same tools and can lead to successful cross-sell and up-sell initiatives.

HOW IS THIS BENEFIT COMPUTED?

This benefit is a negotiated number. The negotiation is between you and the owner of this business function. Start with your company's current annual sales revenue. Reach an agreement with the vice president of sales or other senior sales executive regarding the anticipated boost in sales that an effective up-selling and cross-selling initiative might provide. A boost of 2–5 percent is commonly suggested. From this suggested number, you negotiate to arrive at an acceptable benefit estimate. Remember to factor in the current cost of sales percentage before arriving at a benefit number (revenue minus the costs to generate that revenue yields the benefit number).

WHAT IS A REASONABLE RANGE?

A reasonable starting range for this benefit would be 2–5 percent of total revenue.

DETAILED BENEFIT CALCULATION EXAMPLE

Variables:
a. Current annual sales revenue, in dollars
b. Net profit margin, as a percentage
c. Anticipated growth in revenue from cross-sell and up-sell initiative (% of total revenue)

Formulas:
d. Annual profit, in dollars (A*B)
e. Estimated benefit, per year (C*D)

BENEFIT OCCURRENCE

This benefit occurs annually and in perpetuity.

DUPONT MODEL ALIGNMENT

This benefit, like all revenue enhancement benefits, aligns to the income statement.

Billing for Previously Unbilled Services

WHAT DOES THIS MEAN?
In rare instances, companies provide services that should be billed to customers but, for whatever reason, do not get billed to the customer. This benefit is rare and typically happens only in companies that provide post-sale warranty service.

WHY IS IT IMPORTANT?
Companies that provide warranty service do not bill the end customer unless the warranty has expired. A small percentage of work that is done after the warranty has expired goes unbilled. This is work that the company has performed, and for which it has incurred costs, but for which it does not collect its rightful revenue. Collecting this revenue is a very valuable benefit because it is realized as a gross receipt, not as a net profit number, because the costs associated with this revenue have already been incurred.

HOW DOES THE COMPANY REALIZE THIS BENEFIT?
Tools and processes can enable a company to better track and bill for these services. Knowing when a customer's warranty has expired can ensure rightful billing for non-warranty services.

HOW IS THIS BENEFIT COMPUTED?

This benefit is a negotiated number. You must gain agreement on two things from the executive responsible for warranty billing. First you must gain agreement that some non-warranty work goes unbilled. Then you must gain agreement that some of the unbilled work is worthy of billing (some companies might refrain from billing certain customers as a matter of goodwill). Once agreement on both issues is obtained, you can suggest a possible benefit. It would be reasonable that the company is properly billing for a large majority of its non-warranty work so you should start your negotiation with 1 percent or less. The real beauty of this benefit is that you do not have to deduct costs after you compute the potential revenue boost. Those costs were already incurred. So your equation begins with the current revenue from post-sale services. Revenue from other sources is not included in this equation. Then you determine the percentage of this service work that goes unbilled. Finally, you agree on a future percentage of unbilled work. A common practice would be to reduce the unbilled percentage by half. For example, if the current unbilled percentage is 3 percent, the future target for unbilled work might be 1.5 percent. The value of the benefit is to subtract the future percentage from the current percentage and multiply that number by the annual revenue from out-of-warranty services. Remember, the profit margin, which is used in every other revenue benefit, is excluded from this calculation.

WHAT IS A REASONABLE RANGE?

A reasonable starting range for this benefit would be 1–2 percent of post-sale, out-of-warranty revenue.

DETAILED BENEFIT CALCULATION EXAMPLE

Variables:
    a.   Annual sales revenue from post-sale, out-of-warranty services
    b.   Estimated percentage of work performed but not billed
    c.   Estimated future percentage of work performed but not billed

Formulas:
    d.   Current unbilled revenue (A*B)
    e.   Future unbilled revenue (A*C)
    f.   Estimated benefit, per year (D−E)

BENEFIT OCCURRENCE
This benefit occurs annually and in perpetuity.

DUPONT MODEL ALIGNMENT
This benefit, like all revenue enhancement benefits, aligns to the income statement.

One Percent Revenue Increase

WHAT DOES THIS MEAN?

This is a catchall category that is rarely used but often can help make your point when selling a revenue-improvement solution. You would not use this category if you have already used other revenue improvement benefits, as including this benefit with those would amount to double-counting your benefits (a fast way to have your credibility questioned). If you are unable to isolate a specific revenue benefit from the choices on the previous pages, sometimes you can propose that your solution will drive an increase in revenue by 1 percent (or more if you have evidence to support a larger percentage).

WHY IS IT IMPORTANT?

Additional revenue means additional revenue, simple as that.

HOW DOES THE COMPANY REALIZE THIS BENEFIT?

The company realizes this benefit based on the implementation of your recommendations. You can feel free to use wording from the other revenue benefits to better articulate your proposed benefit.

HOW IS THIS BENEFIT COMPUTED?

This benefit is a negotiated number. This benefit should only be used when other, more specific, revenue improvement areas cannot be articulated. Be aware that using this benefit in addition to other revenue-improvement benefits will typically be viewed as double-counting of benefits. Double-counting is to be avoided.

WHAT IS A REASONABLE RANGE?
A reasonable starting range for this benefit would be 1–2 percent of total revenue.

DETAILED BENEFIT CALCULATION EXAMPLE
Variables:
a. Current annual sales revenue, in dollars
b. Net profit margin
c. Anticipated growth in revenue from this recommendation (% of total revenue)

Formulas:
d. Annual Profit, in dollars (A*B)
e. Estimated Benefit, per year (C*D)

BENEFIT OCCURRENCE
This benefit occurs annually and in perpetuity.

DUPONT MODEL ALIGNMENT
This benefit, like all revenue enhancement benefits, aligns to the income statement.

APPENDIX D

EXPENSE REDUCTION BENEFITS

An Overview of Expense Reduction Benefits

Expense benefits are those benefits that decrease any expense item in your organization's operations. The three most common expense reduction categories for IT projects in commercial enterprises are:

- Reducing the cost of production materials (called "direct material").
- Reducing the cost of nonproduction materials (such as office supplies, cleaning supplies, and the like, which are called "indirect materials"). This expense reduction strategy is often called "Reduce Maverick Spending," as the cost controls are implemented to enforce buying within established—and well-negotiated—company contracts for such items.
- Reducing the costs associated with annual IT system maintenance and annual software license, and support costs, usually through some exercise in system consolidation, application rationalization, outsourcing, or other similar exercise.

Beyond those three common expense reduction strategies are a litany of potential expenses that can be evaluated and reduced, including payroll and overtime costs, power and utility costs, routine factory maintenance, and postage costs. Reducing expenses is a wonderful benefit because the company was already paying that money, so when you can show a reduction in that expense, it is a one-to-one benefit (if you exclude a consideration for depreciation and taxes).

In this appendix, five expense reduction examples are provided. Those examples are:

- Reduce direct material costs.
- Reduce maverick spending.
- Reduce costs due to system consolidation.
- Reduce payroll and overtime costs.
- Reduce costs of external services.

Reduce Direct Material Costs

WHAT DOES THIS MEAN?

Manufacturing companies convert raw material into some finished product. This raw material is called direct material, as it goes directly into the production of the final product. Numerous other items are purchased by a company that do not go into the production of a final product. That spending is called indirect material spend and is not part of this calculation.

WHY IS IT IMPORTANT?

For manufacturing companies, the purchase of raw materials is often their single largest buying category. Reducing the amount spent on raw materials can often yield a significant cost savings for the company. For example, car manufacturers buy sheet metal and convert that into body parts for their vehicles. This same company might also buy other metal products for use in other components of their vehicles, such as axles or steering columns. Some companies manufacture different components of their products in different locations. All of these considerations can complicate the buying process. If the company currently buys these materials separately or by individual location there are likely some potential savings they could realize by consolidating their purchases and negotiating the price using that aggregated purchase value for improved negotiating leverage.

HOW DOES THE COMPANY REALIZE THIS BENEFIT?

The implementation of tools and procedures that centralize and consolidate the purchasing process—such as improved mechanisms for manufacturing, planning, and scheduling—frequently yields significant benefits. Additionally, forethought in the product development process can aid in the more frequent use of common parts. All of these considerations help the company analyze their requirements before they place a purchase order and can provide rich negotiating leverage with the supplier as the company seeks to gain a discount for volume buying.

HOW IS THIS BENEFIT COMPUTED?

This is a negotiated number. You start with your company's annual direct material spend number. You multiply that number by the agreed-upon reduction potential, say 2 percent. That's the benefit. Your company might elect to exclude certain things from the calculation, as they might suggest that they have already negotiated excellent terms on selected items. If that's the case, simply subtract that number from the total spend and multiply the new, reduced spend number by the acceptable reduction percentage.

WHAT IS A REASONABLE RANGE?

A common starting range for this negotiation is 2–4 percent for discussion purposes.

DETAILED BENEFIT CALCULATION EXAMPLE

Variables:
a. Total annual spend on direct material (or amount subject to calculation if less than total spend amount)
b. Potential savings achieved through consolidation and improved procedures (as a percentage)

Formulas:
c. Estimated benefit, per year (A*B)

BENEFIT OCCURRENCE

This benefit occurs annually and in perpetuity.

DUPONT MODEL ALIGNMENT

This benefit, like all expense reduction benefits, aligns to the income statement.

Reduce Maverick Spending

WHAT DOES THIS MEAN?

Companies often invest a lot of effort in negotiating special prices for routine items such as office supplies, personal computer parts, and common maintenance and cleaning supplies. Maverick spending, often called off-contract spending, refers to the purchase of items outside of the specified contract. Such transactions often occur because the purchaser is impatient and wants an item urgently or wants a specific brand of an otherwise approved item; as a result, the purchaser bypasses the standard procedure and, regrettably, costs the company more money. This spending category refers to all companies, not just manufacturing companies.

WHY IS IT IMPORTANT?

Any time an organization spends money, they'd like to spend as little as possible for the goods that they want, while still maintaining the quality that they desire. To that end, most purchasing organizations negotiate vigorously with their vendors to achieve the most favorable pricing possible. Many vendors write purchase requirements into their contracts. The buying organization must buy a certain volume every year, and an annual audit is conducted to ensure that the terms of the contract are fulfilled. If during the audit the vendor determines that the company has not purchased as much as was agreed to, the vendor assesses a "true-up" value that the company must pay. When individuals buy items outside of the established contract, two things tend to happen. First, the company runs the risk of falling short of its purchase requirement and subjects itself to an annual up-charge. Second, the individual purchase is likely more expensive because the purchaser is not taking advantage of the existing favorable pricing that the company receives when buying on that contract.

HOW DOES THE COMPANY REALIZE THIS BENEFIT?

This benefit requires tools and enforcement procedures to be fully realized. Companies that have more than one buying location really benefit from consolidated purchase contracts. But for a company to truly realize this benefit, enforcement procedures must be put in place to ensure compliance and must discipline those that violate the policy. For example, if employees buy office supplies and then submit receipts via the travel expense reimbursement system, it is very likely that those purchases were off-contract. Refusing to reimburse such transactions is one way to stop maverick spending.

HOW IS THIS BENEFIT COMPUTED?

This is a negotiated number. There are two variables to negotiate—the percentage of indirect spend that is off-contract and an estimated premium paid for those purchases. You start with your company's annual indirect material spend number. You multiply that number by the agreed-upon reduction potential, say 10 percent. That's the benefit. Your company might elect to exclude certain things from the calculation as they might suggest that they have already negotiated excellent terms on selected items and that there is no chance for maverick spending in that area. If that's the case, simply subtract that number from the total spend and multiply the new, reduced spend number by the acceptable reduction percentage.

WHAT IS A REASONABLE RANGE?

First estimate the percentage of indirect purchases that are off-contract. For that variable, 10–20 percent is a reasonable range. Then estimate the premium paid for those purchases. A range of 15–20 percent is a reasonable starting range for negotiating this variable.

DETAILED BENEFIT CALCULATION EXAMPLE

Variables:

a   Total annual spend on indirect material (or amount subject to calculation if less than total spend amount)

b. Percentage of purchases made off-contract (as a percentage)

   c.   Percentage premium paid on off-contract purchases (as a percentage)

Formulas:
   d. Estimated benefit, per year (A*B*C)

BENEFIT OCCURRENCE
This benefit occurs annually and in perpetuity.

DUPONT MODEL ALIGNMENT
This benefit, like all expense reduction benefits, aligns to the income statement.

Reduce Costs Due To System Consolidation

WHAT DOES THIS MEAN?

Companies often have multiple systems devoted to serving the same or nearly the same need. The consolidation of systems and personnel can frequently save the company significant money.

WHY IS IT IMPORTANT?

As companies grow, especially as they grow through acquisition, they accumulate numerous systems. There is usually a primary IT function, but often they have additional satellite IT organizations, each with their own infrastructure and support staff. Identifying systems that can be consolidated and functions that can be consolidated can frequently yield a very large financial benefit.

HOW DOES THE COMPANY REALIZE THIS BENEFIT?

Realization of this benefit is quite simple—consolidate systems and personnel everywhere such that consolidation reduces costs without reducing service levels. Consolidation of this type provides significant benefits because consolidation often reduces impediments to smooth business process flow. Whenever transactions are handed off between disparate systems, inefficiency can be present.

HOW IS THIS BENEFIT COMPUTED?

This is more math than negotiation. First, begin by compiling all of the recurring costs of the current environment. These costs could be monthly, annual, or some other frequency. Next, diagram a proposed future state of infrastructure and personnel. Then, estimate the recurring costs of the proposed future environment. The difference between the cost of the current environment and the costs of the future environment represent your savings.

WHAT IS A REASONABLE RANGE?

No range can be offered because each customer environment is unique.

DETAILED BENEFIT CALCULATION EXAMPLE

This calculation is not universal for all organizations. The table below is presented as a framework for your calculations. Your individual situation may vary from this example.

First, document the current environment. Your organization may have one system, or it may have dozens of systems. Document each system as described below. Note that FTE is an abbreviation for full-time equivalent. One person assigned to a task for a full year is one FTE. Your company's IT staff may not all be assigned to these tasks 100 percent of the time. You may have to adjust your FTE value if the employees are assigned less than 100 percent to supporting a specific system. Fully burdened costs represent the full cost of an employee including wages, benefits, overtime and other labor –related costs.

1. System Name	2. System Purpose	3. Number of FTEs currently assigned to supporting this system	4. Average fully burdened cost of each FTE	5. Annual maintenance cost paid to outside vendor(s)	6. Annual capital investment to upgrade and replace

The current cost of the current environment would be computed as #3 times #4 (to compute the payroll and benefit cost of supporting the environment). To the total payroll and benefit cost you would add #5 and

#6. There may be other costs that are specific to your company. Add all of these values together, and the total represents the annual cost of the current environment.

Next, document the proposed future environment for each proposed future system. The expectation is that the future environment will either have fewer systems or require fewer resources to support.

1. System Name	2. System Purpose	3. Number of FTEs estimated to support the future system	4. Average fully burdened cost of each FTE	5. Annual maintenance cost paid to outside vendor(s)	6. Annual capital investment to upgrade and replace

As above, you will compute the projected cost of the future environment as #3 times #4.

BENEFIT OCCURRENCE
This benefit occurs annually and in perpetuity.

DUPONT MODEL ALIGNMENT
This benefit, like all expense reduction benefits, aligns to the income statement.

Reduce Payroll and Overtime Costs

WHAT DOES THIS MEAN?

Payroll costs represent a large financial commitment to any company or organization. Payroll costs, as a concept, actually refer to hourly and salaried workers and can include regular weekly pay, overtime pay, and, in some cases, associated benefits that are linked to payroll (such as the company's contribution to health and retirement benefits). Many of these costs are variable, meaning that they are not contractual, long-term obligations like mortgages or other loans.

WHY IS IT IMPORTANT?

Finding ways to trim payroll and overtime costs helps the company save money. All organizations must find ways to meet the work effort demands with just the right mix of talented people. Too many people for a given task and the company is simply overpaying for its human resources. Too few people for a given task and the company may find that many key tasks are not getting completed in a timely or thorough manner. Striking that balance is a key requirement for effective managers.

HOW DOES THE COMPANY REALIZE THIS BENEFIT?

In many cases, the savings can be immediate, as in the case of terminating an underperforming sales operation. In other cases, it may take some time and severance expense to eliminate a block of employees, such as when the company has employment or union contracts in place. In the case of plant closures, there may be a number of financial considerations before a benefit can be estimated.

HOW IS THIS BENEFIT COMPUTED?

This benefit can be thought of as having two subcategories: payroll reduction and overtime reduction. First, let's explore payroll reduction.

The reduction of payroll is a negotiated number. To reduce payroll, the business case developer needs to create a credible case that shows how a new technology or a new process will be significantly less time-consuming than the existing one. The savings of time is a key variable in this equation. To reduce payroll costs by one full-time person you must save 2,080 hours per year. For example, you may suggest a certain process improvement that saves your company 10 hours per week per individual. If this improvement can be applied across a department of 18 people, it stands to reason that your improvement will yield a savings of 8,640 hours. (10 hours per week * 48 weeks per year * 18 people.) The figure of 48 weeks is used here as it is assumed that employees get two weeks of vacation per year plus roughly ten additional days of holidays and sick days. It would be inaccurate to compute time savings against days when the employee was not actually working. By dividing 2,080 (number of hours in a year—you could also use 1,920, which factors only the working hours for a full year) into 8,640 (the hours that we computed above resulting from our productivity improvements) we get a result of 4.15. That means that trimming 8,640 hours from the workload could reduce the staffing requirement by 4.15 people. Since we can't eliminate 0.15 of a person, we would say that this improvement could facilitate the reduction in staff by four people. That is the number you must negotiate with the business owner of this process that stands to lose these people. You then estimate the cost of each person. The typical cost elements are annual salary, benefits paid by the company (estimated to be an additional 60 percent of annual salary), and other compensation variables such as bonuses and car allowances. Multiply the cost of each employee by the number of jobs eliminated by the new, improved process or technology, and that becomes the value of your benefit.

Overtime reductions work similarly, but have a few differences. First, there must exist an excessive amount of overtime. Determining what constitutes an excessive amount is a negotiation between you and the supervisor responsible for the people who currently work overtime. Second, unlike the calculation for payroll deduction, this calculation simply looks at hours (and dollars) for overtime. There are no additional considerations for non-salary compensation items such as benefits and bonuses, as they are typically a function of base salary and not increased based on additional pay from overtime. Reductions in overtime are typically localized to one department or one facility (such as a warehouse or maintenance facility). A common negotiating approach is to suggest that your improved technology and processes can reduce overtime in a certain department by some percentage, say 25 percent. If that number is deemed too high by the supervisor, engage in negotiations until a suitable compromise can be reached. Once agreed upon, you simply multiply the agreed-upon percentage by the dollars currently spent monthly or annually on overtime in the targeted area and you have your benefit.

WHAT IS A REASONABLE RANGE?

There is no range estimate for this benefit. Each staff reduction and overtime reduction calculation is unique to each situation.

BENEFIT OCCURRENCE

This benefit occurs annually and in perpetuity.

DUPONT MODEL ALIGNMENT

This benefit, like all expense reduction benefits, aligns to the income statement.

Reduce Costs of External Services

WHAT DOES THIS MEAN?

Companies pay for numerous external services from professional services such as accounting, banking, audit, and legal services as well as general services such as advertising, recruiting, contract maintenance, and similar services. There are numerous solutions that can be proposed that can reduce these fees.

WHY IS IT IMPORTANT?

Reducing costs is a constant focus of all organizations. External services have a way of growing and expanding to the point that they consume larger and larger budgets. Implementing new procedures or new technologies can often enable organizations to reduce their need for the full breadth of these services. And when the need for a service can be trimmed, it is reasonable to expect that the corresponding fees can be trimmed, too.

HOW DOES THE COMPANY REALIZE THIS BENEFIT?

Reducing the costs of external services is rather simple. There are two ways to reduce these costs: either the company can re-negotiate its current fee structure on existing services or it can reduce the amount of those services that it needs. This benefit focuses on reducing the amount of services needed. The company realizes this benefit by implementing tools and/or processes that replace previous external services. For example, an improved financial accounting system might reduce the annual external accounting and audit fees, assuming the new system can provide better, more reliable data to the accountants. Better accounting systems might reduce bank fees if bank statement reconciliation can be made easier and more reliable. Similarly, an updated HR system might enable better recruiting capabilities and might, therefore, enable a lesser demand on external recruiters and their corresponding fees.

HOW IS THIS BENEFIT COMPUTED?

This benefit is a negotiated number. The negotiation is between you and the primary business owner of this business function. Discuss your hypothesis with the business owner and negotiate an acceptable reduction in the appropriate usage of a service. Once you can agree that the company will use less of a given service, you can then discuss how that reduction in service translates into a reduction in corresponding fees.

WHAT IS A REASONABLE RANGE?

There is no "one-size-fits-all" range for these services as the services cover a wide variety of business functions. You could consider a 10 percent reduction to be conservative and a 50 percent reduction to be ambitious. From those starting points, you should be able to negotiate an agreeable number with the appropriate business owner.

DETAILED BENEFIT CALCULATION EXAMPLE

Variables:
a. Annual cost of specific external service to be reduced
b. Negotiated reduction (as a percentage)

Formulas:
c. Estimated benefit, per year (A * B)

BENEFIT OCCURRENCE

This benefit occurs annually and in perpetuity.

DUPONT MODEL ALIGNMENT

This benefit, like all expense reduction benefits, aligns to the income statement.

APPENDIX E
WORKING CAPITAL
OPTIMIZATION BENEFITS

An Overview of Working Capital Optimization Benefits

Working capital is that portion of the balance sheet that can most readily be converted to cash. These are short-term assets such as cash, accounts receivable, and inventory. Additionally, a short-term liability, namely accounts payable, is frequently included in the working capital discussion. Benefits that come from optimizing working capital frequently affect cash flow. For our purposes, we will focus on three areas: reducing days in inventory, reducing days sales outstanding, and increasing days payable outstanding. Each of these benefits can present substantial material reward, but since these benefits affect assets rather than expenses, they only yield a single benefit, not a recurring, year over year benefit. Once you reduce the inventory balance or collect outstanding invoices, you have saved that cash for that year. It would be incorrect to suggest that this benefit has a recurring reward. Some business case professionals will compute the interest on the money saved and present that as a recurring savings in carrying cost. We will not do that in these examples as the current low interest rates make the calculation nearly irrelevant.

These three items are also the three components of the cash conversion cycle which was presented in Appendix B.

Reduce Days in Inventory

WHAT DOES THIS MEAN?

Manufacturers buy raw materials and convert them into finished, saleable goods. Reducing the time it takes to convert the raw materials into finished, saleable goods means that the company's cash is tied up for a shorter period of time—which is a good thing. A smaller number of days in inventory means that the company has been effective at converting its purchases into cash. Faster is better (or fewer days are better).

WHY IS IT IMPORTANT?

This measurement refers directly to cash that is tied up and not recoverable. The goal of any company is to convert the raw materials into finished, saleable goods as quickly as possible, while at the same time maintaining a safe production environment and producing quality products up to their existing product quality standards.

HOW DOES THE COMPANY REALIZE THIS BENEFIT?

There are many ways to reduce the number of days that material is still in the conversion stage. The company can find places in the production process where materials sit idle waiting for the next production step. When such idle moments are discovered, the company can put new procedures in place (or hire additional laborers) to move the material to the next production phase more efficiently, thus reducing the wait or queue time. Likewise, bottlenecks create the same opportunity for improvement. Eli Goldratt has written eloquently about the impact of bottlenecks in his book *The Goal*. In the book, Goldratt explains a concept he calls "theory of constraints," which explains how addressing bottlenecks effectively moves product through the production process swiftly and with very favorable impacts on queue time and lower production time. Each day counts. Additionally, the company could work with vendors to have them engage in a program called "vendor managed inventory," where the raw or unfinished parts are stored at the company but are not the company's property until the latest possible moment. Such programs work because vendors are willing to warehouse parts at the company and only bill the company when the parts are taken out of the inventory bin and used in actual production. Such moves can reduce the number of days certain parts are on the company's books by as much as a week.

HOW IS THIS BENEFIT COMPUTED?

This is a negotiated number, but you can influence the number using some common suggestions. This benefit is determined by computing the current days in inventory value, then determining (or negotiating) just how many fewer days could be achieved using the tools and procedures recommended in your business case. Additionally, you can compare your company's performance on this metric against the performance of peer companies. Where those peer companies outperform your company, you can use those other companies as target benchmarks for your company. If the target benchmark of a competitor/peer is five days better than your own, you can suggest that with the right tools and process improvements your company could achieve a similar performance level (translation: you could suggest that your company could reduce days in inventory by the same five days to be on par with your competitor/peer).

WHAT IS A REASONABLE RANGE?

A reasonable range is a 2–5 day improvement, especially if you have identified competitors/peers whose performance is even better than that.

DETAILED BENEFIT CALCULATION EXAMPLE

Variables:
  a. Year-end inventory balance from balance sheet
  b. Annual cost of goods sold value from income statement

   c.   Days covered in your calculation (for one year, use 365)

   d.   Number of days improvement sought (can be fractional days)

Formulas:

   e.   Current days in inventory: (A/B)*C

   f.   Value of single day in inventory: A/E

   g.   Estimated one-time benefit: E * F

BENEFIT OCCURRENCE

This benefit occurs once. It can span multiple years. For example, it is common for the benefit to be divided in two, with one portion of the benefit occurring in the first year and the remaining portion of the benefit occurring in the second year.

DUPONT MODEL ALIGNMENT

This benefit, like all asset optimization benefits, aligns to your company's balance sheet.

Reduce Days Sales Outstanding

WHAT DOES THIS MEAN?

Companies sell their goods on credit. The balance sheet entry is called accounts receivable. This is money that is due (or receivable) from your customers (or accounts). This measurement is based on the number of days from the time an invoice is generated for the credit sale until the company receives full payment from the customer for this invoice. Reducing the time it takes to collect outstanding accounts receivable means that the company's cash is tied up for a shorter period of time—which is a good thing. A smaller number of days sales outstanding means that the company has been effective at collecting the money due in from customers. Faster is better (or fewer days are better).

WHY IS IT IMPORTANT?

This measurement refers directly to cash that is tied up in debts owed to the company by its customers for goods and services that the company sold to the customers on credit. The goal of any company is to collect their outstanding accounts receivable as quickly as possible.

HOW DOES THE COMPANY REALIZE THIS BENEFIT?

There are many ways to reduce the number of days from invoice to collection. The primary ways are as follows: First, ensure that invoices are accurate. Errors on invoices create disputes. Disputes take time to resolve, even if only a few days. Another way is to consolidate invoices across business units so that your customers receive fewer invoices, thus reducing confusion on the customers' end. If your company still produces and mails written invoices, migrate to an electronic system in which invoices are sent via email, thus reducing the lag time of the US Postal Service. Such moves, and others, can work to reduce the number of days that invoices remain unpaid.

HOW IS THIS BENEFIT COMPUTED?

This is a negotiated number, but you can influence the number using some common measures. This benefit is determined by computing the current days sales outstanding, then determining (or negotiating) just how many fewer days could be achieved using the tools and procedures recommended in your business case. Additionally, you can compare your company's performance on this metric against the performance of peer companies. Where those peer companies outperform your company, you can use those other companies as target benchmarks for your company. If the target benchmark of a competitor/peer is five days better than your own, you can suggest that with the right tools and process improvements your company could achieve a similar performance level (translation: you could suggest that your company could reduce days sales outstanding by the same five days to be on par with your competitor/peer).

WHAT IS A REASONABLE RANGE?

A reasonable range is a 2–5 day improvement, especially if you have identified competitors/peers whose performance is even better than that.

DETAILED BENEFIT CALCULATION EXAMPLE

Variables:
a. Year-end accounts receivable balance from balance sheet
b. Annual sales revenue from income statement
c. Days covered in your calculation (for one year, use 365)
d. Number of days improvement sought (can be fractional days)

Formulas:
- e. Current days sales outstanding: (A/B)*C
- f. Value of collecting cash one day sooner: B / C
- g. Estimated one-time benefit: D * F

BENEFIT OCCURRENCE

This benefit occurs once. It can span multiple years. For example, it is common for the benefit to be divided in two, with one portion of the benefit occurring in the first year and the remaining portion of the benefit occurring in the second year.

DUPONT MODEL ALIGNMENT

This benefit, like all asset optimization benefits, aligns to your company's balance sheet.

Increase Days Payable Outstanding

WHAT DOES THIS MEAN?

Companies buy raw materials and other supplies on credit from their vendors. The further they can push the payment out, the better it is for corporate cash flow. Increasing the number of days from receipt of vendor invoice until payment means that the company holds on to its cash that much longer—which is a good thing.

WHY IS IT IMPORTANT?

This measurement refers directly to how long a company holds onto its cash before paying its obligations to its vendors. The goal of any company is to conserve the cash as long as possible without offending or injuring the vendor relationship.

HOW DOES THE COMPANY REALIZE THIS BENEFIT?

The company realizes this benefit by simply delaying payment to its vendors by a few days. There is a delicate balance here, as extending the payment too long can injure the vendor relationship and adversely affect the buyer-seller relationship and future payment terms and delivery commitments.

HOW IS THIS BENEFIT COMPUTED?

This is a negotiated number, but you can influence the number using some common measures. This benefit is determined by computing the current days payables are outstanding, then determining (or negotiating) just how many more days could be achieved using the tools and procedures recommended in your business case. Additionally, you can compare your company's performance on this metric against the performance of peer companies. Where those peer companies outperform your company, you can use those other companies as target benchmarks for your company. If the target benchmark of a competitor/peer pays, on average, five days later than your company, you can suggest that with the right tools and process improvements your company could achieve a similar performance level (translation: you could suggest that your company could delay payment by the same five days to be on par with your competitor/peer).

WHAT IS A REASONABLE RANGE?

A reasonable range is a 2–5 day improvement, especially if you have identified competitors/peers whose performance is even better than that.

DETAILED BENEFIT CALCULATION EXAMPLE

Variables:
a. Year-end accounts payable balance from balance sheet
b. Annual cost of goods sold value from income statement
c. Days covered in your calculation (for one year, use 365)
d. Number of days improvement sought (can be fractional days)

Formulas:
e. Current days payable outstanding: $(A/B)*C$
f. Value of single day of outstanding payables: B / C
g. Estimated one-time benefit: $D * F$

BENEFIT OCCURRENCE

This benefit occurs once. It can span multiple years. For example, it is common for the benefit to be divided in two, with one portion of the benefit occurring in the first year and the remaining portion of the benefit occurring in the second year.

DUPONT MODEL ALIGNMENT

This benefit, like all asset optimization benefits, aligns to your company's balance sheet.

BIBLIOGRAPHY

Charan, Ram. *What the CEO Wants You to Know*. New York: Crown Business/ Random House, 2001.

Epstein, Lita. *Reading Financial Reports for Dummies*. Hoboken, NJ: Wiley, 2009.

Goldratt, Eli. *The Goal*. 3rd ed. Great Barrington, MA, The North River Press, 2004.

Keen, Jack M. *Making Technology Investments Profitable: ROI Road Map to Better Business Cases*. 2nd ed. New Jersey: John Wiley, 2011.

Khalsa, Mahan, and Randy Illig. *Let's Get Real or Let's Not Play: Transforming the Buyer/Seller Relationship*. FranklinCovey, Rev. ed. New York: Penguin Group, 2008.

Miller, Robert B., and Stephen E. Heiman, with Tad Tuleja. *The New Successful Large Account Management: Maintaining and Growing Your Most Important Assets—Your Customers*. Rev. ed. New York: Hachette Book Group USA, 2005.

Page, Rick. *Hope Is Not a Strategy: The 6 Keys to Winning the Complex Sale*. New York, Nautilus Press, 2002.

Paulk, Mark C., Weber, Charles V., Curtis, Bill, and Chrissis, Mary Beth. *The Capability Maturity Model: Guidelines for Improving the Software Process*. New York: Addison-Wesley Publishing Company, 1995.

Rackham, Neil. *SPIN Selling*. New York: McGraw-Hill, 1988.

Read, Nicholas A. C., and Stephen J. Bistritz. *Selling to the C-Suite*. New York: McGraw-Hill, 2010.

Scalia, Antonin, and Bryan A. Garner. *Making Your Case: The Art of Persuading Judges*. St. Paul, MN: Thomson/West, 2008.

Schwarz, Roger. *The Skilled Facilitator: A Comprehensive Resource for Consultants, Facilitators, Managers, Trainers and Coaches*. San Francisco: Jossey-Bass, 2002.

Stinnett, Bill. *Think Like Your Customer*. New York: McGraw-Hill, 2004.